Essays in Honour of

Sir Brian Neill

The Quintessential Judge

ESSAYS IN HONOUR OF

Sir Brian Neill

The Quintessential Judge

Edited by

Mark Saville

and

Richard Susskind

LexisNexis™ UK

Members of the LexisNexis Group worldwide

United Kingdom	LexisNexis UK, a Division of Reed Elsevier (UK) Ltd, Halsbury House, 35 Chancery Lane, LONDON, WC2A 1EL, and 4 Hill Street, EDINBURGH EH2 3JZ
Argentina	LexisNexis Argentina, BUENOS AIRES
Australia	LexisNexis Butterworths, CHATSWOOD, New South Wales
Austria	LexisNexis Verlag ARD Orac GmbH & Co KG, VIENNA
Canada	LexisNexis Butterworths, MARKHAM, Ontario
Chile	LexisNexis Chile Ltda, SANTIAGO DE CHILE
Czech Republic	Nakladatelství Orac sro, PRAGUE
France	Editions du Juris-Classeur SA, PARIS
Germany	LexisNexis Deutschland GmbH, FRANKFURT, MUNSTER
Hong Kong	LexisNexis Butterworths, HONG KONG
Hungary	HVG-Orac, BUDAPEST
India	LexisNexis Butterworths, NEW DELHI
Ireland	Butterworths (Ireland) Ltd, DUBLIN
Italy	Giuffrè Editore, MILAN
Malaysia	Malayan Law Journal Sdn Bhd, KUALA LUMPUR
New Zealand	LexisNexis Butterworths, WELLINGTON
Poland	Wydawnictwo Prawnicze LexisNexis, WARSAW
Singapore	LexisNexis Butterworths, SINGAPORE
South Africa	LexisNexis Butterworths, DURBAN
Switzerland	Stämpfli Verlag AG, BERNE
USA	LexisNexis, DAYTON, Ohio

A CIP Catalogue record for this book is available from the British Library.

ISBN 0 406 97033 5

Printed and bound in Great Britain by Antony Rowe Ltd, Chippenham, Wilts

Preface

The origins of this book can be traced to Café Lazeez, an incomparable Indian restaurant in St John Street, London. Every few months, we meet there for dinner and an informal chat. At one such meal, in early 2000, our discussion turned, as so often it does, to Brian Neill, for whom we have always shared a strong admiration and affection. That evening, we were reflecting on how active he continued to be, even at his age. But at precisely what age, we wondered? We realised, after some approximate calculation, that he must soon be 80, even though, as we agreed, he was more astute and vital than most men half, indeed one quarter, of his age. We resolved over coffee that we should determine the exact date of his transition to octogenarian and should recognise this milestone in some way. The idea of a *festschrift* followed naturally – for a man, so masterful with the written word, we could think of no better token of our respect than to produce a collection of essays in celebration of Brian. Better still, we thought it would be wonderful to have the book published in stealth, so that, at some auspicious moment, we might present the end-product to Brian as a surprise.

The following day, we confirmed that Brian's 80th birthday was on 2 August 2003. Although time was therefore on our side, we immediately set about contacting a number of his friends and colleagues to engage their support in the publication project. Our proposal was met with unbridled enthusiasm and so this book was born – conceived as a warm tribute to a great man from a group of long-standing peers, collaborators and friends.

As to the subject-matter of the book, we took the view that we should concentrate on two fields that seemed to us to be closest to Brian's heart: the impact of information technology on the law; and the law of defamation.

This book is neither a biography of Brian nor an analysis of his contribution to the law. That said, a few words of background are surely in order, by way of brief summary.

Brian was educated at Highgate School, London, and Corpus Christi College, Oxford, and was called to the Bar in 1949. He was appointed a QC in 1968, as a judge of the High Court (Queen's Bench Division) in 1978, and to the Court of Appeal in 1985, where he sat until 1996. On retirement (a misnomer, of course), he began to sit as an arbitrator and, from 1997, sat in the Court of Appeal for Gibraltar, of which, from 1998, he was President until recently.

Neither of us knew Brian as a barrister. One man who did was David Hirst, a contemporary of Brian and a former Court of Appeal judge. According to David: 'Brian was an extremely skilful advocate, dispassionate, persuasive, unruffled, and backed in court by a gift for the most thorough and meticulous preparation of his case; all round he was a very formidable opponent.' David goes on: 'Brian is an outstanding lawyer, with an innate grasp of the essential principles. This is well exemplified in the 1978 publication of Duncan and Neill's *Defamation*, of which Brian was the leading author and moving spirit. This slim little book, now in its second edition, has proved a godsend ever since to judges when embarking upon (for them) the previously uncharted waters of a libel or slander case.'

As to Brian's work as a judge, we need do no more than draw attention to the sub-title of this book, which captures our sentiments. Solomonically wise, prodigiously diligent, profoundly perceptive, unarguably expert and scrupulously impartial, Brian was indeed the quintessential judge. Indeed, we can think of no finer role model in the judicial world.

David Hirst offers this supplementary overview: 'As a High Court judge Brian was a leading member of the Commercial Court, over which he presided with great distinction shortly before his elevation to the Court of Appeal in 1985. From then on he gave several important judgments, often displaying his special gift of presenting a clear and succinct summary of the relevant legal principles in short concise paragraphs. He became an excellent presider, and set a valuable example to colleagues, including myself, who sat with him'.

On a lighter vein, we note also that Brian is even judicial in appearance. Tall, imposing, with a shock of white hair, a face that exudes wisdom, experience and gravitas, and a rich booming, bass voice, Brian looks and sounds as though he might have been first choice by central casting to play the part of a senior judge in a play or film. Indeed, some years ago, when Sky Television interviewed Brian about the first trial in this country of computer-assisted, real time transcription of court proceedings (a then radical but now mainstream technique), the director later confessed he could not credit his good fortune in being presented with so palpably judicial a figure. (We do accept, of course, in seeking to align themselves with Brian's example, that aspiring and serving judges can do little to alter their physical appearances or vocal strains!)

Turning now to the production of the book, we are very grateful to our fellow contributors – Henry Brooke, Colin Tapper, Charles Gray, David Eady and Desmond Browne. Although each is enormously busy, none needed any prompting or cajoling to deliver drafts or proofs on time. This partly reflects their own remarkable industry but also reveals, of course, their commitment to the project and to Brian himself.

Particular appreciation is due to Harry Woolf and Tom Bingham. There can be very few busier people in the land and with more onerous work-loads than the Lord Chief Justice and the Senior Law Lord. And yet they devoted many hours to crafting the introduction to this *festschrift* – a handsome tribute, followed by a crisp preview of each of the succeeding chapters.

Penultimately, we thank Valerie Bath. Unflappable, highly organised, tolerant and kindly, this project would have faltered badly had it not been for her formidable administrative talents.

Finally, we wish to thank Brian's wife Sally for supporting the production of this volume. It cannot be easy to conceal a surprise of this magnitude from a husband of almost 50 years, but she was characteristically enthusiastic and supportive.

To both Brian and Sally, we extend our very warmest wishes for the future.

Mark Saville
Richard Susskind

May Day 2003

Contents

The contributors

Harry Woolf

Lord Woolf was born in 1933 and educated at Fettes and University College London. He was called to the Bar in 1954 and, after a period as First Treasury Counsel, appointed to the High Court Bench. He has served as a Lord Justice of Appeal, Lord Appeal in Ordinary and the Master of the Rolls, before becoming Lord Chief Justice in 2000.

Tom Bingham

Tom Bingham was called to the Bar in 1959 and took silk in 1972. He became a judge of the High Court and the Commercial Court in 1980 and was appointed to the Court of Appeal in 1986. In 1992 he became Master of the Rolls, in 1996 Lord Chief Justice and in 2000 Senior Law Lord.

Henry Brooke

Lord Justice Brooke has been the Judge in charge of modernisation since 2001. He was appointed a High Court Judge in 1988, and a Lord Justice of Appeal in 1996. He has been involved with Information Technology and the Law since 1985. He was formerly President of the Society for Computers and Law. He is now the judicial member of the Court Service's Courts and Tribunals Modernisation Board.

Desmond Browne

Desmond Browne has practised in defamation and media law for some 30 years from chambers which are now at 5, Raymonds Buildings, Gray's Inn. He took silk in 1990. Readers who think they detect the sound of axes being ground should know that he acted for claimants in the Elton John, Berezovsky, Kiam and Loutchansky cases and for the media in Spycatcher, Derbyshire CC, Ashworth Hospital, Wagstaff and Persey. He has no one but himself to blame for the failure of the defendants to raise Article 10 in *Goldsmith v Pressdram*.

David Eady

David Eady is a former pupil of Brian Neill. He served on the Neill Committee on Defamation and on the Calcutt Committee on Privacy. He is also the co-author of a textbook on Contempt of Court. Having practised at the bar in the field of media law for many years, he still regularly encounters the law of defamation in his current capacity as judge in charge of the jury list

Charles Gray

Charles Gray was called to the Bar in 1966. His practice was principally media law. He took silk in 1984. Clients included the *Sunday Times* in the *Crossman Diaries Case* and the thalidomide litigation (led by Brian Neill), the *Guardian* and the *Observer* in the *Spycatcher* case, Lord Aldington, Ian Botham and Jonathan Aitken. He became a High Court Judge in 1998. His judgment in *Irving v Penguin Books* was published in paperback.

Mark Saville

Lord Saville is a Lord of Appeal in Ordinary. Since 1998 he has been conducting the Bloody Sunday Inquiry. He has interested himself for many years in promoting the use of Information Technology in the Court system. Lord Saville is currently President of the Society for Computers and Law and Chairman of ITAC (Information Technology and the Courts).

Richard Susskind

Richard Susskind OBE is an independent adviser to professional firms and national governments. He is IT Adviser to the Lord Chief Justice, Chair of the Advisory Panel on Crown Copyright, and holds law professorships at Gresham College, London and the Centre for Law, Computers and Technology at Strathclyde University. He is a law columnist at *The Times* and the author of five books on legal technology.

Colin Tapper

Colin Tapper MA, BCL; of Gray's Inn barrister at law, is Emeritus Professor of Law in the University of Oxford, and Emeritus Fellow of Magdalen College. He was a Founder Member of the Society for Computers and Law. And he is author of *Computers and the Law* (1973) and *Computer Law* (1978–1991).

Sir Brian Neill

Tom Bingham and Harry Woolf

Introduction

This book is a unique tribute to one whose achievement, as all would agree, fully deserves so unusual an accolade.

The essays collected here are very largely devoted to two aspects of Brian Neill's career: his unrivalled contribution to the law of defamation; and his far-sighted, pioneering and determined work to apply the new world of information technology to the old world of traditional court practice.

We say a little on these subjects below (although these excellent essays leave little to say). But we have one advantage denied to the other contributors to this volume. This is not just that we count ourselves among Brian's friends, a privilege which we doubtless share with all the other contributors. It is that we have, through longevity alone, had the cumulative pleasure of knowing him longer than others, of appearing against him in court, and of sitting with him as a judicial colleague. This experience, we hope, entitles us, as it certainly enables us, to range somewhat more widely than the contents of the book.

Libel was of course the legal field in which Brian specialised at the Bar, and libel trials are perhaps the nearest that forensic practice comes to show business. This is partly because those who have earned their title to celebrity by public performance not infrequently feature in such trials as protagonists or witnesses on one side or the other, and partly because (despite the technicality of much of the relevant law) the issues often lend themselves to presentation in a simple and seductively adversarial way. Not surprisingly, advocates regularly appearing in such cases may themselves acquire something approaching celebrity status, their *bon mots* savoured, their jokes retailed, their demeanour studied, their scoring record noted as if they were fashionable strikers. This can lead to a certain showiness.

Brian was not a showy advocate. He can never have been the darling of the headline writers. But he was a prime choice of newspaper solicitors, legal managers and editors who wanted to win or, at worst, lose inexpensively. In Brian they recognised an advocate who was highly erudite, very intelligent, immensely well-prepared and so persuasive that it always seemed unreasonable to disagree with him. He was an opponent with whom it was impossible to quarrel, however badly one's case was going. No wonder the clients came back again and again.

On appointment to the Queen's Bench Division in 1978, Brian would have been a natural choice to take charge of the defamation list. But the law has always aped the old Foreign Office tradition of posting Arabic speakers to Peru, and such was not his destiny. Instead he was plunged, almost at once, into presiding at a very long criminal trial, a task which he discharged with characteristic professionalism and conspicuous success. And in 1980 a perceptive Lord Chancellor appointed him to the Commercial Court.

There have been many judges of the Commercial Court whose professional practices had given them greater familiarity with the intricacies of WWDs, BLADINGS and NAABSA berths than had Brian's. But all the qualities which had earned him distinction as an advocate quickly led to his becoming a widely-admired commercial judge. Anyone listed before him could be confident of a hearing that would be courteous, open-minded, rational and transparently fair. Not for him the record of being slow, rude and wrong. His court was a show-case for the British system at its exemplary best.

As a member of the Court of Appeal for 11 years from 1985-1996 Brian's exceptional qualities were at a premium. Whatever (almost) the subject-matter of an appeal, Brian was an obvious member of the ideal constitution to be invited to hear it. Defamation? Yes, of course. An appeal from the Commercial Court? Certainly. Employment? Yes, his service as a judge of the Employment Appeal Tribunal for three years had given him an invaluable expertise. Judicial review? His judgments in this burgeoning field impressed judicious observers as sound and well reasoned. In a high profile case calling for particularly sensitive handling, Brian's were recognised as the safest pair of hands in sight. Increasingly, as time went on, Brian presented the administrators with an inescapable dilemma, as the former Registrar of the Civil Division would be the first to testify: the intractable laws of nature forbade his inclusion in more than one constitution at a time. The inevitable result was that, even by the standards prevailing in the Court of Appeal, his workload was formidable.

Such a workload would have led, in most mortals, to an evident sense of strain. But if strain there was, it never surfaced. He was always superbly prepared. His contributions to the Socratic dialogue with counsel were always courteous but pertinent. In private discussion his approach was eminently collegiate, seeking an agreed solution where possible, ready to give and take up to a point, but unwilling to compromise on important matters of principle. His reserved judgments were models of promptness, thoroughness and clarity. It was a dark day for London, but proved a sunny day for Gibraltar, when in 1996 Brian retired from full-time membership of the Court of Appeal before becoming (shortly thereafter) a Justice of Appeal, and then the President, of the Court of Appeal for Gibraltar. No wonder the citizens there value their British connection.

Brian's contribution to the law of defamation and related subjects is amply attested by the essays in this book. We draw attention to one aspect of this contribution only: the small but invaluable textbook on *Defamation* written in collaboration first (1978) with the late Colin Duncan, then (1984) with Richard Rampton, and now (as all will hope) awaiting a third edition. There are textbooks and textbooks. In some, weighty and learned though they doubtless are, the inquiring reader may find much information but no answers to the particular problem which vexes him. In others, the author has with uncanny prescience foreseen the questions which will be asked, and answered them. *Defamation* falls triumphantly into this second category: in its conciseness, its erudition, its accuracy and its distillation of experience it has few peers.

And so to the IT revolution. It was Disraeli who famously observed that this is a hard country to move. What is true of the country at large is not less true of the legal profession. So introducing modern electronic techniques into the traditional handling of court business was never likely to be easy. Some of Brian's most active and authoritative collaborators and successors have contributed essays which fairly acknowledge Brian's pioneering role, at any rate in judicial circles. So rapid (if incomplete) has been the transformation over the last 20 or so years, that it is now hard to recall that Brian's was once a voice crying, not in the wilderness perhaps, but in judicial and administrative corridors where most of the doors were closed.

The whole profession of the law owes an immense debt to Brian Neill. We are very pleased to have such a good opportunity to add our stone to this cairn, erected by his friends and admirers as a monument to his achievement.

The essays

Henry Brooke is particularly well qualified to assess Brian Neill's contribution to the introduction of technology into the judicial process since Henry Brooke is the first person to hold the office of *Judge in Charge of Modernisation*. Henry Brooke identifies Brian Neill as one of the first members of the judiciary to recognise the potential that the application of technology had for the judiciary. As early as 1985 Brian Neill presided over the Bar's Society for Computers and the Law. He formed and chaired the Information Technology and the Courts Committee, which studied the place that technology could play in our court system. From 1990 he chaired the Judicial IT Help project which helped the court service to identify ways in which computers could be used to help judges. Brian Neill had the vision to press for greater investment in technology to support the judicial function. He confronted reactionary attitudes among the judiciary and administrators. Having set out Brian Neill's contribution, Henry Brooke details the huge strides that have since been made, building on that contribution, to provide the technology that the judiciary today requires. He does, however, give a stark warning as to what remains to be done and explains why it is essential that the government provide the massive resources required to complete the job.

Mark Saville's belief that information technology had the potential to make great improvements to the administration of justice was fostered by Brian Neill. In his essay, he describes how his appointment in 1998 as Chairman of an Inquiry into the happenings in Londonderry on Sunday 30 January 1972, gave him the opportunity to demonstrate the potential of the application of information technology. Information technology was the key to making the long inquiry a truly public process, which was imperative given the controversy that surrounded the original inquiry. The essay describes how the tribunal's use of technology enabled statements from over 1,500 witnesses as well as tens of thousands of other documents, to be shared with all parties concerned, including the media and those in the public galleries in London and Londonderry (who were connected to the London proceedings by video-link), and internationally, via the tribunal's website. Advanced technology was also used, in the form of a virtual reality model of Londonderry as it was in 1972, to assist witnesses to describe events in a city which had changed shape in the intervening 30 years. It clearly emerges that technology is indeed radically affecting the nature, and capabilities of a tribunal. Technology makes it possible for the public to be truly involved in this Tribunal's search for justice in the most difficult circumstances and at the same time for a great deal of public expense to be saved.

Richard Susskind has made the subject of the contribution which information technology can make to legal practice and the administration of justice his own. Here he provides a valuable insight into the challenge of managing the judiciary as a workforce. He discusses the judiciary's need to communicate both with the public and among themselves and the contribution technology can make to this. He also assesses the contribution that IT can make to training. Richard Susskind worked closely with Brian Neill in the early 1990s while he was Chairman and Brian President of the Society for Computers and Law. Richard Susskind reflects on his years of association with Brian Neill. He describes with great warmth Brian Neill's openness to fresh ideas, his vision and his role as a mentor and a wise advisor.

Colin Tapper recalls a time when solicitors were so averse to the use of new technology that they were reluctant to accept typed opinions from counsel. He notes that Brian Neill's enthusiasm and support for the application of modern technology to law and law reporting, reflected in his membership of countless working parties and research groups, contributed greatly to the alacrity with which English lawyers later greeted the advent of the personal computer. He assesses the interaction between the changes in the use of technology that Brian Neill helped to bring about and the means of legally regulating these changes. His essay considers the intellectual property rights of which law reporters have historically been able to avail themselves and the challenges posed as reporting technology has advanced to the creation by legal publishers, at substantial cost, of the online case law and statute databases which are today an essential practitioner's tool. There is also a discussion of the degree of protection offered to the creators of such databases by the law of copyright, and the database right introduced by the EU's Database Directive.

Desmond Browne QC is an advocate who has been regularly engaged in litigation involving freedom of expression. His article examines the impact Art 10 has had in UK domestic law, both before and after the Human Rights Act 1998 came into force. He notes that as an advocate, Brian Neill, as early as 1973, unsuccessfully attempted to persuade the House of Lords to adopt an Art 10 approach in the case of *A-G v Times Newspapers*, which involved the contempt proceedings relating to the litigation arising out of the marketing of thalidomide. He traces the developments that took place over the following years. Another particularly significant contribution of Brian Neill, which Desmond Browne identifies, is Brian Neill's judgment in the case of *Rantzen v MGN* in 1994. In this case he 'tackled head-on' the submission that the ECHR was not part of English domestic law. He stated, '[w]here freedom of expression is at stake ... Art 10 has a wider role and can properly be regarded as an articulation of some of the principles underlying the common law.' In *Rantzen*, in an effort to overcome the long-standing problem of excessive awards of libel damages, Brian Neill introduced new guidelines for juries to ensure that awards of damages conformed with the requirement of proportionality. The article proceeds to chronicle the influence of Art 10 on particular principles of domestic law, including 'the public's right to know', the confidentiality of journalistic sources and the public's right of access to information.

David Eady and Charles Gray are the two most experienced defamation judges on the High Court bench. Charles Gray contributes the next article. Here David Eady focuses on another area of the law on which Brian Neill had a significant influence, this was practice and procedure. Brian Neill was the chairman of the Supreme Court Procedure Committee for many years.

In 1990, Lord Mackay of Clashfern, the then Lord Chancellor, appointed Sir Brian to chair an investigation into defamation practice with a view to suggesting improvements. The Neill Committee presented its recommendations in July 1991. Among those which were adopted were such important innovations as the claimant's obligation to plead by way of a detailed response to a defendant's particulars of justification and a provision (now found in CPR 53, PD, 4.1) enabling the parties to obtain a judge's ruling on whether the words complained of were capable of bearing a certain meaning or meanings. David Eady traces the developments in important issues identified in the Neill Committee's report. He considers whether there should be a special common law privilege for the media, whether the burden of proof should be placed on the claimant where the defendant pleads justification, and whether the committee's recommendation that exemplary damages in libel cases be abolished should be looked at afresh. He also charts the route taken by the courts in recent years in bringing order to the system of compensatory damages in defamation cases.

Charles Gray's article begins by discussing two celebrated cases in which Brian Neill acted as barrister for the defendants. These cases each made a significant contribution to the judicial and statutory recognition of the importance, if not primacy, to be afforded to freedom of expression. The first, the Crossman Diaries Case, marked the first occasion on which an injunction was sought to restrain the publication of public or governmental information, here in relation to discussions which had taken place in cabinet. This case was significant in that it recognised the right of government to invoke a private law right to prevent the dissemination of governmental information. The second landmark case identified is *A-G v Times Newspapers*, the thalidomide case. *The Times* was successful in arguing before the European Court that the legal rule that it was contempt of court to make any comment on proceedings before the court which could interfere with the proceedings was outdated and more weight must be given to freedom of speech. It is explained that this case has provided the stimulus for radical changes to the law of contempt. These changes have largely eliminated the chilling effect which the law of contempt once had on freedom of expression. Included in the article are a discussion of the influence of Art 8 on a right to privacy, its relationship with a right to confidentiality and the tension between Arts 8 and 10.

Technology and the judicial process

Henry Brooke

On 15 July 2002 the Government announced its spending plans for the next three years. After 15 years of travail, we had just embarked on a well-designed programme of court modernisation, in which IT was to play a central part. Judges and the civil servants who served them were working together towards common goals as never before. And then the bubble burst. No extra money at all was earmarked for modernising our civil and family courts, although the strains caused by years of under-investment were most obvious in that corner of the court system. Again I had to comfort the walking wounded. I had a very strong sense of deja vu.

I came onto the law and technology scene in 1985. I had just spent two years away from legal London as counsel to the Sizewell Inquiry, where I had seen the benefits which well-planned applications of modern technology could bring. Soon after I returned to my practice as a barrister, I was invited to help form the Bar's first ever computer committee. Our first chairman was a silk who knew what computers could do from his experience as a director of a regional newspaper company. One of the committee's other members was a young barrister who worked for Rank Xerox. He told us of the advantages of the work station which brought electronically to his desk draft documents, letters and memoranda from his company's outposts.

One of the committee's early successes was a series of workshops run for barristers and barristers' clerks by members of the Society for Computers and Law. The society had been formed in 1973, with Lord Justice Scarman as its first president. Twelve years later Brian Neill had taken over as president.

When I went to see him in his room in the Law Courts I remember he told me that he thought he had joined the movement far too early. Since 1973 the cause of technology and the law had gone backwards almost as often as it had gone forwards, particularly with one over-ambitious project. In 1985 the Bar's resistance to computerised accounting systems was fuelled by over-zealous salesmanship by vendors who did not understand the idiosyncrasies of barristers' charging systems. Fee notes were still sent out manually from barristers' clerks' rooms throughout the Temple and Lincoln's Inn.

He said, however, that things were now going forward again. He had nearly persuaded the Lord Chancellor (Lord Hailsham) to approve the creation of a joint committee of civil servants and practising lawyers who would study the place which technology could play in our court system. This led to the formation of the Information Technology and the Courts Committee (ITAC), with eight delegates drawn equally from the Lord Chancellor's Department (LCD), the Home Office, the Bar and the Law Society. Brian Neill was our first chairman, and he told us at our first meeting in December 1985 that the general justification for our existence was the need to improve the running of the courts and to reform the costs of legal services by establishing better chains of communication between government departments and the legal profession.

One early opportunity for us arose out of the consultation processes being conducted by the Civil Justice Review. A powerful inter-disciplinary team, headed by an experienced businessman, had been appointed by the Lord Chancellor to advise him how 'to improve the machinery of civil justice in England and Wales by means of reforms in jurisdiction, procedure and court administration, and in particular to reduce delay, cost and complexity.'

In February 1986 the Review published a consultation paper on personal injuries litigation. We set up a small working party to respond to it. The paper expressed the view that the present arrangements were 'inefficient, dilatory and disproportionately expensive'. I suggested that we should look forward over a 15-year time span when considering how sensible use of modern technology could help, rather than propose any instant solutions.

Some of the ideas we canvassed – for instance, the use of expert systems to help the high street litigation solicitor advise his clients with accident claims – were perhaps too visionary for a real world. Others, such as legal information databases, computerised judicial case control, and widespread use of electronic communications, are today's accepted wisdom. Ten years before Lord Woolf's final report, and 16 years before the Government declined to give significant support to the embryo civil and family court modernisation programme, I wrote:

> 'The advantage of looking at personal injuries litigation as a discrete topic is that this approach is building on what have been the success stories in court administration on the civil justice side in the last 20 years, where an individual discrete topic (employment disputes, commercial disputes, building contract disputes, administrative law disputes) is assigned to a particular group of judges with their own supporting staff: there is no reason why a comparable technique should not be carried over into personal injuries dispute resolution.
>
> If a judge, assisted by a team of all the talents comparable to the Advisory Committee in the Civil Justice Review, emerged from the review process with the personal responsibility of overseeing and putting into effect the ideas for harnessing modern technology in support of personal injuries litigation which are ultimately approved, and clear lines of communication were established with court users, lay and legal, and the suppliers, such a structure would probably ensure that the new thinking was smoothly implemented up and down the country.'

In the end ITAC submitted two papers to the Review. In July 1986 we drew attention to all the different ways in which technology could help solve some of the issues with which the Review team was grappling in the field of personal injuries litigation. A year later we advocated greater investment in debt recovery systems and in listing, case management and management information systems. No doubt driven by Law Society caution in the search of a consensus we were hesitant about advocating over-rigid systems of computerised case control from the centre.

The Review team's views were clear. In their final report, published in 1988, they said crisply that computer facilities for the management of court lists and individual cases should be made available as a matter of priority. They were equally crisp in expressing their view that judges and administrators each had a role to play in running the civil court system. They recommended that a major programme should be mounted with the aim of improving the quality and quantity of management information available to both judges and administrators, particularly at circuit and local level.

Very little was done to implement either of these recommendations, so far as the judiciary was concerned.

I have in my possession many of the papers which record the meetings and discussions over the next 10 years. Throughout that time far-sighted judges, led by Brian Neill and, later, Lord Saville, pressed for greater investment in technology to support the judicial function. It is easy with the benefit of hindsight to see what went wrong.

LCD was a small department. It had grown up haphazardly. The Lord Chancellor's Office was originally formed to support the judges, although the Lord Chancellor had also had a traditional responsibility for the condition of our civil and family law. Over the years there had been accretions to its functions. The most notable of these had been in 1971, when it took over the responsibility of running all our criminal courts, and in 1988, when the state took over from the Law Society the responsibility for running a demand-led legal aid scheme whose finances were running out of control. In comparative terms, however, the department spent so little money that it was only quite recently that it was considered appropriate or necessary for the Lord Chancellor to be supported by a junior minister in the House of Commons.

In those days the judges were generally content that the Lord Chancellor could obtain sufficient resources from the Treasury to meet their needs. In turn they respected the convention that because they could not be accountable for the expenditure of public money it would be inappropriate for them to be anywhere near the place where decisions on spending priorities got taken. In any event most judges possessed little by way of administrative or management skills, and nothing at all was done to help them acquire them. On the whole judges were agnostic about issues relating to the appropriate way to run the courts. Two cultures co-existed side by side in the courts, the judicial and the administrative, each dependent on the other, but with few points of well-informed contact in the places where policy was being formed.

Another tradition was that there was very little cross-fertilisation of staff between LCD and other departments of state. While investment in IT steadily increased across Whitehall, the court system remained an oasis of manual records and manual accounting. In any event there was very little money for forward investment. The department only knew for certain what money was allotted to it for a year in advance, and IT projects had to justify themselves by being able to pay for themselves quickly in terms of the savings they achieved. While it was wise to avoid rushing into major spending projects without careful small-scale piloting, no strategic plan existed to support future investment in court IT systems, or at any rate none which the judiciary was invited to take part in devising. Year by year in the early 1990s I had to comfort the head of the department's small IT branch after its fairly modest request for increased resources had been turned down.

In February 1989 a working party of the Society for Computers and Law prepared a powerful paper advocating the use of computers in the Official Referees' courts. These courts were chosen for special treatment because the six Official Referees were all housed together in a newly refurbished court building, and the courts' clientele contained many for whom the use of modern technology in their businesses was a commonplace. Most of the recommendations in this report formed part of the thinking behind the court modernisation plans developed by the Court Service a decade later. Its message was summarised in these terms:

> 'We conclude that the computerisation of the administration will:
> (i) provide the court with the ability to monitor and report on the state and progress of all cases in the Official Referees' list, and take appropriate early action;
> (ii) improve trial listing performance;
> (iii) encourage early settlement of cases by monitoring compliance with orders such as a costs estimate order, or other orders requiring action to be taken which is directed to be notified to the court.
> (iv) speed up the production of formal orders and certificates;
> (v) cater for cashless payments of fees;
> (vi) remove the need for stamping of documents to be carried out in the Royal Courts of Justice;
> (vii) automate accounting procedures.
>
> Further, if the proposed computerisation of the administration is linked to an external network accessible to solicitors, this would:
> (i) provide for electronic issue of writs;
> (ii) provide for the electronic issue of summonses, and the fixing of dates for the hearing;
> (iii) enable electronic communication with court staff or court clerks, to supplement the use of the telephone and fax'.

Very little came of any of this. The report, however, coincided with the development of a legal information communication system called LIX by a barrister, Sean Overend, and a solicitor, John Mawhood. This was later to be adopted as the basic tool for electronic communications and conferencing between members of the judiciary, a role for which it is still in use today.

At this time two major projects were consuming most of the resources available to LCD's planners, so far as IT support to the courts was concerned. The first was called CREST, a project designed to automate the back-office systems within the 90 or so Crown Court centres. The other was the construction of a Summons Production Centre, coupled with a Computerised Bulk Claims Centre, at Northampton. This provided an electronic debt recovery service to a number of major creditors. They would post their unpaid final invoices to Northampton, which would issue court process electronically, and follow up with the issue of a default judgment electronically if the debtor showed no inclination to defend the claim. The department hoped at that time that it might be able to reinvest the savings in court staff which these projects would achieve in other IT investments which might not be able to show such dramatic short-term savings.

A 1990 departmental IT strategy identified the need to give priority to products which had the potential for making the most effective contribution to the department's business needs. Strategic thinking was inevitably inward-looking, because this is what the Treasury required. LCD's business managers were charged with evaluating IT projects by criteria which included 'return on investment', 'strategic match', 'policy analysis review effectiveness' and 'management information for operational effectiveness'. The judges were not invited to take any real part in the creation of these strategies. Savings in judicial time, or greater efficiencies in the services the courts could render to litigants (other than by back-office efficiencies), did not seem to feature. The quality of justice was not an attribute which civil servants were mandated to measure in money terms. It did not therefore appear in their calculations.

How different things were in Australia. Among my papers is the April 1990 newsletter of the Australian Institute of Judicial Administration. In Western Australia the Chief Justice was taking the lead in organising case management seminars. In that jurisdiction a local area network linking judges and masters of the Supreme Court was already being installed. A similar tale was told by a member of the Supreme Court of South Australia. There was also a meeting in Melbourne of 24 Australian and New Zealand judges, summoned for the purpose of comparing notes on the state of computerisation in the courts in each of their jurisdictions. The New World was forging ahead of the Old. It has been in the lead ever since.

In 1990 the Head of the Court Service invited the Deputy Chief Justice to help the Service identify the ways in which computers could be used to help judges.

For this purpose a small, broadly based group of judges, chaired by Brian Neill, met three or four times a year to examine the possibilities. One of the driving forces behind the Judicial IT Help ('JUDITH') Project that emerged from this initiative was Judge Michael Mander, of Shrewsbury county court, who had attracted national media publicity by using his laptop PC to take notes when sitting on the bench for a jury trial. Another was Judge Anthony Thorpe, later the resident judge at in the Chichester Crown Court, who was aghast on his appointment as a civilian judge to discover the lack of the IT support for judicial officers which had been taken for granted within the Armed Services. Sean Overend, now a circuit judge, was also a tower of strength in those early days.

To launch this new initiative the judiciary was allocated one-tenth of one civil servant's time and two-tenths of another and, crucially, enough money to hire a consultant, Mr Peter Hardie-Bick, whose task it was to go out into the field and prepare a report on the way in which the provision of computers could help the judiciary do their jobs better.

His report, delivered in 1992, was positive. In addition to a word-processing function, he identified a communications function as one of the possibilities we should explore. Judges do lonely jobs. A lot of them are on the move from court to court, with quite limited library facilities available, and some High Court judges have to be away from their base, and their homes, on circuit for weeks at a time.

The report provided the necessary leverage for the release of money for a pilot scheme, embracing 25 judges, to try out the possibilities. WordPerfect 5.1 for DOS was chosen for word processing, since this was what the Court Service used at that time, and LIX developed into FELIX, with a variety of open and closed conferences, a messaging system which allowed for the attachment of files, and the facility for posting longer files centrally, available for draw-down by any judge who wished to read them. The laptops, supplied by Siemens Nixdorf, who provided helpdesk support, had a 186 central processing unit, which seemed at that time to be powerful enough for any foreseeable judicial future.

This pilot scheme was a success, and with the help of a convincing business case JUDITH in 1993 chopped off the head of Holofernes, in the form of Treasury scepticism, and sufficient money was allocated to provide for a total of 300 judges over a three-year period. During this time an additional tranche of money enabled the Project to acquire 120 more powerful Pentium desktop computers, equipped with Windows software and CD-Rom drives. The Court Service had by now changed to Word for Windows, so that this was supplied as well. The Pentiums were allocated to computer-literate volunteers who thought they could cope with this equipment without training support. This freed up most of their laptops for redistribution to judges on the steadily increasing waiting list.

Towards the end of 1995 the Project started running into difficulties. It had been a huge success, so far as most of the participants were concerned, but certain problems were already evident, and the Government required a new consultants' report, and a business case based on the consultants' recommendations, to justify any further expenditure. At the same time the newly created Court Service Agency was having to turn to the equally new Private Finance Initiative ('PFI') to support investment like this, and 1996 was consumed by the consultants' investigations and the tendering process aimed at identifying the new PFI supplier.

In the meantime, about 100 more judges who possessed their own computers were supplied with the FELIX software and a modem. By this time FELIX had been developed for Windows users, and WordPerfect 6.1 for DOS was supplied to the JUDITH judges who still possessed their original laptops. By the end of 1996 380 judges – one third of the total – had their JUDITH computers. There were another 200 on the waiting list.

The consultants, Joyce Plotnikoff and Richard Woolfson, stated, in unqualified terms, that the achievements of the Project to date had been impressive. Everybody they had met was of the view that it had made a significant and valuable contribution. Descriptions of it included the epithets 'resounding', 'brilliant' and 'tremendously valuable'.

Two innovations which potentially had wide application in both the civil and criminal process were the ability of some judges to generate copies of their orders and directions in court and to distribute them to the parties on the spot, and the use of computers to expedite the process of releasing cases from a High Court judge to a circuit judge approved to handle High Court cases.

They also reported that the arrival of FELIX had had a profound effect on judges' ability to communicate with each other, particularly for those judges who sat outside London. The Project had been instrumental in changing many judges' attitudes to the use of technology from scepticism to enthusiasm. Until July 1996 it had cost only £1.6m (excluding Court Service staff costs), or rather less than £4,000 for every judge involved.

The consultants also identified a number of concerns which had long been obvious to many of us. First among these was the need to provide resources for training, since the Project Board had never been resourced for training judges (some of whom had very limited computer skills) in a properly structured and professional way.

Other criticisms related to the Project's lack of structure or focus (which was inevitable owing to the comparative lack of staff support), problems created by the wide variety of different applications which individual judges added to their systems, and problems connected with the use of helpdesk support, lack of user discipline, the poor motivation of some of those to whom equipment was initially issued (leading to its non-use), and a number of different types of concern about security.

Many of the computers allocated to the Project in its early days were incapable of being upgraded. By 1997 these could be treated for all practical purposes as obsolete. The power and capacity of the Pentium desktops provided a clearer indication of the likely scale of judges' computer needs in future.

The reason why things stood still between 1995 and 1999 was not for want of judicial enthusiasm. The impasse stemmed from factors wholly outside judicial control – the hiatus created by the switch to the PFI as the means of financing public sector projects of this type, the Treasury's curious belief (never, it seems, debated in Parliament) that subject to a few exemptions the whole of the civil and family justice systems could reasonably be expected to pay for themselves, and the adoption of cost-benefit formulae much more suited to measuring the value of back-office as opposed to front-office systems.

Perhaps more important was the realisation that future provision for the judiciary should lie in the creation of an Intranet, with the judges' terminals being serviced from central sources, rather than a proliferation of standalone PCs, each equipped with their own software and their own CD-Roms. Although this need was clearly perceived in 1996, very little progress was made towards networking the courts until 2002, and eventually an expensive new generation of standalone PCs had to be ordered, following a four-year standstill.

It was appreciated from the outset that the adoption of policies based on an Intranet would throw up its own set of problems, since judges are not deskbound office-workers. They spend much of their days in court, and many use their computers for judicial duties at home in the evenings and at weekends. Any forward planning had to take these considerations on board. Of 79 judges who answered a survey in 1996, 27 said they used their computers in court, 69 in chambers, 9 in judges' lodgings, 11 while travelling and 71 at home: these figures were not, of course, cumulative. 81% of those who responded said they made use of the portable nature of their machines.

In 1997 the main judicial needs were summarised as:

- word-processing and note-taking in court
- communications with other judges and court administrators
- access to on-line databases (or, for the time being, CD-Roms)
- judicial case-management

So far as word-processing and note-taking were concerned, many judges could not now do their job without their word-processor, and a small, but increasing, number were using their laptops for taking notes in court. None of the 550 circuit judges, the 330 district judges or the other members of the full-time judiciary below the High Court bench were provided with clerks or secretaries, and for many of them the computer had become an essential part of their working kit. At this time we had to plan for a change from DOS-based WordPerfect software to Windows-based Word software, with all the transitional difficulties this would bring, particularly when resources for training in the past had been so scarce.

When I sat in the Court of Appeal for seven weeks in April-May 1997 to clear 130 outstanding appeals and applications concerned with Ord 17 r 11 of the County Court Rules, we used FELIX to obtain useful information from district judges about the continuing problems they were encountering over the application of this difficult rule. In the continuing absence of a network at the Royal Courts of Justice, we also used FELIX to circulate drafts of our judgment (in *Bannister v SGB plc*) to each other, and as one of the three tools we used (the others being the Internet, and the despatch of hard copies of the 70-page judgment to every main county court centre in the country) to ensure that every judge exercising civil jurisdiction in the county court would have access to a copy of the judgment within a week after it was delivered.

The consultants had also prepared a complementary report in 1997 which described the way in which technology might be harnessed in aid of judicial services in future. They said that the challenge now was to create the organisational structures to realise this vision of the future. Some fundamental issues had to be resolved first:

> Who should speak for the judiciary and how could they represent the whole range of judicial opinion within a single coherent view?
>
> What priority would be given to judicial needs in discussion with the new PFI contractor given that the funding must come out of the Court Service budget?
>
> How would the needs of the legal profession and other justice system agencies be taken into account?

They observed that in an integrated approach the services to be provided would have to be costed and prioritised according to the benefits they delivered to the justice system as a whole. These benefits might take the form of cost savings or speedier case processing, but they might also result from improvements in the quality of justice. The discussion of these issues would have to encompass, in particular, the ways in which judges could work more effectively alongside court and administrative staff. It should also take account of the examples of good practice encountered during their study. The courts' library services and the Judicial Studies Board would have to be included in the discussion. They said, correctly, that integrating these different strands into a coherent strategy would require an understanding of the court environment, the judicial function and the technological options.

The scale of the continuing cultural difficulties we faced was recorded in a long paper I wrote in the autumn of 1997, soon after I succeeded Lord Saville as the Court of Appeal judge responsible for identifying and championing the judiciary's short- and medium-term needs. By this time the Court Service had appointed two of its senior officials as project sponsors (for civil and criminal justice respectively), and each had a projects evaluation team reporting to them. The job of these teams was to identify the requirements of their business in sufficient detail to provide the basis for discussing an overall strategy for IT developments with the Court Service's newly appointed PFI contractors.

In 1996 a judges' group had been formed with the aim of providing some judicial input into the work of these teams (for example, explaining what was needed to ensure compliance with the Rules of Court). In its early days at least, the extent and effect of this consultation was patchy, although things improved as Court Service staff got used to the quite novel idea of judges working with them. In the autumn of 1997 a new Judicial Technology Group (JTG) was created under Lord Saville's chairmanship. This had the aim of providing a more sharply focussed vehicle for collaboration. At its first meeting the two Court Service project sponsors affirmed their conviction that effective consultation with the judiciary in IT matters affecting the delivery of judicial services was absolutely essential. This positive declaration, made 11 years after ITAC was created, marked a milestone in the relations between the judiciary and the staff who served them.

Within the US federal judicial system, and in many other comparable jurisdictions, a high level IT sub-committee of the Court Service Board would be chaired by a senior judge. Judges would also head the teams selecting and overseeing the different projects. Under the arrangements we were devising any judicial input would have to come to the Court Service's IT sub-committee indirectly via the judicial members of JTG. These were very busy judges, some of them with a good deal of IT know-how but with no effective staff support and no budgetary responsibility for any of the decisions that were to be made. I described in my 1997 paper how the experiences of ITAC and its Civil Litigation Working Party (which I founded and chaired between 1991 and 1996) showed clearly that arrangements like this left the judges, who are at the apex of the system which delivers judicial services to the citizen, with a very superficial and unsatisfactory role. Those who took part in liaison meetings with Court Service staff were given no administrative backup at all. They were expected to do all the necessary work (apart from attending meetings) in their own time. The documentation they were asked to read and comment on could be quite bulky. Much of the next four years was spent in a search for solutions for these difficulties.

Examples abounded of the problems stemming from the absence of effective liaison in the past. Things had sometimes gone badly wrong when the development of IT systems for the courts took place without proper consultation with the judiciary. There was, for instance, a serious lack of liaison between Court Service staff and a group of district judges who had been involved in developing a system called DataCase. These judges had been assured that this system would be closely examined and that full advantage would be taken of the work they had done and the solutions they had found. They would also be consulted before any final decisions were made.

In the event they were not consulted at all, and they later discovered that the installation of DataCase which they had put in place at the Court Service's headquarters had never even been run, let alone studied. Events then conspired to rob their efforts of any real value. Despite an early spectacular failure of the new 'system' called CASEMAN, which was then being piloted for use in the back offices of county courts, it was by now too late to modify the pilot version to any meaningful extent before its roll-out. As soon as it was rolled out, the Private Finance Initiative was in place. As a result only a few further modifications could be made, so that the PFI contract, which embraced over 200 county courts, was based on the system's existing functionality. Modifications the judges had been assured would be put in place had still not been made a year later. Immediately after this, what the Association of District Judges described as 'the Attachment of Earnings fiasco' occurred.

These events give me the opportunity to pay tribute to the enormous contribution made by a few highly skilled district judges, in particular Richard Stevens OBE, Bill Vincent, Stephen Gerlis, Stephen Greenwood and Geoff Edwards, to the development of technology for our court system over the last 10 years.

Another long-running difficulty resulted from the fact that CASEMAN's order production systems from time to time generated orders which departed from the requirements of the Rules or from the intention of the judge who made the order. This was because those who designed the templates and the logic for using them were not lawyers, and they did not take advantage of the advice from experienced judges which they knew (or ought to have known) was on offer. The correction of these mistakes turned out to be a slow and expensive business. At the first meeting of the new Judicial Technology Group judges and senior officials alike resolved that they would learn from these mistakes. We agreed not to dwell on them any longer in the new collaborative atmosphere that had now emerged.

Between 1997 and 1999 two major processes were under way. The first was the development of the plans for what became known as the JT (judicial technology) project. Treasury sanction was obtained towards the end of 1998 for the provision of 1,000 modern laptop computers, to be supplied to the judiciary by the PFI contractors under three-year leases. The specification was superior to that of the old JUDITH laptops, and on this occasion the arrangements included the provision of three days' initial training for every judge, unless it was obvious that this was not needed. Windows NT and Word 97 were the main features of the new specification, together with the indefatigable FELIX, some of whose features proved difficult for novice judges to master. Sadly, no provision was made for follow-up training for these novices.

The first tranche of 1,000 PCs were delivered between January 1999 and July 2000. By this time the approach of the Human Rights Act 1998 had led the department to approve arrangements whereby the judiciary was provided with Internet access via a specially designed portal. By this means judges, wherever they were sitting, could access the database of judgments of the European Court of Human Rights, and a very large volume of case law and statutory material. This development excited the interest of many judges who had not hitherto chosen to join the scheme, and approval was given for the purchase of a further 200 JT laptops. Since then, arrangements have been made for the surrender of laptops by judges when they retire, and for the provision of JT laptops, together with initial training, to new judges within a few months of their appointment to the bench.

At the same time valiant, but in the end wholly abortive, efforts were made by the Court Service to deliver IT systems in support of Lord Woolf's civil justice reforms. The then Head of Civil Justice, Sir Richard Scott, believed strongly that these reforms should not be implemented until IT systems were in place to give the procedural judges the support they badly needed if they were to maintain effective judicial control from the centre. This wish was never susceptible of fulfilment. For one thing, the new rules and practice directions were forever being changed, and IT systems designers needed a period of stability in which to do their work. For another, there was insufficient know-how available on how to design an intricate set of new systems without the risk of another very expensive failure.

The judges on JTG, advised by Professor Richard Susskind, became increasingly anxious about what might happen. The systems that were being designed could not possibly have supported the more sophisticated modern systems that were bound to be needed in future. We feared that designers might be planning another one-storey building, like CREST and CASEMAN (and its half-sister FAMILYMAN), with shallow foundations on which nothing could be built on top. Our vision was of a 12-storey building, in which an electronic court file, serving the needs of the trial judge, would in due course take pride of place.

Eventually the Government decided to implement the reforms on 26 April 1999 without waiting for the IT systems to be put in place. Minor enhancements were made to the existing (wholly inadequate) systems, and for a short time additional court staff were allocated to help with the increasing load of paper the reforms would bring in their wake. In the Central Office at the Royal

Courts of Justice, for instance, case files had to be created for the first time since those courts were opened in 1882. The paper mountain then grew and grew.

In the event, it turned out to be a wise decision to implement the reforms without waiting for the IT. In April 1999 the Court Service Board, led by their new chief executive, Ian Magee, bravely decided to stop all the development work and to devote their energies instead to some fundamental thinking about the way the civil and family courts should be delivering their business, and the role IT should play. Their decision was undoubtedly correct. Inevitably, however, it created a situation in which those courts faced very serious problems indeed because the judges applying the new procedural rules did not have the IT support they badly needed.

By now the gospel ITAC had been preaching ever since its formation in 1986 had become the accepted wisdom. The delivery of justice to the citizen in the modern world required the support of integrated IT systems. Initially the Court Service set out to deliver these systems piecemeal, with one set of arrangements being made for the criminal courts through what became known as the Crown Court Programme, and another set of arrangements being made for the civil and family courts. In addition, the 12 groups of administrative tribunals for which the Lord Chancellor was responsible were being managed under quite separate arrangements.

It was now taken for granted that there would be proper judicial involvement in all this planning. In its early days the projects within the Crown Court Programme were quite modest. They involved testing the capabilities of electronic presentation of evidence ('EPE'), digital audio recording, and video conferencing within the Crown Court setting. Plans were also prepared for the IT infrastructure needed by a modern Crown Court. Three circuit judges with great experience of criminal justice were on the boards overseeing these projects. A different project, financed by the Home Office, piloted the use of video links between a few criminal courts and their local prisons, a concept in which I had tried to interest the Home Office as long ago as 1986.

So far as civil and family justice was concerned, the new Court Service review threw up some challenging ideas about the way that local justice should be administered in future. Our civil and family court system has grown up and developed in a very haphazard way since a network of 497 county courts was first introduced in 1846. There have been huge shifts in population movement.

New towns have grown up. Densely populated city centres have been deserted. Often a court closure occurred for no better reason than the expiry of a lease. There was little strategic thinking about the optimal location, or the essential function, of the courts.

The review compelled us to think whether our civil and family courts were in the right place, and whether they were all accessible by public transport. Were all the functions they performed a necessary part of the functions of a court? Could their advisory role be performed more effectively, and inexpensively, by other means? Were the links between the family jurisdictions of the magistrates' courts and of the county courts working sensibly? How should the courts in the Royal Courts of Justice complex relate to the other civil and family courts in the Greater London area and beyond?

Then there were questions about the roles the judges were now required to play. Overall, there are many more judges in the lower level of the judicial hierarchy than there were 15 years ago. Judges are an expensive resource: far more expensive than the staff who serve them. Were we really making best use of judges' times and skills? A clear message emerged that judges were spending far too much of their time sorting out muddled court files, or waiting for the information they needed, or doing things that could be done just as well by court staff or by technology. One then had to ask whether court staff were being provided with the training and the technology they needed, and what could be done to improve job satisfaction, for staff and judges alike, throughout the court system.

All these early questions threw up another set of questions. What are the best ways in which information and communications technology can help judges and court staff? How can judges obtain secure electronic access to court files and lists and diaries so that they can manage their cases more effectively? What is the future of tele-conferencing and video conferencing and e-mail conferencing? What about voice-activated word-processing? On the back office side of things, how much court information can be sent to a central databank (which does not take up expensive space in a prime downtown location), to be called up by judges and court staff when needed? What are the confidentiality problems over public access to electronic court files? How much time and money will be saved if information is stored electronically and not manually? What are the implications for staff morale and motivation?

During the course of 2000 I joined the Court Service's Modernising the Civil Courts ('MCC') Programme Board. A senior judge had never previously been appointed to an executive board of this type. It was symbolic of an immense culture shift within a single decade whereby the power of IT had forced judges and administrators to work so much more closely together. My appointment stemmed from a request made in June 1999 to Ian Magee by the then Lord Chief Justice, Lord Bingham, to the effect that judges should be brought closer to the centre of the Court Service's decision-making processes. During 2000 a number of pilot projects were initiated in civil courts, along the same lines as the pilot projects in the Crown Courts, but with greatly reduced financing, and early in 2001 a public consultation paper sought views on the way the Court Service's thinking was moving. The response to this paper was very encouraging.

In August 2001 a representative judicial working group, led by Mr Justice Cresswell (who had led the Bar's response to the Civil Justice Review 14 years earlier), published a report called 'The Judges' Requirements'. These five judges had been provided with a small amount of consultancy help, and they were given appropriate 'judge-release' time so that they did not have to do all their work in the evenings and at weekends. At the beginning of their report they described some of the problems every judge in the country faces every day. The list began: 'Insufficient staff – high staff turnover leading to the use of inexperienced staff – missing or chaotic files – court orders take too long to be drawn and are often drawn incorrectly – lack of proper administrative support for the judiciary'. Later on in the list they said that very few members of court staff had real IT expertise, and that there was a chronic lack of funds even for basic equipment. Senior Court Service managers would not disagree with the broad thrust of this analysis. Indeed, the MCC consultation paper had spoken in similar terms.

These judges concluded that there was a pressing need for common computerised information systems to be introduced as soon as possible across all the civil and family courts in England and Wales. They added that these common information systems should extend to criminal business. They also described the need for our administrative tribunals to benefit from this common approach. In a very important part of their report they described the four interlinked systems which lay at the heart of their proposals: the electronic case record; the electronic case management system; the electronic diary; and the electronic file.

In a speech I made at the Foundation for Science and Technology towards the end of 2001 I described the central message of this report in these terms:

> 'Court administrators know all about the back-office problems. We judges know all about what I will call the "front-office" problems. Under court modernisation, the front office and the back office will be jointly networked for the first time. If at the end of a hearing, the judge wants to fix the next appointment for a hearing, he will be able to call up the diary system from his computer on the bench and fix a new date there and then. In Appendix 5 of their report the five judges gave three worked up examples of how this provision would enable them to provide a much better service for litigants.
>
> In one of these examples, a five-day case settles unexpectedly a week before the hearing date. The electronic diary is then used to interrogate the system to see if there are any over-bookings at that court or at neighbouring courts to fill the judge's list. Three possibilities are identified. E-mail messages are sent to the solicitors in each case to ask whether the cases are still effective. When told that they are, the system spots that there is a disabled litigant in one of them, and earmarks a ground floor courtroom for that case. The system can also check that the new cases will be assigned to a judge who is appropriately qualified to hear them. The court diary arrangements are updated to show the new listing arrangements. The parties' solicitors are then informed by e-mail of the new arrangements.
>
> At present every step in that process is done slowly and inefficiently by telephone and a card index system. In a modernised court every step could be taken automatically. Alternatively, some of these steps could be made subject to judicial decision, or the decision of a court administrator of appropriate seniority. If a more senior judge has to be involved, his authority can be sought and given electronically from the faraway court at which he is sitting. All of this is light years away from the present ways of doing these things.'

In the meantime, and in part driven by the logic emerging from the judges' work, the different strands of the Court Service's modernisation plans were woven together into what became known as the Courts and Tribunals Modernisation Programme. Lord Woolf, now Lord Chief Justice, gave me the formal title of 'Judge in charge of Modernisation', with the authority to speak for the judges of England and Wales, and the new Programme Board met for the first time in the early summer of 2001. It had been allotted about £160m for the 2001-2004 period. One of its early tasks was to prepare the case to the Treasury for the funding needed to drive the modernisation programme forward between 2003 and 2006.

Judicial involvement in all this planning was achieved by the creation of five new judicial advisory groups, each dedicated to a different aspect of the programme: training and knowledge management, hardware and infrastructure, in-court technology and so on. Two large 24-hour judicial conferences (the second led by Lord Woolf and the other Heads of Division) were arranged to achieve a measure of judicial 'buy-in' to the programme, and in February 2002 the 30 (or so) members of the new advisory groups met for an all-day seminar, in order to understand how the work of their group fitted into the wider picture.

I have described another part of the programme in these words:

> 'An important part of the new strategy is concerned with handling much more of this undefended back-office work electronically. Many more actions will start electronically, and will be dealt with electronically unless and until resistance is shown. At that stage the electronic file will be sent electronically to a place where staff and judges will also handle it electronically.
>
> We are also now starting to test what is called e-filing in pilot schemes. There has been a lot of American experience with this. The essence of it is that anyone will be able to issue a money claim from his home computer or his business computer. He will pay the fee and send the claim off electronically to the Court Service at any time of the day or night. The Court Service will then authenticate and issue the claim, so that many more people and businesses will have the benefits now only available to major creditors. This will take quite a load off court staff.'

A few pilot schemes involving court technology were by now under way. The PREMA project, an early experiment in electronic communications with a court, was launched at Preston in the spring of 2001. The only court-based IT equipment at that large centre consisted of the networked dumb terminals used for CASEMAN and CREST, and the judges' standalone laptops. The MCC programme provided funding for four networked PCs. Solicitors could now correspond with the court by e-mail for a variety of simple applications. In the event the service was greatly under-used. One local firm of solicitors were enthusiastic devotees of PREMA, and within 18 months three other users (including the Blackpool office of the Official Receiver) had each used the service more than 10 times. In general, however, there was the same cultural reluctance to embark on the unknown as has characterised English lawyers' approach to most technological innovations over the last 15 years.

It may well be that this service will become more popular once it can be used for a wider range of solicitors' work. It is surprising, however, that the value of arrangements whereby solicitors can obtain a consent order releasing their clients' funds in less than two days as opposed to 20 (under the current manual arrangements) has not become more widely appreciated.

In September 2001 a new information system called XHIBIT was launched at the Chelmsford Crown Court. This had been developed as a result of discussions between the different criminal justice agencies, all of whom have an interest in knowing the progress a Crown Court trial is making. Witnesses need to get to court at the right time, police officers who have to give evidence should not be taken away from their other duties for too long, those who are concerned in the next case in the list have an interest in knowing whether the current trial is running to time, and so on.

XHIBIT is a web-based system which depends on someone keeping a log of events in court. These events are then transmitted instantaneously to the XHIBIT screen. By way of example they may include: prosecution opening speech; prosecution lay evidence; police evidence; defence evidence; closing submissions by the prosecution; judge's summing up; jury in retirement; verdict; sentencing. The information on XHIBIT is accessible on monitor screens in the public parts of the court building, and also on the website of the Crown Court. Text messages can also be sent to people who need to be warned when to attend court. In due course XHIBIT was extended to two other Crown Courts in the Essex area. In March 2003 it is likely to be installed at the Snaresbrook Crown Court centre in north-east London, where a full IT infrastructure has now been installed, and where digital audio recording is currently being tested.

For some time now, evidence has been presented electronically in very long criminal trials. Anyone visiting the trial of Kevin and Ian Maxwell, for instance, would have seen two monitor screens. The first showed the raw Livenote transcript scrolling up a few seconds after the witness's words were uttered. The other generally showed the witness's face (because it was a very large court), but when use was made of the facility to exhibit a document on the screen, everyone in court could read it, too. Zoom facilities enable the operator to highlight those features which a party wants the jury to see, such as a signature, or the manuscript writing on a document. Juries like this kind of presentation. Its use also saves an immense amount of court time. If any of the parties want the document printed and put in the jury bundle, this can easily be done.

In American courts it is now becoming very common to demonstrate the effect of evidence by the use of PowerPoint or other similar technology. Those who use it know how much more quickly the eye (as opposed to the ear) absorbs complicated information.

The possibilities of EPE are now being addressed in a systematic way. Nine Crown Courts were originally earmarked for trials of this equipment, and although some of the cases for which its use was planned ended quickly with pleas of guilty, an increasing volume of practical know-how has already been built up.

Under the MCC programme four civil court centres were equipped with video-conferencing facilities, and a few other courts paid for it out of their own resources. Experience is already demonstrating its value for a number of different types of case. For trials it is being used where a witness is abroad, or is seriously disabled, or is a long way away from the court and it would be disproportionately expensive for him/her to travel there. For pre-trial hearings it is being used where one of the party's lawyers is a long way from the court where the hearing is being conducted, or where an urgent order has to be sought from a judge at a distant court.

In criminal courts video-conferencing is being increasingly used for links with prisons. A successful pilot experiment between four courts (including a Crown Court) and their local prisons led to this facility being extended to magistrates' courts throughout the country in 2002. This technology has also been used for some time for the evidence of child witnesses, and for foreign witnesses in criminal fraud cases. In July 2002 its use was extended when legislation was implemented whereby vulnerable or intimidated witnesses were permitted to give evidence in a criminal court by a video link.

Experience has shown, however, that unless the equipment is very good, the evidence of a witness over a videolink for the purposes of a trial does not have the same immediacy as when the witness gives evidence in court. Some criminal judges believe that juries have acquitted in cases where they might well have convicted if they had actually seen the complainant child witness give evidence from the witness-box. In September 2002 the relevant judicial advisory group published a paper which demonstrated the value of this technology, but advocated the adoption of a more strategic approach for developing its use in our courts, instead of the piecemeal arrangements which have dominated the scene so far.

An e-filing project called MCOL ('Money Claims On-Line') was launched in February 2002 for the purpose I described in my Foundation speech. An individual creditor could now obtain a default judgment and apply for a warrant of execution on-line through this service. Claims of up to £100,000 could be issued against up to two defendants, and within six months 75 claims were being processed through this service every day. Plans are now in train to make it easier for solicitors to use the service, with monthly invoicing rather than insistence on the use of a credit card for each transaction, and to enable defendants to respond to the claims on-line.

At Walsall, the Court Service is developing a pilot business centre close to the county court. In September 2002 all that was visible there were large stretches of unoccupied carpet and about 30 networked workstations, fitted with basic CASEMAN, FAMILYMAN and Microsoft Office systems in a Windows environment. The purpose of this project is to test the concept of a business centre, separated in distance from a court hearing centre, which would deal with all the correspondence and accounting work of the court, and relieve the staff at the hearing centre from all their responsibilities other than those involved in assisting judges to hear defended cases. In due course this pilot centre will also take over the business functions of some neighbouring county courts as well.

An important part of these plans involves the creation of an electronic diary, accessible to judges and court staff alike (save that the private sections of the judges' diary will be barred from general access). In this early experiment Microsoft Outlook will be used to provide this functionality in a fairly basic way. For how many more years judges and court staff will have to wait for the vital help described by the judges in their August 2001 report is at present unclear.

In May 2002 I delivered a public lecture about our modernisation plans. During the course of it I said:

> 'Far and away our greatest need is to introduce software systems which will enable court staff and judges to manage court business better in the civil and family courts. Today the courts are not networked. CREST and CASEMAN link dumb computer terminals with a court database,

> but we are miles behind most government departments and modern private sector businesses. Our aim is to lop off the business sections of the civil courts, and to enable those courts to concentrate on their real purpose: hearing defended cases. The back-office business will be diverted to new business centres, linked to the courts by IT. The first of these business centres will start on a pilot basis in the Midlands this autumn.
>
> In the autumn we also hope that testing will have begun for the new software systems we will use in future in all our courts. At present we rely on paper filing systems. It is not always easy to retain and motivate staff when files go missing, or get into a muddle quite so often. Nowadays court users have every reason to complain about some of the delays and inefficiencies that occur. Once modern software is in place, court staff and judges with case-management responsibilities will be able to handle cases far more efficiently before trial than is possible today. A modern electronic diary and listing system will enable trial dates to be fixed more quickly and judges' time to be more effectively used.'

On St Swithin's Day 2002 the Government published its spending plans up to April 2006. Very significant sums of money were earmarked for IT in the criminal justice system. Within the next three years IT infrastructure should be installed in all our Crown Court centres. Attention has also been paid to the need for information to flow more easily between the different agencies in the criminal justice system, a need first trumpeted by ITAC in 1986. But it is not at all clear to me how the courts will be able to accommodate this information if their much-needed 'enabling applications' cannot be developed for lack of finance.

So far as our civil and family courts are concerned, after all this careful planning we seem to have struck that long snake close to the top of the Snakes and Ladders Board. We have been sent back a long way, and the morale of the judges and of the staff who serve them so devotedly is bound to be badly affected. On the evening of the spending review announcement the Treasury published a description of the objectives of the Lord Chancellor's Department. It did not even mention the modernisation of our civil and family courts. How much progress can be made from the general funds allotted to the department will become clearer later in 2002. But most of the relief we hoped that technology would bring to our very hard-pressed civil and family court judges and their staff will not be available. Whether 'jam tomorrow' will ever turn into 'jam today' remains to be seen.

In other words, within two months it had become clear that the central hopes I had expressed in my May lecture had been dashed. As things stand, for the next four years none of our courts will have the benefit of the technology described in the judges' report, other than in a fairly rudimentary form. Those who develop our pilot business centre will probably be able to go no further than doing their best to adapt a common form Microsoft Office product instead of installing the much more sophisticated electronic systems the judges said were necessary. It is common knowledge that the old back-office 'systems', CREST (whose initial design goes back to 1986) and CASEMAN, simply do not possess the functionality to serve the linked diary and electronic case file, case management and case record systems that today's courts so desperately need, although I understand that efforts are being made to provide some kind of link.

It would be wrong, however, to despair too much. In this chapter I have described the huge strides forward that our relatively conservative judicial and administrative cultures have made since Brian Neill's voice in the wilderness first cried of the need for clear, joined-up thinking about the value of applied technology in the court system. Those who were then fast asleep have now become half ready to meet these challenges. In July 2002 other social needs were adjudged by our rulers to have a higher priority than the need to provide a system of justice for the citizen which is not totally overwhelmed by mountains of paper. Perhaps in my lifetime, if not now in my judicial lifetime, a brighter future will really arrive.[1]

Addendum

The editors have allowed me to write a short addendum to this essay. The plans to install an IT infrastructure into all our Crown Courts are now rolling forward, and valiant efforts are being made to assemble sufficient resources to carry out a similar exercise in all those civil courts that have a long-term future. On the bright side, the Court Service is doing its best to maintain its long-term goals, although we will now have to muddle along in all our courts for a few more years with case-handling software which is not up to the job. More depressingly, there are indications that a scattergun approach is now being adopted to meet the case-handling needs of our criminal courts, instead of the integrated approach that was central to our planning. There is still a very long way to go, but the future is not all dark.[2]

1 30 September 2002.
2 30 November 2002.

Information technology and a public inquiry

Mark Saville

Some years ago I came to believe that information technology properly applied had the potential to make great improvements to our justice system. In great measure my belief was fostered by Brian Neill, who long before me became convinced of this, at a time when most others were indifferent if not indeed sceptical.

Time has proved Brian Neill to have been right; for though budgetary and similar considerations have slowed progress, there is now general acceptance of the proposition for which he fought so hard and for so long.

It is of course very easy to be carried away by information technology. It is a most exciting development and I rejoice that I live in times when its progress is at such a remarkable and increasing speed. However this means that it is easy to get overwhelmed with that excitement, so it is vital that we constantly have in mind the end result that we are trying to achieve.

This again is something that Brian Neill has always emphasised. In the context of justice systems, indeed in the context of any form of human activity, doing something in a new or different way is not an end in itself. 'If it ain't broke, don't fix it' is a sound rule.

Justice is one of the most important parts of a democratic society. But however good our substantive laws may be, and however independent and impartial our judges, justice is not done if legal processes take too long, if they are too expensive for people to use, or if they are not sufficiently accessible. The fact is that these shortcomings have existed and continue to exist in our justice system. Delay, cost, and inaccessibility are in fact injustices and thus things that need fixing. What Brian Neill appreciated before most others was that the proper application of information technology could provide a new and better way of tackling these faults in our justice system. He also appreciated that by this means justice could not only be done but be seen by all to be done.

It so happens that over the last five years I have been given a unique opportunity to demonstrate what can be achieved. In 1998 I was appointed as Chairman of a public inquiry into something that happened in Northern Ireland over 30 years ago. That inquiry is still continuing.

To put the inquiry into context it is necessary to set out some of the background to the particular events with which we are concerned. This can only be done in the most general of terms, since there are aspects of that background that may be in dispute in the inquiry, and on which I cannot form any final view until we have heard and considered all the evidence and submissions.

Northern Ireland is part of the UK. It is a small part of the island of Ireland, about the same size as the state of Connecticut. The rest of the island is the independent country of Ireland; also known as Eire or the Irish Republic. The whole of the island used to be part of the UK, but in 1921 Eire became an independent state.

The island of Ireland has had an unhappy history, with an unhappy relationship with Great Britain. One result has been a division in that island along sectarian lines. This is known nowadays as the sectarian divide, but what in truth that means is that between Catholics and Protestants there has been great fear, hatred and mistrust; and a significant lack of tolerance or willingness to compromise.

The majority of people in the island of Ireland have been Catholic, but for historical reasons there is in the north a substantial and majority Protestant population. These people did not want to be independent. They wanted to remain part of the UK and did not want to become part of a Catholic country. So when after the First World War the British Government decided to give Ireland its independence, it was confronted with the problem of what to do about the people there who did not want it. This was a serious problem, because this part of the population was so opposed to leaving Britain that any attempt to make them do so would undoubtedly have led to a civil war in Ireland.

The solution that was adopted was to divide the island into two parts, leaving the six counties in the north that had a predominately Protestant population as part of Britain. That is why the present full name of the country is the United Kingdom of Great Britain and Northern Ireland.

This division may have been the only solution at the time, but it was far from perfect. The Irish in the south thought it wrong that part of what they regarded as their island should remain British. Furthermore, though in a minority, there was a large Catholic population in the north, who thought the same. The Protestant majority in the north held the view that they were and should remain British. Since they were the majority, they dominated the provincial government of Northern Ireland and were determined to do everything in their power to keep Northern Ireland part of Britain. The Catholic population regarded itself as the subject of religious discrimination, treated in effect as second class citizens in many respects, including the areas of housing and jobs.

The problem did not go away. There were those in Ireland who thought that if they used violent methods, they could achieve union with the rest of the island. They believed that Britain was clinging onto Northern Ireland as one of its colonies and that they could and should use force to fight the colonial power (as other colonies had done) in order to achieve their aim of a united independent Ireland.

Matters came to a head in the 1960s. That was a decade when the concept of violent action in support of civil rights swept across the world. Northern Ireland was no exception. The Irish Republican Army (terrorists or freedom fighters, depending on your point of view) grew in strength and engaged in increasingly violent and deadly activities.

This violence grew. The police began to lose control and in 1969 the Northern Ireland Government asked the British Government to send troops to help to keep order. This was done and at first the Catholic population in Northern Ireland welcomed the soldiers, thinking that they would act to protect them from what they perceived to be a government and police force intent only in keeping them subjugated. But the violence continued and in the course of it a number of Catholics were killed and injured, leading the Catholic population in the main to believe that the soldiers were simply the agents of the Northern Ireland Government, no better than the police.

In August 1971 the Northern Ireland Government decided to introduce internment without trial of suspected terrorists, expressing the view that this was the only feasible means of reducing violence and restoring law and order.

The Northern Ireland Government introduced a ban on marches. This infuriated both sections of the sectarian divide. The Protestants were prohibited from conducting their traditional marches; while those who wished to march in support of civil rights were also prohibited from doing so. The reason given for prohibiting all marches was to reduce the opportunity for the violence which, sadly, so often accompanied these events.

Notwithstanding this prohibition, the Northern Ireland Civil Rights Association decided to hold a civil rights march in January 1972, in the city of Londonderry. This small city, which many call Derry, lies in the far west of Northern Ireland, close to the border with the Republic.

It appears that the authorities decided to stop this march from reaching its publicised objective, the City Guildhall, using the army to do so. The city had been the scene of violent riots over the preceding months and of deadly attacks by the IRA on the security forces. Much of the city lay in ruins. The authorities used the army to set up barriers, so as to keep the march in the Catholic areas of the city, known as the Creggan and the Bogside.

The march took place on Sunday, 30 January 1972. It would seem that many of those who marched that day were intent on making a peaceful protest, but there were others, mostly young people, who engaged in rioting and stoning the troops manning the barriers. Between about ten to four and twenty past four that afternoon a number of people were killed and injured through army gunfire on the streets of the city. The circumstances in which this occurred are matters of great controversy and form the subject-matter of the present inquiry.

Within a very short time the British Government announced that there would be a public inquiry into the matter, to be conducted by Lord Widgery, then the Lord Chief Justice of England. In a matter of weeks this inquiry produced a report, which many on the Catholic side of the sectarian divide categorised as a cover-up and whitewash of the actions of the soldiers. They expressed the belief that in truth the soldiers had deliberately shot dead innocent people, some indeed alleging that this had been done on instructions from those in government.

The years passed. The violence continued. There were many atrocities. Over the last 30 years people continued to be killed and injured, as the result of violence not just by the IRA, but by those in the Protestant population who also thought that violence was the way to solve the problem as they saw it, as well as deaths and injuries arising from the actions of the security forces. The British and Irish Governments made attempt after attempt to try and work out a peaceful solution, acceptable to all. Finally in 1998 a peace agreement was reached, though on both sides of the sectarian divide there remain those who are violently opposed to this peace process.

Over 3,500 people have died violently over the last 30 years as a result of the troubles in Northern Ireland. But to the Catholic population that Sunday in January 1972, which immediately became known across the world as 'Bloody Sunday', remains of particular and special importance, not just because of the deaths and injuries on that day, but also because of the belief that the inquiry held immediately afterwards was an unforgivable denial of justice. Many continued to campaign for a new inquiry and finally, in 1998, the British Government, as part of the peace process, agreed to set one up. That is the inquiry that the British Government asked me to chair, and which I am now conducting with the assistance of two judicial colleagues, one from Canada and one from Australia.

This Inquiry was set up by Parliament and is running under the provisions of the Tribunals of Inquiry (Evidence) Act 1921. Its terms of reference are:

> 'to inquire into the events of Sunday, 30 January 1972 which led to loss of life in connection with the procession in Londonderry on that day, taking account of any new information relevant to events on that day.'

With the exception of the last 12 words, the terms of reference are identical to those for the previous inquiry.

There have been about 21 public inquiries under the Tribunals of Inquiry (Evidence) Act 1921. There are also many public inquiries conducted under the provisions of other statutes, for example planning inquiries and the like. It is interesting to note that the 1921 Act started life as a Bill designed to deal with a specific matter (allegations against certain officials in the then Ministry of Munitions) and it was only during its passage through Parliament that it was decided to adapt it so that it could be used in the future in order to set up an independent tribunal to inquire into any matter of urgent public importance.

This was in theory a good idea, since in the past previous inquiries into alleged misconduct by public servants had usually been conducted by a Select Parliamentary Committee or Commission of Inquiry, with the result that there was a tendency for party political considerations and loyalties to play a part in the conclusions reached. This tendency came to a head when a Select Committee was appointed to investigate what was known as the Marconi scandal. In 1912 the Liberal Government had accepted a tender from the English Marconi Company for the construction of a chain of state owned telegraph stations throughout the Empire. There were rumours that the Government had corruptly favoured this company and that certain of its prominent members had improperly profited from this contract. The result of the inquiry was that the majority Liberal members of the Committee produced an exonerating report, while the minority members found that there had been gross impropriety. When the report came to be debated in the House of Commons, the House divided along strictly party lines, with the result that the majority view of the Committee was accepted.

This was the last time a matter of this kind was investigated by a Select Committee. But the haste with which the 1921 legislation appears to have been drafted and passed through Parliament meant that the Act in a number of respects was defective.

In 1966 Lord Justice Salmon (as he then was) was asked to report on inquiries and his report contained a number of recommendations for improvements, (as well as a fascinating summary of the history of inquiries), but the 1921 Act has not been amended and remains as it was originally enacted. However, Lord Justice Salmon also expressed his views on how the proceedings of an inquiry under this Act should be conducted, principally so that the procedure should be fair to all concerned, particularly those in respect of whom serious allegations were being made. These views have become known as 'the Salmon Principles' and as often happens in the law, have tended to become words writ in stone and to take on an almost statutory importance. However, in my view the importance of what Lord Justice Salmon said lies not so much in the procedures he suggested should be adopted, but in the reason for such suggestions, which is to ensure that public inquiries are conducted fairly as well as thoroughly and impartially. I myself believe that the correct procedures for ensuring fairness often depend on the subject matter and form of the particular inquiry in question; and that slavishly to apply the same procedures without regard to their efficacy in any given case is to lose sight of the wood for the trees, and to confuse the means with the end.

Public inquiries of the present kind are inquisitorial in nature, rather than adversarial. As I said in my opening statement in the inquiry, from the point of view of the tribunal, unlike ordinary litigation, there are no sides, nor, again unlike ordinary litigation, is the task of the tribunal to decide which side has put up the better case, acting as sort of referee to ensure that the litigation is conducted within the rules and giving the result at the end of the day. In contrast the task of a tribunal conducting a public inquiry under the 1921 Act is to try itself to seek the truth, in the present case about what happened on Bloody Sunday. It is for the tribunal to take the initiative in trying to discover what happened, by collecting the relevant material, deciding such matters as who should be asked to give oral evidence and (through its counsel) being the principal questioner of the witnesses.

It has sometimes been difficult to maintain the inquisitorial nature of the present inquiry, since there is of course a very sharp division between the families of those who died and the wounded on the one side; and the soldiers (and certain government departments) on the other. The families believe that their relatives were shot and killed or wounded without any justification at all. The soldiers insist that they were reacting to incoming fire from paramilitaries and were, in effect, simply seeking to defend themselves in a proper and lawful way. In addition the families felt that they were allowed neither to be properly represented at the previous inquiry nor given all the relevant evidence available at that inquiry, and so came to the present inquiry with an understandable anxiety that matters should be conducted differently this time round. However, we are convinced that the inquiry must remain inquisitorial in nature, since we alone start with no preconceptions save for our duty to seek the truth with fairness, thoroughness and impartiality. To allow the inquiry to drift into an adversarial battle would, we consider, gravely hamper the search for the truth and leave the tribunal with the risk of deciding instead who had made the better case before it; something that may not correspond with the truth at all. Thus we are not engaged in determining whether the families or the soldiers are right, but in what in fact happened, which may or may not correspond with what they believe and assert took place on that day.

This particular public inquiry has raised formidable problems. Our basic task is to try and discover what happened in those few minutes 30 years ago, but we cannot confine ourselves to the actual incident, since to our minds it can hardly be understood unless it is placed in the context of the overall situation at the time. The present position in Northern Ireland is far from perfect, but it is entirely dissimilar to the situation in 1972, where there were daily bombing and shooting incidents, rioting and arson and violent confrontations with the security forces. Thus we must look at the situation as it developed in Northern Ireland over the months preceding Bloody Sunday, including the plans and actions of the Northern Ireland and British Governments and of the way in which the police and army were used to try and keep order. We must also look at the plans and actions of those who decided to organise a march on that day, as well as the plans and actions of the soldiers. We must also investigate the activities of the paramilitaries, they having been on any view engaged in deadly violence in the city in the days and weeks preceding Bloody Sunday; and, it is alleged, on the day itself. We must of course listen to many of those who took part in the march, to the many journalists who were present, and to the soldiers who were there. We must look at the many photographs and the footage that was filmed on the day; and examine the statements that were taken soon after the event, as well as the evidence that was given to the previous inquiry. We must always bear in mind that with the passage of so much time, memories in nature of things are often likely to become dim or distorted.

Above all, and particularly because there had been an earlier inquiry which many regarded as flawed, it was clear from the outset that to the greatest degree possible, this must indeed be a *public* inquiry, so that all concerned could see how we were conducting it, and have access to the evidence and materials that we are examining, as well as to our proceedings, to the greatest degree possible.

I believe that without using information technology we would simply have been unable to achieve this aim of conducting what can properly be called a public inquiry. We have tens of thousands of documents and photographs, tens of hours of video footage, statements from well over 1,500 witnesses, and hearings that are now approaching 300 days. Those days started with counsel to the tribunal presenting to us at a public hearing the documentary and other material and drawing our attention to the most important statements of evidence, having necessarily taken many months to prepare that presentation. The size of our task can perhaps be gauged by the fact that it took our counsel nearly 50 days to make this presentation. It was followed by submissions from the lawyers acting for the families of those who were killed and the wounded and the soldiers. We then embarked on hearing oral evidence (which we are continuing to do) though on a number of occasions we have had to spend substantial periods of time hearing arguments and then preparing and giving rulings upon a variety of interlocutory matters. We have already heard oral evidence from hundreds of people and as I write intend to hear evidence from many more.

In addition to the general need to hold a public inquiry, it is clearly of prime importance that the relatives of those who died should be given a full opportunity of seeing how we are conducting the inquiry, since under Article 2 of the Human Rights Convention they have a right to a proper inquiry into deaths at the hands of state agencies.

Simply to hold the inquiry in public would not suffice. In any legal proceedings involving documentation of any size, the public will have very little understanding of what is going on, since it is simply not feasible to provide them with copies of the documents.

What we have done in this regard is to scan the documents, photographs and films, together with the statements of evidence that we have taken, and which were taken at the time, into computers, so that they exist in digital form. This then enables us to do a variety of things that would otherwise be impossible.

In the first place, those who attend the inquiry are able to see the material in question, as it is presented to the tribunal and examined with the witnesses, because it is put on large screens for the public to see. It is also made available in like form to the media.

As I write, the inquiry is taking place in London, since the courts directed that for security reasons the evidence of the soldiers and some others should be taken here, rather than at the Guildhall in the city where Bloody Sunday occurred. Not all who live in that city and have an interest in the proceedings are able to come here to watch and listen, so we have a link which enables the material being considered by us to be seen on screens at the Guildhall, where we had previously been conducting the inquiry, together with a video link to enable people there to watch what is going on at the inquiry while it is in London.

Public interest in the inquiry is not, of course, limited to those who are able to attend the hearings in London or the Guildhall. Bloody Sunday is of international interest and concern. So we have a website on the Internet. On this site much of the evidential material may be found, together with a daily transcript of our proceedings and such things as the many rulings that we have had to make during the course of the inquiry.

By these means we have, I believe, really been able to make this inquiry public, to a degree that formerly would simply have been impossible. At present there are 120 gigabytes of electronic evidence, 60,000 pages of digitised documents, 2,500 digitised photographs and 20 digitised videos. Each of these pieces of evidence is uniquely indexed, using the system we have developed for referencing documents, and may be retrieved and displayed in the manner that I have described in a matter of a second or so.

Also by this means we have reaped many other advantages. This inquiry has already taken nearly five years, and is still far from finished. But the task we were given was immense. We had to interview and take statements from a very large number of people, some of whom now live abroad. We had to retrieve documents from the Public Record Offices of both Great Britain and Northern Ireland and from numerous government departments and other sources. We have employed experts in many fields, ranging from the historical to the forensic. We have had to examine the whole of the evidence and material submitted to the previous inquiry, so as to be able to form a view as to the reliability of the testimony given on that occasion. We have had to collate and analyse all that we have gathered and, through our counsel, present it in public in the clearest way possible. This formidable task of preparation, before we could begin to take oral evidence, itself took two years.

Without information technology, I believe that the time needed would have been far greater than we are likely to take. For example, there are many interested individuals who are legally represented at the inquiry. The lawyers of course must be provided with all the material relevant to their clients so that they can properly represent them. It is simply impracticable for them all to attend with paper bundles of the documents. It would in any event mean that whenever a particular document was to be examined, each of the lawyers would have to select the appropriate bundle and turn to the appropriate page. The tribunal and the witness would have to do likewise. Anyone who has conducted litigation with an appreciable number of documents will know how time consuming this exercise can be. Some will be unable to find the right bundle or the right document. The numbering or referencing system often breaks down, with some having a different system from others. The witness will have to be helped to find the right bundle and the right document. Much of the day will be spent in taking out the appropriate bundle, finding the document, then replacing the bundle and doing the same exercise with another bundle, rather than examining the document and asking questions about it. Over the course of a hearing day the time taken for these purposes would be very long indeed. This is truly wasted time; which by digitising we have reduced to insignificance.

The team needed to conduct an inquiry like this is substantial. The tribunal is assisted by counsel, who present the evidence to it. This, of course, involves a very large and time-consuming amount of preparatory work. Our counsel have divided between themselves the work of actually questioning the witnesses before the tribunal, but obviously they must be constantly aware of what is taking place, even if they are elsewhere preparing for the next witnesses. They must also have access at all times to the evidence and material. They therefore have access to CCTV as well as to the computers holding the evidence and materials, so that they are never out of touch with the proceedings. The same applies to the lawyers acting for the interested parties.

The overall administration of the inquiry is in the hands of a senior civil servant. This person has responsibility for the staff, for managing the financial provisions, for dealing with government departments and outside contractors, for matters of security, for organising the accommodation required for the inquiry, and for a variety of other matters. She and her assistants again must have the means to be able to follow the proceedings, having no time to attend the hearings themselves. This could not be provided without the use of information technology.

We are also served by the solicitor to the inquiry. He is primarily responsible for the gathering of evidence, to be the main interface between the inquiry and the interested parties, to liaise with government departments and other organisations over the collection of evidence and like matters, to deal with ancillary litigation connected with the inquiry, together with a host of other duties. He and his assistants again must be constantly aware of what is going on, so again they are provided with electronic means of following what is taking place at the hearing.

Because the inquiry has had to move to London from its primary site at the Guildhall, we have offices in and near the Central Hall, Westminster, as well as in and near the Guildhall. Apart from counsel, the secretary and the solicitor to the inquiry, there are many others in our staff who can only function properly if they have full access to what is going on at the hearing, as well as the ability to communicate swiftly with each other, notwithstanding the hundreds of miles that divide them.

The ability to communicate has been of inestimable advantage. We use internal e-mail to the greatest possible extent. By this means the staff can keep constantly in touch with each other. Furthermore, unlike most legal proceedings, the tribunal is also able to use this means of communication while actually sitting, so that it is not isolated from everything else. By way of example, I get messages during the day informing me of the progress of matters of current concern so that I can, if appropriate, give an immediate response with my colleagues. Again, something may arise during the course of a hearing day which leads my colleagues and me to decide that some further action should be taken. I can immediately communicate what we want to counsel or the inquiry solicitor or other members of the staff, so that the necessary action can be taken without delay. I can do this whether the person concerned is counsel sitting in front of me, or someone in an office on the other side of the Irish Sea.

A hearing day of course requires a great deal of advance preparation by all concerned. The way we have chosen to proceed is to take written statements from potential witnesses, in the main using an outside firm of solicitors who can provide a sufficient number of properly qualified and experienced lawyers for this task. Those giving statements have of course the right to have a solicitor of their own present during this exercise, in order to see that their rights are properly protected. In view of the number of potential witnesses, the statement taking process has taken a very long time; indeed it is a continuing operation as I write.

The written statements are scanned into the system and distributed to all the interested parties, who in the main comprise the families of those who died and the wounded and of course the soldiers. The tribunal and its counsel then consider which witnesses should be called to give oral evidence, and draw up a programme for attendance at the inquiry, taking account to the greatest degree possible of the convenience of the witness.

In this latter regard we have developed what we call the witness liaison team. They are responsible, among other things, for arranging for the attendance of the witnesses; but do much more.

Those who attend court as witnesses are very often critical of the process as it applies to them. They are not kept informed of events and are often kept waiting an inordinate length of time with no adequate explanation for the delay. Giving evidence can be a nerve-racking experience for those who are not used to the courts, but in the main scant regard is paid to this.

In this inquiry the witness liaison team meet the witness upon arrival at the hearing. We have a witness suite where the witness can relax and where the procedures are explained. For those witnesses who were present on the day, we have developed a computer program to assist the witness in giving evidence.

The city is nowadays very different from 1972. In particular there were three large high rise flats in the Bogside, near which much of the action took place. These have long since disappeared. What we have done is to create a virtual reality representation of the city as it was on the day in question, using contemporary photographs and computer models of the buildings as they were. The program starts by showing a map of the city with a number of hotspots (some 80 in all) marked on it. The system is interactive so by touching a particular hotspot the scene as seen from that position appears. It is possible then by touching the screen to expand the view and look round 360 degrees from the position chosen or indeed to *'walk'* through the scene. The witness can thus explain with the aid of the program his location and what was happening and where, if necessary by touching the screen to draw a line or other mark, which can then be recorded electronically as part of the evidence of that witness.

This virtual reality program has been designed so that it can be used by all, even those with no previous experience in using computers. It only takes a few minutes for the Witness Liaison Team to show the witness how to work the program; and it has proved to be a most useful tool.

The witness liaison team do all they can to ensure that the witness is comfortable. Some request a mid-morning break for medical or other good reasons, and this request is communicated to the tribunal together (often by e-mail) with any other relevant details about the witness which it is important for the tribunal to know in order to make the experience of giving evidence as comfortable as possible.

Witnesses are called to give oral evidence in cases where the tribunal considers the witness to be of particular importance, or where it appears that the witness could usefully expand upon his written evidence; though we have made clear that the written testimony of a witness (whether or not called to give oral testimony) is and remains part of the material that the tribunal will consider in making its report.

In many cases the witness will have made previous statements; some indeed gave evidence to the previous inquiry, some have given interviews to the press or taken part in television programmes dealing with Bloody Sunday. Many also made statements immediately after the events in question. In the case of a number of those who took part in the march that day, we traced to New York a series of tape recordings that were made only a few days later, when people were asked to recount what they saw and heard. Where these recordings exist, they are played to the witness concerned by the witness liaison team before giving evidence. Many had forgotten about these recordings and were amazed to hear their own voices from 30 years ago. Those recordings now form part of our digitised record. Statements and evidence of the witness (including any such recordings) are electronically filed so that there is a complete dossier for each witness, readily accessible at any time.

In order properly to question the witness, it is necessary to ensure that all relevant documents and statements are brought to the attention of the witness. We have made clear that we are conducting an open inquiry where witnesses are not to be taken by surprise and must be given proper advance notice of matters that concern them, particularly of the details of any allegations of misconduct or wrongdoing. Those in respect of who such allegations are made are, of course, entitled to legal representation, so that their interests are properly protected.

When the witness has been sworn, counsel to the inquiry starts the questioning. Here we take advantage of the LiveNote method of transcription. This is a well-known and respected form of real time transcription where everything that is said to or by the witness appears virtually instantaneously in typescript on the laptop computers used by all the counsel involved as well as the tribunal. One of the advantages of LiveNote is that each individual user (including the members of the tribunal) can make private notes on the laptop as the hearing proceeds, and ascribe these notes to particular issues or in any other chosen way, so that they can be retrieved at any later time, and if necessary resorted to. LiveNote also has an automatic indexing system. It is a tool of very great value. Every evening the transcript for the day is posted on our website, and so is available for anyone to read anywhere in the world.

The basic technology we are using is not today's cutting edge state of the art, for we have been using the elements of it for some years. But what we have done (and are among the first to have done) is to bring all these elements together into one integrated system for use in a courtroom environment. We have, of course, taken advantage of improvements in the basic technology as they have been developed, for example the increase in the storage capacity of computers, including laptop machines. The present position is that we can store on each laptop the entire transcript and will continue to be able to do so, with the result that everything said during the course of the hearings can be easily transported and will be instantly available. We are engaged in doing the same with all the documents and other evidential material that we have gathered.

We make an audio record of the proceedings. We have used technology which enables us easily to retrieve what was said at a particular moment on a particular day. This recording is of very high quality and thus is likely to avoid any disputes as to precisely what was said, or even the tone of voice being used. It may also have some historical value. At the outset we decided, however, not to have a video recording of the hearings, since it seemed to us that this might well inhibit the witnesses. However, in some cases it appears that it will be necessary to take oral evidence by means of a video link to another place, for example where the witness is abroad and unable or unwilling to come to the inquiry; and where there are no means of requiring him to do so.

In general terms the IT systems we use are as follows. The PC network spans the two hearing sites and the two sets of inquiry offices. There are approximately 100 PCs and laptops and some 20 servers, using Compaq and Fujitsu Siemens equipment. The PC network is managed by Fujitsu Services and uses Microsoft Windows 2000. For the evidence display (which spans five sites) we use Trial Pro Version 4, with the evidence controlled and manipulated by legal teams using touch screen technology. For the Real Time Transcription we are using Version 7 of LiveNote. The virtual reality program was supplied by the Northern Ireland Centre for Learning Resources. CCTV and the audio (the latter managed by MK Audio) also span five sites, broadcasting the proceedings in the hearing chamber save where the tribunal has ruled otherwise for reasons of security. In total these systems require some 17 skilled staff.

The inquiry has cost to date a vast sum of money, and much more will have to be spent. It has been the subject of great criticism for this reason, though this has come in the main from those who were opposed to instituting a new inquiry at all. Every effort is made by the staff of the inquiry to satisfy themselves that money is properly spent and not wasted and all expenditure has to be properly recorded and accounted for to the department involved, which in this case is the Northern Ireland Office.

Much of the money has gone on paying the fees of the many lawyers attending the hearings. But any public inquiry is going to be very expensive. To achieve its purpose it must be thorough, but it must also be fair and open. Fairness dictates that those who face allegations of serious misconduct (in the present case, many of the soldiers face allegations of murder and others of either complicity in murder or of conduct which they must have appreciated was likely to lead to the death of innocent people) must have legal advice and assistance so that their rights are properly protected. Similarly, the families of those who died have (as already observed) a statutory right to a proper open inquiry where death has been caused at the hands of state agencies, so they too in my view should have the benefit of legal representation in order that their interests are properly protected. Those who were wounded may not have the same statutory rights, but to my mind are also, as a matter of fairness, entitled to be legally represented for the same reasons.

In the course of the inquiry, the tribunal has had to consider and make rulings upon a number of matters of great importance, where the views of the families and those of the soldiers have been in very sharp conflict. Among other matters, we have made rulings on whether the soldiers are entitled to anonymity when they give evidence, and on whether they should give their evidence in London or at the Guildhall. These rulings have been successfully challenged by way of judicial review in the courts. Court challenges to interlocutory rulings of a tribunal of inquiry are very time consuming and expensive, but are really inevitable in an inquiry of the present kind, especially where human rights are involved.

The successful challenges to our rulings on anonymity and venue have themselves entailed substantial delay and expense. All the documents have had to be examined and re-examined so that soldiers' names are redacted and ciphers put in their place, while the move to London has meant the setting up of a new hearing room together with arrangements to enable representatives of the families to stay in London so that they can continue to observe the proceedings. The cost of that move alone has been some £15m.

The two rulings successfully challenged involved the question whether to any and if so what degree the public nature of the inquiry should give way to other considerations, including human rights, in particular the right to life given by Art 2 of the Convention on Human Rights. In addition we have made a number of other rulings on the right to life which have not been the subject of successful challenge, for example that some of the police should give their evidence screened, since they had reasonable grounds for fearing that their lives (and those of their families) would be put at risk from paramilitaries were this not to be done. We have also had to grapple with questions concerning journalistic privilege and applications by government departments for public interest immunity protection.

All in all, the inquiry has turned into a massive exercise, taking a great deal of time and costing a great deal of money.

To my mind, however, the decision to use information technology is one that has saved and will continue to save substantial sums of money. Of course the technical staff we employ and the hardware and software that we use cost considerable money, but the efficiency gains are very great. It is impossible to provide a precise estimate of the savings we hope to achieve through the use of information technology, but in terms of time it seems to me that the inquiry would have taken months if not years longer had we not been able to employ these tools. The daily cost of the inquiry runs into many tens of thousands of pounds, so every day saved means a significant saving of money.

At the end of the day there will be time for reflection, in particular whether there might be different and better ways of dealing with public concern over an incident like Bloody Sunday. But our present task, which Parliament has reposed in us, is to conduct a public inquiry under the 1921 Act into the events of that day. This is what we are attempting to do, to the best of our ability and that of our staff. Whether we shall succeed is something that others will judge, and whether our report will be criticised we shall have to wait and see. But I firmly believe that the use that we have made of information technology has saved substantial sums of money, has given us a tool to enable us to do a better job than would otherwise have been the case and has made this an Inquiry which, whatever its other shortcomings may be, is truly public.[1]

1 November 2002.

Management and judges

Richard Susskind

I first met Brian Neill in the summer of 1986, during a conference at the University of Warwick, organised by the Society for Computers and Law. I had recently completed my doctoral thesis on computers and law and had just enjoyed my first serious publication – an article in the *The Modern Law Review*, travelling under the far from snappy title of 'Expert Systems in Law: A Jurisprudential Approach to Artificial Intelligence and Legal Reasoning'. [1] At a social gathering, after a plenary session, I was introduced to Brian. I was amazed that he recognised my name as the author of the pithily entitled piece just mentioned. More remarkable still, given just how dry the article was, he seemed to have read it in its entirety, evidenced by a couple of tricky queries he put to me about deductive legal reasoning. As a young academic, it meant the world to me that a senior judge had taken the time to look at my work. Then, as in later years, he was kindly, encouraging and wise.

In the early 1990s, we worked closely together: he was President of the Society for Computers and Law for most of my term as chairman. My fondest memories are of council meetings that he attended while I was supposedly in the chair. In the squabble one invariably finds when a diverse group of senior individuals assembles round the table as the committee of a voluntary organisation, Brian's presence dominated in the most benevolent of ways and his great sense would always prevail. After frenetic debate on given issues (all of which seemed to be contentious), I would turn to Brian for help. When he spoke, all others remained silent. In his deep, mellifluous tones, he would succinctly summarise all sides

1 Vol 6, No 2, March 1986, 168.

of any given argument and then move compellingly but with a lightness of touch towards outlining his own position. Persuasive, diplomatic and quintessentially judicial, he would settle discussions with authority. It was a joy, as chairman, to have an instant appeal process to hand.

Brian was also a mentor to me, always ready to offer guidance and encouragement. What perhaps surprised me most over the years was his openness to new ideas, his capacity to take seriously even my most extreme ideas about the long-term impact of IT on legal practice and on the administration of justice. Indeed, having read an early draft of my book, *The Future of Law*, [2] he encouraged me to be braver in my predictions than I was originally inclined. He saw greater potential for the use of IT in judicial decision-making than any legal technologist I have met.

Brian was always keen, of course, that judges should make use of new techniques and ideas that were being deployed to good effect in the private sector and in other industries. It is in that spirit that I have written this chapter. It concerns various aspects of the discipline of management and their applicability, especially in England and Wales, to the work of judges.

In preparing this article, I have drawn heavily on two sets of personal experiences. First, I have had the good fortune to have worked closely with many English judges for over 10 years and, since 1998, have been IT Adviser to the Lord Chief Justice. Through innumerable meetings, seminars, conferences and online discussions, I have been exposed to judges at all levels of the English judiciary. Second, since the mid-1980s, I have advised countless law firms across the world, many of whose partners have viewed management with a similar distrust to that expressed by some judges today. In having being exposed over the years to the impact of management and having often come to see its benefits, I believe the experience of senior partners can help us explore and exploit management for judges.

Judges and management

Many judges consider management to be anathema to the business of judging. Management, one version of the argument runs, imposes constraints, procedures and standards to which independent and impartial arbiters should not be subject. At the same time, the jargon of management often gives rise to

2 Oxford University Press, 1996.

judicial intolerance – many judges have little truck with terms such as total quality management, business process re-engineering, SWOT analysis, Boston Grids or the like. (It is ironic that judges, whose own world is so laden with jargon that often confuse the laity, should not recognise in other disciplines the need for technical terms on the one hand and short-hand on the other.)

In any event, my thesis here is that the discipline of management and the work of judges, certainly in England and Wales, overlap and interrelate in numerous important ways and that the overall performance of the judiciary would be greatly enhanced by the more systematic and intensive application of management principles.

I should say a word or two at the outset about what management is. While it is the kind of discipline whose very nature and scope itself often stimulates fierce debate, most working definitions suggest we are talking about the science (or art) of achieving results, of getting things done, through the organisation and motivation of people. When seeking to attain objectives, the theory and practice of management holds that we should be systematic rather than haphazard, focussed instead of vague. The discipline in question embraces issues as diverse as strategy and policy, human resources, finance, working processes, IT, information systems, marketing, project management, performance appraisal, communications and training.

With respect to judges and management, an important distinction should be drawn at the outset. One way in which the discipline of management and the work of judges overlap is to the extent that *all judges are managers* of sorts, even if they do not always recognise this. In their daily work, judges are frequently engaged, for example, in the management of people (in organising and motivating individuals and teams), documents, cases, timetables, events, projects, computer systems, the media and all manner of other resources. All of these tasks are over and above the job of substantive judicial decision-making (listening to evidence and legal argument, undertaking legal research, reflecting, reasoning, drawing conclusions and drafting judgements). While the illustrative management tasks just outlined might easily be dismissed as mere administration, a necessary evil perhaps, experience in other fields suggest there is immeasurably more to management than number crunching and the organisation of data. Indeed, as Peter Drucker, the father of modern management, puts it: 'The Manager is the dynamic, life-giving element in every business'. [3] It is my belief, but not substantiated here, that judges who

3 *The Practice of Management* (Harper Collins, New York, 1993) p 3.

develop their management skills will, in the end, actually improve the quality of their substantive legal decision-making.

It is not my purpose in this chapter to discuss the topic of judges as managers. There is, no doubt, much that can and should be written on this matter (not least about how much training judges should receive in the discipline of management), but my purpose here is broader and that is to explore a second, distinguishable connection between management and judges. I have in mind the challenge of *the management of the judiciary as a workforce*, albeit a unique one. Judges are a vital and core group of individuals in any modern democracy, independent in their decision-making from both the elected legislature and all executive bodies. Nevertheless, judges are a human resource of sorts. They belong to what can be looked upon as a community of sole practitioners, constitutionally and fiercely independent and yet bound by a common social and jurisprudential purpose – the delivery of formal, procedural and substantive justice in all cases that come before them, leading through their decisions to the development of a coherent, consistent body of common law.

Although judges operate as individuals (unless sitting together in the hearing of given cases), their need to maintain independence in particular cases should not lead to isolation, given their shared objectives. As a human resource, they have talent, reputation, a working environment, research facilities that need to be nurtured and developed. Judges should, I believe, be organised, motivated, developed and measured. They require regular communication and they should have clear objectives to which they can aspire. All of this calls for active management of the judiciary as a workforce. In this chapter, I hope to give a flavour of the nature of this management challenge by addressing the following six questions:

- should the performance of judges be appraised?
- how might the external perception of judges be managed?
- how might internal communications be improved?
- what modern training methods might be used for judges?
- what is the relevance of IT?
- who should manage judges?

This is in no sense exhaustive of the scope of management of the judiciary. But it is a start upon which others can build.

Performance appraisal of judges

One area of management that is of some considerable potential sensitivity is that of appraising or reviewing the ongoing performance of the work of judges. I can immediately recognise and sympathise here with some judges' intuitive misgivings and concerns. If judicial work is constantly being assessed, this might be said, at the very least, to be a distraction; or, much more serious, a threat to independent decision-making. Judicial work is demanding enough, it might be argued, without having to worry about being subject to evaluation and scrutiny that does not naturally form part of the judicial process. No matter how able the judge, it would be hard not to be in some way affected by the shadow that an appraisal system might cast. And, in any event, who is competent to assess substantive judicial decision-making?

Beyond such formal concerns, I understand too that judges may feel that they are at the stage in their career that any kind of ongoing assessment is unnecessary and even insulting to their status.

These feelings are frequently shared in the private sector – in major law firms, for example. Over the past few years, many of the world's leading practices have introduced performance appraisal for partners, including the most senior of lawyers. At first, this development has not been welcomed and has been considered to be a mix of threatening, inappropriate, wasteful of resource, and even misconceived. However, those firms that have introduced partner appraisal professionally and systematically have generally come to recognise a wide range of benefits – for the individuals concerned, for their firms and, crucially, for their clients.

In summary, if a partner is performing well, that is to the satisfaction of his peers, his teams and his clients, then it is reassuring, motivating and productive for all concerned to have that satisfaction articulated and often even rewarded. Conversely, if a partner is under-performing in some relevant respect, then it is surely vital for all affected that the various shortcomings are identified and discussed and remedial precautions are put in place.

I am convinced, as a general matter, that a well-conceived and skilfully-managed appraisal system can valuably highlight the strengths and weaknesses of most professionals. In the commercial world, it must make business sense to ensure the best people are performing to the best of their abilities. In the public sector, there is an analogous and perhaps even more compelling reason to accept the proposition that the performance of public servants be subject to review; and that is that public servants (including judges) are accountable to society generally for their work. In the context of judges, I can see strong arguments that this accountability, in turn, requires that their work is neither shrouded in secrecy nor masked by traditions which render their activities opaque to many non-lawyers. Further, in an era when most of central and local government are coming to be subject to appraisal, it is hard to find compelling reasons to exclude judges entirely from any kind of ongoing assessment.

That said, I do not believe that all of the work of judges should be assessed and appraised in the ways currently favoured in the private sector and in many parts of government. Most importantly, it does not seem to me that the substantive decisions made by judges – their judgements – should be subject to any new kind of new performance review. Quite apart from the difficulty of identifying suitably qualified and experienced lawyers to undertake the task, I feel that the entire balance of the judicial system could be disturbed by the addition of a new review process. This is clearly a complex matter and I could spend some considerable time assessing likely imbalances and anomalies that might arise. However, I would like instead to stress a related point – that, quite unlike most other environments in which performance appraisal takes place, there is, in the judiciary, a well-established, tried and tested system of evaluation already built in. I am referring to the appeals processes. Poor or defective decisions rarely go unnoticed in the justice system and we can surely rely on our lawyers in this country to identify judicial decisions that are inadequate in some relevant way; and to invoke appeal procedures accordingly.

Of course, the fact that a particular judge's decisions are frequently overturned does not, of itself, establish the incompetence of the judge. On the contrary, over the years, some outstanding if iconoclastic judges (Lord Denning springs naturally to mind) repeatedly had their judgements and arguments criticised and rejected on appeal; only to find their positions affirmed some years later. Nonetheless, it is entirely foreseeable that less able judges may simply under-perform and that evidence of this will emerge through the results of regular appeals. If 'performance appraisal through appeals' is to function, the public should want reassurance that judges whose decision-making is repeatedly defective (in terms of fact-finding or legal reasoning), should be monitored with a view to their receiving counselling or support.

All of that said, I do see considerable scope for reviewing other aspects of the performance of judges, beyond their substantive judicial decision-making.

One area where judicial work might productively be evaluated with a view to improvement (which might take the form of training) is in the areas of interpersonal skills, listening skills and skills of oral expression. In relation to interpersonal skills, for example, judges should strive to be courteous, empathetic and helpful. Regarding listening skills, they should be (and be seen to be) attentive, receptive and not bored with proceedings. And when they speak, judges must be readily understood and keep unnecessary jargon to a minimum (even if others, such as management theorists, do not). Inadvertently, human judges are all capable of failing to exhibit such skills. Crucially, although they might believe they do not suffer from failings in the areas just mentioned, those who appear before them may legitimately think otherwise.

Unnerving though it may be for them, if judges were occasionally observed, then constructive evaluation could lead to better judicial service. This is not mere packaging. The public's perception of judges (and I will say more on this later) may in large part be created by their behaviour in court rather than the erudition and eloquence of their judgements.

I see no reason in principle why their *efficiency* as judges should not also be subject to scrutiny. If some judges take demonstrably longer than others to progress court business or write their judgements or complete their administration, then that is a matter of concern. It is not unreasonable that these aspects of their work be monitored in the public interest.

One final area of potential application for performance measurement arises in England from the ongoing civil reforms. Further to Lord Woolf's *Access to Justice* Inquiry, [4] many judges now have considerable case management responsibilities. There are new demands and new techniques to master here. I see considerable scope here for formally assessing how judges are coping – in scheduling, planning, communicating and monitoring progress of cases, for example.

I can imagine that all of these suggestions of assessing judicial performance may disturb or even offend some judges. But, just as in the private sector, where I have noted that firms are keen to know if they are doing well or badly so that they can build on strengths and address weaknesses systematically,

4 See Lord Woolf's Interim Report (June 1995) and Final Report (July 1996) at www.lcd.gov.uk

then so too in the judicial context. If judges aspire to being part of an outstanding and respected judiciary, then it is unlikely that they will evolve and improve as much as they might if they are left unmanaged. They must surely expect that they will need a light (or indeed a heavy) hand on the tiller; but if these adjustments are to be focussed and productive, they must surely be based on rigorous investigation and analysis rather than anecdote, supposition or speculation.

In this connection, I am convinced that other techniques also deserve serious thought and discussion. The notion of 'peer group review' holds potential for the judiciary. In the government, and in the academic world too, it is not uncommon for senior figures from other countries to visit and observe and in other ways investigate organisations and the people who work in them. This leads to their reporting (informally or writing) on their impressions of their object of study and the making of suggestions on the basis of their experience in their own jurisdictions. Thus, I could imagine a team of senior overseas judges visiting the courts, observing judges in action and giving their thoughts on how they might improve.

Internationally, it would also be useful if there were 'benchmarks' for judges and courts – standard measurable criteria which would allow the assessment of judicial performance as against similar jurisdictions. This might be confined to the throughput, efficiency and costs of courts and cases; but might also look at specifically judicial issues (for example, the average time that judges take to write their decisions).

Other possibilities to explore, again derived from the private sector and some parts of government, are 'mentoring' whereby senior judges would support the development of junior judges, offering them impartial counsel and a shoulder to cry on; and 'personal development plans' for judges, so that they can formally manage their own progress, perhaps identifying on an annual basis what they want to achieve in the coming year (for example, increased specialist knowledge in some area of law or improved skills of some kind).

I can envisage the day when there might even be 'user satisfaction studies' of judges and courts. Again, there are analogies here in the private sector where law firms now ask their clients whether or not they are providing a good service. And once again, whether or not the answer is positive or negative, they want to know, so they can act accordingly. So too with the judges and courts. If judges really want to be perceived as outstanding, this is not simply a matter of how they believe they are performing. Users should also have a say – the lawyers and litigants who come before judges. This leads naturally to the issues of external perception and external relations, to which I now turn.

Marketing and the external perception of judges

There are surely a set of standard, stereotypical accusations that are levelled at the judiciary. We sometimes read, for example, that judges are too old or out of touch or excessively conservative or impatient. The list of accusations, if fully articulated, would be a daunting one indeed.

Judges must not be complacent or in denial in this regard. There are no doubt some judges who do suffer from some of the above defects. In passing, I think it important to say that I do not look upon old age as a defect – so long as judicial minds remain agile and judges have considerable energy, then theirs is a field, above all others perhaps, where genuine experience and wisdom is so very valuable.

Nonetheless, I am of the view that most of the stereotypes are inaccurate, certainly in relation to the lion's share of English judges. While the *reality* of matters is, in my view, encouraging, I think it crucial for judges to recognise that *perception* is also extremely important. It is not enough that judges are independent, fair, open-minded, legally robust, forward-looking and creative. They must also be seen to exhibit those characteristics, if they wish to win the complete trust and confidence of the public and the legal professions. Alien though it may seem for many judges, they should, I submit, consciously work on their image.

Some empirical evidence is helpful here. Professor Hazel Genn, in her seminal study of 'what people do and think about going to the law', reports that an attitude question posed to her respondents gave rise to rather negative responses. Respondents were asked whether or not they agreed that most judges were out of touch with ordinary peoples' lives. About two-thirds agreed or strongly agreed with the statement. [5] Crucially, however, there is also some suggestion that those (relatively few) who have actually appeared before judges have a generally more favourable view than those who have not (whose views seem largely conditioned by various media). The best that can be said, in light of these research findings, is that perception is out of kilter with reality.

5 See *Paths to Justice* (Hart Publishing, 1999) pp 239-240.

This does not lead me to advocate the engagement of image consultants to recommend so-called 'make-overs', extending to judges' choice of clothes, hair-style and preferred degree of sun tan! They may safely leave such measures to others, for whom these issues might genuinely matter. Nor am I proposing an advertisement campaign, extolling the virtues of the judiciary, complete with a suitably flashy '21st century' brand and logo! Nor indeed do I recommend a sustained media campaign, during which judges proactively solicit the attention of the press.

However, I do think each and every judge, by way of training, should be made more aware of how they might appear to the world at large – to members of the public and to the legal profession. All judges are ambassadors for the judiciary and should be conscious that the perception of each and every judge is important and can colour society's views of their competence and suitability.

In this context, I would strongly encourage judges, subject of course to the already considerable demands on their time, to get out and about a bit more. I do not just mean attending or speaking at lawyers' functions but penetrating more deeply into our communities. One very positive recent step is that some judges very valuably give speeches at schools. Here is a chance to show how user-friendly they can really be and, at the same time, to educate the young and engender greater confidence in the justice system in future generations.

Clearly, judges must be conscious of avoiding political and other sensitive social issues, when their observations on these might be perceived as diluting their independence or impartiality. But there is much that judges can say that is non-contentious, even if they do not all manage to steer clear of all troubled waters.

Press handling is an art in its own right. Top judges have become increasingly conscious that any statements they might make in public, however well intentioned, might find their way into print even if not entirely in their full and original context. To some extent, this is a hazard of their positions. That said, much of what is reported is both accurate and helpful. Media awareness training might be of enormous assistance to those senior judges who are regularly in the public eye. Many newly-appointed senior partners of law firms are given such training, invariably with some reservation or even reluctance on their part. But most will later report how practical and helpful it can be. At the very least, judges must be fully prepared and briefed before speaking to the press. And journalists should want it no other way.

Clearly there are many occasions on which judges are simply unable to speak to the press, because the issues of interest are before them in court. On other occasions, however, it may be helpful all round for judges to express a view in public but I think greater thought needs to be given as to how they can do this more systematically from their own point of view and more helpfully for the media.

Finally, on external relations, I have two proposals for projects that, in my opinion, are of sufficient merit to deserve further examination. The first is that the judiciary might produce an annual report, summarising their performance and key achievements in the past year, complete with statistics and relevant news.

Second, they should consider, in England and Wales certainly, the development and maintenance of a dedicated judicial website – an online resource devoted to news and information about the judges, accessible by the entire community. This topic provides, for me, a very useful case study on judges and their reactions to external relations. For some time, I have been recommending the establishment of such a website but many judges do not seem to see the need. For me, this reflects, if I may say so, a shortcoming in their appreciation of the ramifications of marketing and external relations.

Underpinning my recommendation that there should be some sort of new judicial site is my belief that an independent judiciary should have its own independent website. Almost all public sector entities now have their own websites and I can see no reason why the judiciary should be different. As it stands, in England, the current online presence of the English judiciary is nested within the Lord Chancellor's Department's website, residing at the rather lengthy and instantly forgettable address of www.lcd.gov.uk/judicial/judgesfr.htm and entitled 'Judges and QCs'. For non-lawyers who are browsing, judges are seen to be part of the Lord Chancellor's Department and related to QCs in a way that is not at all clear.

I would greatly prefer to see a distinct judicial website (not shared with QCs), living at an address such as www.englishjudiciary.gov.uk (with links to this site, of course, from the Lord Chancellor's site). My recommendation is that all the materials relating to the judiciary on the Lord Chancellor's website be excised from there and inserted into a newly created site – an independent site for an independent judiciary. No new materials need be added and this would be a short afternoon's work for a competent web developer. In all, this is a low risk, low cost proposal which, aside from the constitutional arguments in its favour, would also bring strong practical and public relations benefits. The main practical benefit I have in mind is that the site itself and materials on it would be easier to find. For example, speeches of judges are today located at www.lcd.gov.uk/judicial/speeches/speechfr.htm whereas, on the new site, they would be but one click from the home page, a resource that would, I believe, become better known and more frequently perused than the current materials, tucked away as they are. Many judges give first rate speeches that are worthy of publication and yet never appear in print. As for the speeches of the most senior judges, these are often crucial statements of policy that should be in the public domain and deserve far wider audiences than the hundreds who gather to hear their presentations. Such material is valuable, if not for the public directly, then for the media, academics and students and as well as for practitioners.

Regarding public relations, the very existence of this distinct website that I am proposing would surely send out a very positive signal, within and beyond the legal profession, that we have a progressive, forward-looking judiciary that is at once supportive of new technology and is seeking to be more accessible than ever before. The launch of such a site is precisely the kind of event that I write about in my regular column in *The Times*; and I am confident, from the thousands of e-mails that I receive in the context of that column, that readers would be impressed and interested.

That many judges do not support the need for an independent judicial website, with all its public relations benefits, indicates just how much more management is needed.

Internal Relations and Communication

While it is important that judges improve their many external relations, it is equally vital that they strive to communicate more effectively within judicial communities. Historically, this has not always been easy, because the judges are often geographically dispersed so that they have fewer opportunities for face-to-face meetings, or indeed chance encounters in the corridor, than those who work together under the one physical roof. It is here that I see particular potential for the use of IT, as I will touch upon later. I am hugely enthused by the idea of developing an 'Intranet' for judges – a private website to which judges could enjoy exclusive access. It is here, among other facilities, that interesting and important news could be made readily available – not just legal updates such as new decisions; but notices of other developments, such as new appointments or initiatives in the Court Service or Lord Chancellor's Department. I believe it imperative that judges feel better informed and they must harness new technology in this context: to establish new and different facilities that enhance the quality and efficiency of their working lives.

Beyond communications among themselves, it is also important that judges enjoy positive and constructive relationships with court officials: in England and Wales, in the Court Service and the Lord Chancellor's Department. In many dimensions, I believe that judges enjoy good relations with officials at an unprecedented level but they must work hard to maintain these. Just as they would wish to be kept up to date with government projects that bear on their working environment, then they should recognise also a reciprocal responsibility to inform officials of their own initiatives, views and aspirations.

Modern training methods for judges

I think it fair to say that, conventionally, the training of judges has involved the gathering together of judges in one physical location, often for what I term 'just-in-case' education – the judges are exposed to new developments or emerging issues (such as civil reforms or human rights or judicial case management), through face-to-face sessions with trainers (other judges or experts), thus equipping them with insight and knowledge that they *might* need at some future stage. This model, of classroom training, has dominated in the world of paper and print. In the era of the information society, in broad terms, IT can augment this conventional training of judges in three ways.

First is the use of IT as a new channel for the delivery of training. I have in mind here the use of *distance learning* techniques. In England, the Judicial Studies Board has already experimented with this approach (for example, through the production of a CD-Rom containing five seminars on possession claims). At Strathclyde University, I have been heavily involved in distance learning since 1995, when we launched one of the world's first online masters degrees in law. Aimed at busy full-time lawyers, it has been enormously successful and has convinced me that there is huge scope for far wider exploitation among lawyers and judges. It is not necessarily a substitute for conventional training but is wonderful where access to training services would otherwise not be available. Distance learning can involve anything from providing collections of useful documents online through to sophisticated online web-casting, a technique for playing video clips online with which I have been experimenting to good effect over the past year.

The flexibility of distance learning techniques – especially its availability at all hours – has led many commentators and trainers to take a step back and reflect on the very nature of training. Some have concluded that just-in-case training is often inherently inefficient and so have worked on the development of what I call *just-in-time* training – a second use of IT in support of training. For judges, the idea here would be that, on many occasions (but emphatically not all), online training facilities should *not* simulate the attendance at a seminar for some just-in-case edification but should be regarded as an instant online resource. When a judge is confronted with a subject beyond his range of knowledge, he should be able to go online and benefit from an immediate training session – perhaps an interactive multimedia web-cast of a leading judge.

The third use of IT for judges is for the purposes of *knowledge management*, a subject that is attracting major interest and investment in the private sector. Knowledge management refers to the systematic capturing and sharing of the collective knowledge and experience of a group of individuals. Knowledge management need not involve IT but technology unquestionably helps – by providing useful facilities for the delivery of knowledge, such as Intranet systems (see later). Generally, the knowledge that is shared through knowledge management techniques is not conventional, published materials. Rather, it tends to be more practical in orientation, including know-how (guidance on the process of going about some task), know-who (pointers to who knows most about a given topic) and know-where (advice on the best resources to consult). In England, the high level of use of the conferencing facilities on the judges' FELIX system suggest that there is a real need for judges to share their expertise. I suspect part-time judges would also benefit enormously from this kind of knowledge at their fingertips. Knowledge management services are delivered through a mix of systems and services – conferencing (such as FELIX), Intranet (a private Internet facility for judges to browse through), e-mail alerts (when there is important news to impart), and a variety of databases.

I have sought above merely to give a sense that IT offers the opportunity to help educate and train judges in new and improved ways. Classroom training, as it were, will always have its place (if only for attendees to network in the social sense) but distance learning will make training materials more widely available and accessible; just-in-time training will ensure that judges, while working, always have training resources at their fingertips; and knowledge management will ensure that the judicial community harnesses and shares its phenomenal collective wisdom and experience.

How might these new approaches to training be taken forward? In my view, in England, the Judicial Studies Board is the ideal body to pursue and implement these new approaches to training. However, its scope would thereby be considerably expanded – to encompass not just conventional training but also, I would suggest, knowledge management, information and library services, judicial e-mail and conferencing, know-how databases and a judicial Intranet. This would result in a body that is more like a judicial academy or institute. To be clear, I would not suggest that a new-look Judicial Studies Board would be responsible for judicial IT, for the plumbing itself. Rather, this is about content, about what flows through the pipes and ensuring its quality, consistency, coherence and timeliness.

In management terms, a judicial academy or the like would need to be systematic in analysing the learning, information and knowledge needs of judges at all levels. This should be achieved by in-depth 'information needs' analysis. The purpose of focussing on information needs is to try and ensure that any facilities or systems or IT that judges receive do indeed meet their requirements.

A number of lessons can be learned from information needs work in law firms. First, when IT is involved, more attention should paid to the 'I' than the 'T' of IT (less focus on the 'plumbing'). Second, a distinction should always be made between perceived and actual needs of judges (the all-important distinction between what judicial users think they need and what they would want if they knew what was actually possible and available). Third, the actual needs of judges can only be understood if all technical possibilities are appreciated. Fourth, the services of a systems analyst should be secured (a clever, clear, independent thinker). Fifth, for some time there will inevitably be parallel systems (paper-based and IT-based, although it is helpful to distinguish between primary (direct) users of IT and secondary (indirect) users, the latter being those judges who ask officials to use the systems for them). Finally, the information needs of all classes of judge must be assessed (in different levels of courts and different jurisdictions – civil, criminal, family and special; and different levels of sophistication of user).

To give some flavour of the exercise of formally analysing the information needs of judges, the following are the types of questions that should be asked in respect of each of the key tasks (at key moments in time) with which judges may be involved in the course of their work:

- to what information or knowledge do you need ready and immediate access?
- what information, knowledge and materials should be brought automatically to your attention?
- what information or knowledge that you produce should be captured and stored for later attention?
- in what form would you like information or knowledge presented?
- with whom do you need to communicate information and knowledge?

Thus armed with a clearer appreciation of what judges want and need, appropriate systems can be designed and developed. Inevitably, the enhancements to judicial training, learning and knowledge management that I have in mind require funding. In England, some of that funding already exists but is held and managed beyond the Judicial Studies Board. That said, some funding would need to be new. This investment would be modest, however, relative to the likely benefits – in the shape of a more productive, efficient and satisfied judicial community.

What is the relevance of information technology?

Periodically, I have mentioned the application of IT in this chapter. It is a subject very close to my heart. And it is a management topic that has devoured much attention of senior judges over the last few years. It may come as something of a surprise that I regard IT as a management issue. I believe that the successful introduction of information technology to any organisation today is indeed, in large part, a management challenge. Of course, it is a technical matter as well but most of the obstacles (strategic, organisational, cultural, motivational, financial) are management obstacles and are not about bits and bytes.

I cannot hope here to do justice to the subject of judicial IT. My intention is to pick out a few key issues, all of which point to IT becoming a crucial and not peripheral tool of the judge. I start by identifying a few technologies that I expect to be of particular importance in years to come. Thereafter, I address the issue of integrating technology across the justice system, with special reference to judicial needs. And then I close the discussion on IT by identifying the benefits that new technologies can bring.

Before I go any further, however, I think it important to have, by way of context, an insight into the main applications of IT that judges *should* have at their fingertips. These I have summarised in the table that follows.

Judicial applications of information technology

1. Document creation

- an industry standard word processing system
- with a suite of judicial 'macros' to impose uniform format and to provide some basic text to save time
- with a suite of standard documents accessible for adaptation to judicial users
- moving towards automated document assembly (eg, for the production of standard orders)

2. Electronic communications

- secure, reliable, e-mail (and attachments) with other judges, court staff and the outside world
- PC-based fax (outgoing and incoming)
- desktop to desktop video-conferencing
- systems to support electronic meetings, electronic hearings and 'groupware' for team working
- 'remote access' to central systems through laptops

3. Document management

- tools to create and read electronic indexes (simple flat file databases)
- tools to search using full text retrieval systems and to read imaged documents
- tools for browsing through 'hyperlinked' documents
- the use of an industry standard relational database management system
- towards the electronic case file (containing all the documents and materials relating to any particular case, all collected together and accessible on an online basis)

4. Retrieval of external information

- non-subscription systems – (World Wide Web sites)
- online subscription services accessible via the World Wide Web

- online subscription services that are not Web-based
- CD-based subscription services
- distance learning

5. Internal information resources

- a Judicial Intranet (for e-mail and for sharing information)
- shared bodies of online judicial know-how and experience (eg bench book)
- a suite of 'bookmarks' (to guide judges directly to invaluable sources on the Internet)
- online 'virtual' communities or interest groups (akin to FELIX)
- decision support tools (eg sentencing support systems)

6. Case management

- online case tracking and access to and creation of electronic case files
- case planning using project planning tools
- case load management tools and resource management (eg for listing)

7. Courtroom technologies

- laptop or desktop facilities for the taking of notes
- document and exhibit display technology
- digital audio recording
- video simulations and IT-based demonstrative evidence
- computer-assisted real-time transcription
- access to internal information resources and external information
- video-linking for remote evidence

8. 'Promulgation' [6]

- automated uploading of decisions onto a judicial Intranet
- uploading of decisions onto the Internet (with a need for medium neutral citations and paragraph marking)

Although most judges who are enthusiastic about IT would like the full range of applications immediately, the reality is that it will at least take at least 3–5

6 See my book, *The Future of Law* (OUP, 1996 and 1998 (paperback)) in which I argue that promulgation – the formal mechanism by which the public are informed of new laws (or changes in old) – may soon be possible using IT (see pp 18-23 and 99).

years to put all eight in place in England. Two very significant questions arise. First, how should judges prioritise among the eight and, vitally, who should be responsible for setting these priorities? My inclination is that while the prioritising is ultimately a matter of government policy, senior judges should be consulted extensively. By when should we say that all judges will be expected to use IT? My response here is 'within three years' (ie by 2005).

Over the years, while advising English judges on IT, I have become increasingly convinced that there are many ways in which information technology will not only radically improve the workings of the justice system but will also bring about some fundamental changes as well. I have learned, in the public sector, however, that IT projects tend to take far longer to complete than in private law firms. For example, in 1995, I became enthusiastic about the use of video conferencing technology in support of a variety of types of hearings. I had it mind then that some case management meetings or pre-trial reviews might, in due course, be conducted via video conferencing. I also felt that some applications for leave to appeal to the Court of Appeal might more conveniently and less expensively be made by video conference. In the event, it was not until 2000 that the first *pilot* of application-by-video-conference was actually conducted. It took five years from idea to pilot, which is far longer than I would have wanted. This experience is not uncommon.

At the same time, I have discovered that putting in place new systems across the courts is genuinely complex and challenging. I think it fair to say that it has taken several years for the Court Service in England completely to recognise the full impact of the technology recommended by Lord Woolf's civil reforms; for instance, that case management systems of the sort he envisaged could not simply be grafted onto the court systems that were in use in the 1980s and 1990s. Instead, an entirely new approach was required. In this context, I am very pleased that recent analysis and project planning clearly acknowledges the scale of IT that is now needed, even if the funding position is looking rather grim.

It is also pleasing to find that a majority of English judges are now keen to make use of the machines that are now available to all full-time judges. The quality of IT training is steadily improving (although there is still much room for improvement), as are the help and support facilities for those who encounter problems. Over time, as judges become more confident and adventurous and as younger judges are appointed, I have little doubt that they will become more efficient through their use of IT and enjoy richer research resources as well.

From the range of possibilities summarised earlier, I would like here to focus on four applications of IT that seem to me to be especially important for judges in the coming years.

First, there is video conferencing, which I have already mentioned. The quality of such systems is unquestionably improving. Further, video conferencing facilities are becoming far more widely available. Indeed versions of these systems frequently now run on lawyers' desktop computers. Video conferencing is becoming a standard tool of private sector organisations that are located in many places. I continue to see huge potential for their use in law – not only for remand hearings, or for the hearing of evidence by vulnerable witnesses, as is becoming increasingly common today, but for all manner of other meetings where face-to-face congregation is not necessary.

At the same time, we should not forget, these systems' more modest cousin – telephone conferencing. For many years, I have advocated that some classes of meeting could very effectively be conducted by telephone conference, especially those that involve the exchange of facts and basic information rather than the advancement of arguments or the bringing of evidence.

A second set of technologies that I think will be of lasting significance are those that support judicial case flow management. I look forward with great anticipation to the day when judges can track progress on the cases for which they have responsibility, when they can be reminded every day of the tasks which must be discharged before leaving in the evening, when they can generate case plans automatically, complete with automatic diarying and listing.

Thirdly, is electronic mail and conferencing facilities. Many hundreds of judges currently use the FELIX system, both for e-mail as well as for exchanging news and views across the judicial community. I am of the view that FELIX has succeeded in the past in spite and not because of the technology upon which it has rested. In practice, FELIX has not been especially easy to use and although it has been considered to be homely by more experienced users, it has not been welcoming to the novice. English judges need a new e-mail system (whether on a new FELIX or otherwise) – more secure and reliable than past versions of FELIX and one that more easily allows the transfer of documents. More than this, judges would benefit from having the related facility of their own judicial Intranet. As I mentioned earlier, this is akin to a private Internet site, complete with useful news, primary and secondary resources, links and documents and allowing judges to 'talk' to one another online. As a geographically dispersed community, such a resource would greatly help to bring judges together as one group – under the one 'virtual roof'.

Finally, I note that judges are only beginning to derive benefit from the Internet. While, like others, I worry about information overload, I am convinced that the Internet will become increasingly central to their working lives and at the heart also of many of the cases upon which they are called upon to decide. A modern judiciary must seek to understand the potential as well as the limitations of new tools and services and so I would encourage all judges to go online, to experiment and to learn.

Of course, electronic methods will not always be better than manual and conventional approaches. The challenge is to achieve the best blend of electronic and conventional working practices.

But that is not the only challenge. Technically and organisationally, another formidable set of management issues arise when taking a step back from judicial technology and looking at the integration of the systems of different parts of the justice system as a whole. While judges do not have direct responsibility in this arena, it is important that they grasp the underpinning management thinking.

In England today, there are clear overlaps, from an IT perspective, between the current proposals from the Court Service to modernise the civil courts, the ongoing work in bringing together the major information systems across the criminal justice system, and the various other initiatives in the family courts, specialist courts, and indeed in the tribunals.

A crucial task for government policymakers is to identify the interrelationships between the various systems and technology that will come to underpin the civil, family, criminal and tribunal systems and, where necessary, to ensure there is sufficient and appropriate interoperability; or even shared systems.

That there should, to some extent, be interoperability or even shared systems is widely accepted as a general matter of good sense. I think it is necessary now, however, to be far more precise about what systems and what elements of systems can and should be common across the different jurisdictions. As it stands, I know of no work that is specific enough on this subject. There are general demands for common systems (judges are among those who are calling for this) but no full analysis yet (that I have seen) of the nature of that commonality nor justifications for the claim that systems should indeed be common.

As a starting point, it seems to me that the following categories indicate what aspects of systems might be developed or maintained in common across the justice system:

1. the information and data itself;
2. the user interface;
3. the infrastructure; and
4. some applications.

In what follows, I say a little about each of these four categories.

In the criminal system, the main systems (police, prosecution, court, prisons and so forth) should, I believe, share a common pool of information and data (this is much more than mere interoperability where one part of the system passes materials electronically to another). I see less need for this 'unification' of data in the civil and tribunal jurisdictions, but a clear task for policymakers, I suggest, is to identify those parts of the system where the overlap and sharing of data is so pervasive that common data should be advocated. Sometimes, when there is a need to pass data between systems, trying to establish common data is going too far. Instead what is needed, as I say, is interoperability – the capability of systems to pass information easily between one another.

From the judges' point of view, I think there should be a common judicial user interface, so that the part of the system that the judge actually sees and uses is not different across different jurisdictions. Indeed all data from all jurisdictions should feed automatically into this single interface. This leads naturally to the concept of a 'judicial portal'. I suspect a common user interface for many court and tribunal officials would be similarly appropriate.

Some infrastructure should surely be shared across all jurisdictions, such as telecommunications, major file servers, relational database management systems and technical support. It would be potentially very inefficient for the Lord Chancellor's Department and its executive agencies to run similar services (in different jurisdictions) using different infrastructure. This is partly an economy of scale issue; and partly a question of setting up systems so that when interoperability or common data is wanted, then having common infrastructure increases the chances of successful operation.

Some applications should be common. A judicial working group has powerfully argued, for example, that case management systems for civil and family courts should be the same. I am not sure they need to be the same as those for criminal but this needs some further discussion. There are strong arguments, however, for diarying/listing systems to be common – this would help officials with their case load management and, of course, judges who will want one integrated diary (although I accept this could be achieved less elegantly through interoperable systems). The challenge again for policymakers is to identify those applications (software systems, other than operating systems) that, for policy, economic or operational reasons should be common; and, of course, they would need to point to what parts of the system (if not the entire justice system) this commonality applies to.

Finally on IT, it is always important to reflect on the benefits that technology might bring to the judiciary and to the court system more generally. I believe these benefits can be summarised briefly, as in the following table:

The benefits of IT to judges and the courts

- increased efficiency and so cutting of costs
  - networking all participants in the justice system
  - replacing a lot of paper by electronic media
- better productivity and so reduction in delays
  - internal Intranet leading to the sharing of information
- improved justice and access to justice
  - more accessible judges
  - primary and secondary sources on the Internet
  - new tools for satisfying hitherto unmet legal need
- greater public confidence in a modern and forward-looking justice system

These four classes of benefit are well worth achieving. But judicial IT, in particular, will not arise from nowhere. Committed, focussed, relentless management will continue to be needed.

Who should manage judges?

A central theme of this chapter has been that judges and their work would benefit considerably from the introduction of various management techniques that are working well in private sector law firms, such as performance appraisal and knowledge management.

A question that immediately falls to be answered is – who should be responsible for progressing and implementing modern management techniques within a judiciary? Who, in short, should manage the judges? The two most plausible classes of candidate are either professional managers (whether or not these are civil servants) or judges themselves.

Once again, I find it illuminating to reflect on the experience of law firms. Most major legal businesses around the world have experimented with a variety of top management structures, including having their very best lawyers assume the top management roles (such as managing partner), on a full-time or a part-time basis; engaging full-time professional managers who have never been practising lawyers (as chief executives or the like); adopting a hybrid model with senior partners and professional managers working hand-in-hand, dividing management responsibilities; and even giving the leading management roles to mid-range partners, those who are competent but not the best practitioners, thus leaving the outstanding client handlers and advisers to serve the market.

As a backdrop to each of these models, it should be noted as a general matter that most good lawyers, I think it fair to say, prefer advising their clients to managing their firms. On the other hand, most partners within law firms are more comfortable being managed by fellow partners rather than by professional managers. There is some snobbery and overstatement here, I have little doubt, but it is true that fellow lawyers with recent experience of working at the coal face do seem to have better insight and understanding into the practical demands of client work than non-lawyer professionals who have never advised as lawyers. Not only do lawyers tend to prefer being managed by lawyers but they like it best when they are managed by their leading legal practitioners. While some of the latter turn out to be hopeless managers, many are gifted individuals who take to management with flair and good effect, even if with some reluctance. On the question of whether the senior lawyers should work as managers on a part-time or full-time basis, it is a common experience that the part-time management approach works poorly – in the event of conflicting demands, the partners will invariably, and understandably, tend to the needs of clients before addressing internal issues. Clients take priority over management. In consequence, important, internal management responsibilities remain unfulfilled. Part-time management often means no management, or crisis management at best.

Today, reflecting the various tensions and preferences just noted, most of the world's leading firms now have full-time lawyers in top management roles and these are lawyers who have performed outstandingly with clients and so have considerable internal credibility. If they are not natural managers, this quickly becomes apparent and they return to fee earning. The model works well for all, except perhaps for the top partners themselves, these reluctant yet impressive managers who, when they have a spare moment (which is rare), wonder what life holds for them after they complete their terms as managers and whether they will be able to go back to conventional client work.

Turning back to judges, I am confident that they can learn much from the experience of top managers in law firms. As in legal businesses, as this chapter has sought to show, there is much to be managed in a judicial community.

I am inclined to suggest that full-time management roles should be introduced within judiciaries and that top judges should be seconded to these positions for finite periods of time (two or three years, ideally). Full-time senior managers who are not judges, rightly or wrongly, are likely to be ineffective and will struggle to command respect. And among judges, it will be the best judges who are likely to receive the greatest support from fellow judges, precisely because of their outstanding track records. Part-time appointments may disappoint, precisely because, as with senior partners, their judicial commitments are likely to take precedence. The top judges themselves may not welcome the prospect but these reluctant managers would surely make huge progress if applying themselves on a full-time basis, bringing to bear the energy and intellect that they have historically harnessed in their judicial work.

I can well imagine that some judges would regard the deployment of first-rate judicial minds on management responsibilities to be a lamentable waste, and demotivating for those involved. I have four responses to that line of argument. First, such a view tends unjustifiably to underestimate the potential impact of management on judges. As I have tried to show, various management tools can bring substantial benefits to judges and their work. If the change is led effectively, then the impact could be enormous. And the judicial managers themselves may be surprised at how stimulating management can be. To suggest we cannot afford to devote the time of leading judges to management is reminiscent of the ineffective lumberjack who is reluctant to pause to sharpen his blunt axe on the grounds that he does not have time for such a stoppage.

Second, it may well be that for individual judges it would indeed be a disappointing development in their careers – to step away from judging when perhaps at the peak of their powers to assume some management role, no matter how important. There may be a question of sacrifice here, I suppose. When senior partners in law firms leave client work aside to take on key management roles, they often do so not because they want to but because it will be for the greater good of their firm. Similarly, it may that top judges may need to take on management roles in the spirit of doing so for the greater good of the judiciary and society generally. Some may be willing to make such a sacrifice. Others may not.

My third response to those who might be sceptical about senior judges assuming full-time management roles is that there is strong precedent for senior judges taking some time away from judging. I have in mind the judicial conduct of public inquiries. Many top judges in England, for example, have been absent from the bench for many years while they have led such inquiries. While there is rightly some debate over whether or not this is a good use of judicial time, as long as this practice continues, it cannot be said that judges are appointed solely to decide cases. The intellectual abilities and great diligence of senior judges can surely be directed in more than one direction.

Finally, I say to those who seem to claim that judges should judge and do not much else, that many senior judges already spend significant amounts of time on the management of the judiciary, even if they do not perceive themselves as being heavily involved in the business of management. Ironically, many judges in England currently devote much time to reviewing, challenging and refining the decisions of these full-time professional managers (civil servants) who currently enjoy a wide range of related management responsibilities. Rather than seek to manage the managers, judges might be better employed in managing directly.

One problem today with senior judges' periodic engagement on management issues is the generic difficulty, alluded to earlier, of part-time managers tending to give priority to their mainstream work, so that management issues are not always given the immediate attention they deserve. In England, if the amount of time spent on the management of the judiciary by various senior judges were to be added up, the sum total could comfortably be redistributed, I suspect, so that a small number of judges could work full-time on management while the part-time judicial managers could return to full-time judicial duties. I find it hard to imagine a better way of introducing the discipline of management across the judiciary.[7]

7 December 2002.

The law of databases and databases of the law[1]

Colin Tapper

All of the members of the higher judiciary contribute in their judgments to the development of the law, but our honorand is perhaps unique in his contribution also to the way in which such judgments should be made available in a modern society, using modern technology. His boundless enthusiasm and unstinting support for the application of modern technology to law, partly through his work for the Society of Computers and Law, and partly through his membership of innumerable working parties and research groups, has contributed greatly to the, often unrecognised, warmth of the reception to modern technology by what is often popularly perceived to be a somewhat conservative, indeed reactionary, profession. However justified that perception may have been a century ago, when solicitors were reluctant to accept typed opinions from counsel, it has never been the case with respect to the advent of the computer, and our honorand has played a major part in generating such a response. It is appropriate to bring together in this contribution an assessment of the interaction between the techniques that his extra-curricular activities have helped to develop, and the legal means for regulating them, in the context of the products of his professional career.

At present the law relating to databases is divided between the law of copyright, and a newly introduced, and still unfamiliar, database right. The impact of both of these upon the accessibility of judgements will be considered here, but it is first worth a glance at the provenance of these forms of law, and the part played in that provenance by the problems posed by modern technology.

1 For reasons of space attention will be directed more towards databases of cases than towards those of statutory provisions.

Development

It is interesting to note that the law of copyright was itself a reaction to the adoption of a new and radical technology, that of the invention of moveable type, and its use to print books for, by comparison with the preceding period at least, mass consumption. It should also be noted that in its origins copyright was not developed to protect the authors of creative works, but rather to regulate the printing and publishing of more factual publications. Soon after the introduction of printing by moveable type in the last quarter of the 15th century, the Crown claimed to control printing as part of the royal prerogative, and implemented its control through decrees of the Court of Star Chamber. Much of the motivation for this was the desire to suppress the expression of religious and political discussion.[2] By the middle of the next century the administration of this system was passed on to the Stationers' Company,[3] a feature of which was that it was composed exclusively of printers and publishers, and excluded authors. Once again the principal motivation for the move was the regulation of the printing of factual works.[4] One of the very earliest licences[5] allowed by the Stationers' company was for the printing of law books. Upon the restoration of the monarchy after the civil war, the Court of Star Chamber having been abolished some 20 years before, ordinary statutory control was asserted through the medium of the Licensing Act 1662, which distinguished quite clearly between licensing the printing of statutes,[6] and

2 It is interesting to note that one dimension of the current debate about provision for databases is concerned with the extent to which it can be reconciled with the freedom of speech provisions of the constitution of the United States: see Benkler 'Free as the Air to Common Use: First Amendment Constraints on Enclosure of the Public Domain' 74 NYULR 354 (1999); 'Constitutional Bounds of Database Protection: The Role of Judicial Review in the Creation and Definition of Private Rights in Information' 15 Berk HTLJ 535 (2000); Hamilton 'Response' at 605.

3 Chartered in 1556.

4 The Charter explicitly justified itself at the outset by reciting that '...considering and manifestly perceiving that certain seditious and heretical books rhymes and treatises are daily published and printed by divers scandalous malicious schismatic and heretical persons, not only moving our subjects and lieges to sedition and disobedience against us, our crown and dignity, but also to renew and move very great and detestable heresies against the faith and sound catholic doctrine of Holy Mother Church and wishing to provide a suitable remedy in this behalf, of our special grace and from our certain knowledge and mere motion we will, give and grant [the relevant control to the Company].'

5 To Richard Tottle, running apparently with partly retrospective effect from 25 July 1555 to 5 July 1556.

6 S III.2 which required a warrant under the sign manual.

that of 'all books concerning the common law of this realm.'[7] Despite some early cases[8] offering some support to the requirement for a warrant, the situation seems to have decayed soon afterwards,[9] and the Licensing Acts were not renewed after 1694.[10] This set the scene for the enactment of the first Copyright Act in 1709, and the focus on non-fiction can once again be discerned in the preamble which justifies the legislation as being 'for the encouragement of learned men to compose and write *useful* books.'[11] It is worth noting that this legislation initially refers to 'books and other writings', although most subsequent provisions in the statute refer only to books, and that it confers rights on 'authors', but without essaying any definition of an author.

The publication of law books, quite often law reports, continued to provoke litigation,[12] and it is interesting to note that there never seemed to have been much doubt in England that such reports attracted copyright protection, though it was less clear whether this was for the compilation as such, or for the individual reports.[13] It is also interesting to discover that the issue of whether copyright in a compilation was infringed merely by taking a substantial part of

7 S III.4 which delegated such licensing to the 'lord chancellor, or the lord keeper of the great seal of England for the time being, the lords chief justices, and the lord chief baron for the time being, or one or more of them, by their or one of their appointments.'

8 *Stationers' Company v Patentees about the printing of Roll's Abridgement* (1666) Carter 89; *Roper v Streater* (1672) Skinner 234.

9 See *Earl of Dartmouth v Darrel* (1685) 3 Mod 75. It had not been very satisfactory before since as early as 1558 the patentee was complaining that there was no profit in his patent to print the statutes since his predecessors had printed enough copies to last for 20 years.

10 Although not repealed until the Statute Law Revision Act 1863. They survived only in the meaningless recitation of a licence by publishers of reports, for which they were roundly condemned by Burrows in the preface to his reports in 1765.

11 Emphasis supplied. It is worth noting that when the US secured its independence it still retained this concept, and bestowed upon Congress the power to promote 'the progress of science and the *useful* arts' (emphasis supplied) by, in effect, intellectual property law. It is also worth noting, as pointed out by Ginsburg 'Creation and Commercial Value: Copyright Protection of Works of Information' 90 Col LR 1865 (1990) fn 28 that all of the first five petitions to Congress seeking exclusive printing privileges were for factual works.

12 The reported cases include *Gyles v Wilcox* (1740) 2 Atk 143; *Butterworth v Robinson* (1801) 5 Ves Jr 709; *Saunders v Smith* (1838) 3 My & Cr 711; *Sweet v Shaw* (1839) 8 LJ Ch 216; *Sweet v Maugham* (1840) 11 Sim 51; *Hodges v Smith and Welsh* (1840) 2 Ir Eq 266; *Sweet v Benning* (1855) 16 CB 459; *Incorporated Council for Law Reporting for England and Wales v Green* (1912) 4 McG CC 54.

13 See eg *Saunders v Smith* (1838) 3 My & Cr 711.

that compilation, or whether it was also necessary to copy the principle of organisation of the compilation, was itself ventilated in those cases.[14]

There never seems to have been doubt either about the ability of other forms of utilitarian compilations to attract copyright, for example in the shape of collections of maps, or trade directories. In one of the earliest treatises[15] it was said that all that was needed was the product of the claimant's labour, and that his would be satisfied by 'a use of old thoughts, and ideas, and sentiments, or by a new application or use of known and common materials, or a collection, the result of his industry and skill.' In *Kelly v Morris*[16] for example, it was regarded as too obvious for argument that a business directory[17] compiled after 'many years of incessant labour and expense' could be protected, and that a competitor would infringe, unless he went through a similar process to compile his directory:

> In the case of a dictionary, map, guide-book, or directory, when there are common objects of information which must, if described correctly, be described in the same words, a subsequent compiler is bound to set about doing for himself that which the first compiler has done. In the case of a road-book, he must count the milestones for himself. In the case of a map of a newly discovered island...he must go through the whole process of triangulation just as if he had never seen any former map, and, generally, he is not entitled to take one word of the work previously published without independently working out the information for himself, so as to arrive at the same result from the same common sources of information, and the only use he can make of a previous publication is to verify his own calculations and results when obtained.

Similarly a work that simply adds useful material to existing subject matter, such as the traditional telegraphic abstracts and headnotes prefixed to law reports, will attract copyright.[18]

14 In *Butterworth v Robinson* for example the defendant was said to have *artfully* [emphasis supplied] changed the chronological order of the original compilation of cases into an alphabetic order.

15 Copinger *The Law of Copyright* (1st edn, 1870) at 21, quoting verbatim from Curtis *Copyright* (1845).

16 (1866) 1 Eq 697.

17 A street directory in the same litigation was said to have exhibited great ingenuity in its presentation.

18 *Sweet v Benning* (1855) 16 CB (OS) 459.

It may seem difficult to apply the conventional meaning of the concepts of an author, or of originality, to such productions. If a publisher prints a book containing the judgments delivered in the Court of Common Pleas in a given year, he might seem not to be the author of the work, and it might not seem to be very original. However this appears to ignore the fact that what is protected are not the individual judgments, of which he may not readily be regarded as the author, but the composite work containing them. The compiler may much more realistically be regarded as the author of that work, and the decision to publish a particular year's production from a particular court in a particular order certainly originates with the compiler. It should also be remarked that in the 19th century, where reporters listened to the oral delivery of judgment, and did not purport to record every word in its original form, there was considerable scope for attributing authorship even of a single report to the reporter. It is certainly the case that particular series of reports were regarded as reflecting the abilities of the reporter, and many were roundly condemned.[19]

It was partly for that reason that the system of semi-official law reporting was introduced in the UK in the latter part of the 19th century, by means of the Incorporated Council for Law Reporting.[20] This was certainly motivated by the failure of the previous system to make the case law of the realm sufficiently reliably, concisely and cheaply available to the profession and to the public. In other jurisdictions different approaches were adopted. In the US the supposedly[21] older English practice of appointing official reporters was taken seriously, and in *Wheaton v Peters*[22] the battle between successive official reporters provided the context for determining that no copyright should attach to reporting the decisions of the judges. In the wake of that decision, much the same problems of the proliferation, cost and inaccessibility of reports occurred also in that jurisdiction. Market forces resolved the problems there however as the West Publishing Company gradually achieved market dominance, and by the early years of the 20th century set de facto standards as the clear

19 Espinasse is perhaps the most well-known example of a reporter attracting a bad reputation, though he was far from the worst: see Wallace *The Reporters* (1882) for a systematic analysis of the strengths and weaknesses of the old reporters.

20 See Daniel *History of 'The Law Reports'* (1884).

21 As stated by Plowden and Blackstone, but now universally rejected by reputable legal historians: see Maitland *Year Books 1 & 2* (1903) xi-xiii; Holdsworth *History of English Law* II (3rd edn, 1923) 532-536; Baker *The Common Law Tradition* (2000) 144-145.

22 33 US 591 (1834). See, further, Joyce 'The Rise of the Supreme Court Reporter: An Institutional Perspective on Marshall Court Ascendancy' 83 Mich LR 1291 (1985).

market leader.[23] It is worth noticing that the more formal rationalisation in England, as opposed to the competition-driven resolution in the US, combined with other cultural differences produced a different pattern of law reporting. In England reporting was always relatively sparse, and in theory confined to cases doing more than illustrating the application of an established rule, while in the US reporting was always much more comprehensive. This difference was itself reflected in the pattern of citation, and resulted in English citation being smaller in volume, but greater in age.[24] This gap in English reporting led to a renewed problem of chaotic reporting as publishers vied with each other to publish new specialised series, part of the selling point of which was to tap the reservoir of hitherto unreported cases. It also provided a spur to the development in England of the automated systems after the advent of the computer. In the countries of continental Europe, where codified law plays a greater role, and case law is regarded as more illustrative than determinative of the law, it is understandable that the diffusion of such case law is more often regarded as an official function, and one commonly undertaken by agencies of the state, sometimes in an official gazette.[25] A result of that has been that the development of automated services was more often also itself originated through official channels.[26]

23 Outlined in Biscardi 'The Historical Development of the Law concerning Judicial Report Publication' 85 Law Library J 531 (1993), for a more detailed account of the underlying law see Patterson and Joyce 'Monopolising the Law: The Scope of Copyright Protection for Law Reports and Statutory Compilations' 36 UCLALR 719 (1989).

24 Tapper *An Experiment in the Use of Citation Vectors in the Area of Legal Data* NORIS 36 (1982) Tables 1-3 indicates that an American case is nearly 10 times more likely to be cited than an English; and while two-thirds of the cited American cases were from the most recent decade, less than a quarter of the English came from such a period.

25 In England some official reporting takes place, for example in the reports of Patent Cases which is undertaken by the Crown, although currently through a commercial publisher acting as agent, and in the reports of the decisions of some tribunals.

26 This official sponsorship now applies to making the information available in electronic form, see *Green Paper on Public Information in the Information Society* COM(98)585 final (January 1999) citing the EUR-Lex website which makes the law of the EU, including its case law, freely available in an electronic copy of the Official Journal for a period of forty-five days after publication. Thereafter it is available through the CELEX system for a modest fee. Annex 1 contains a description, member state by member state, of the official information made available. In many member states, including the United Kingdom, legal information is said to be available through public and private co-operation.

Impact of technology

The situation described above in which judgments were largely delivered orally, and ex tempore, and then formulated into a report by a listening reporter, changed dramatically in the 20th century. It became more and more common for judgments to be written in advance and, still later, courts were wired for tape recording, which would then be transcribed into a written form. Nowadays many judgments are prepared on a word processor by the judges, and sometimes made available by the relevant court directly in machine-readable form.[27] The widespread use of computer technology in the publishing industry also meant that more and more commercial publication was mediated by an electronic form of the reports, and simultaneously with this development commercial publishers began to make judgments available electronically through subscription-supported information retrieval systems.[28] Still more recently it has been possible to obtain free access to an ever-widening range of original legal materials, including judgments, from internet-based services.[29]

The fundamental change here has been the supplementation of published volumes of printed reports with legal information retrieval systems containing vast quantities of reports in electronic form.[30] The consequences of this change upon the application of the law of intellectual property in this context are potentially profound.

At the present time[31] the availability of material in electronic form means that it can be manipulated, copied, and transmitted with complete accuracy, at enormous speed, and across jurisdictional boundaries at very low cost, and without much prospect of effective physical control. This is an especially serious problem for databases since the whole point of a database is that it should make the obtaining of relevant information as easy as possible. A legal database

27 For example the speeches in the House of Lords when sitting judicially.

28 Such as Lexis and Westlaw.

29 AUSTLII was an early example, and has given birth to a fledgling British system BAILII.

30 These are increasingly being supplemented by CD Rom-based stores of archived information in electronic form to reduce communication costs, now that personal machines have acquired sufficent power and large enough fast storage capacity to conduct efficient searching operations.

31 Development of effective encryption systems may change the situation radically in the future: see Gimbel 50 Stanford LR 1671 (1998); Chicola et al *Digital Rights Architectures for Intellectual Property Protection* (Joint MIT Harv LS Report, 10 December 1998).

will achieve utility to the extent that it makes it simple and speedy to find the relevant primary sources, and to the extent that they are not readily available in hard copy form to the user, to enable him to reproduce them for his own purposes. This will often involve several stages of copying, first to the central processor and the monitor for the purposes of checking relevance, then to some form of less volatile storage, typically on a local hard disk, to preclude the need for repeated communication with the central database, and often to a form of hard copy, given the greater ease of human use of information in such a form.[32]

At first the impact of such developments on the proprietors of commercial electronic legal databases was relatively muted. In part this was because of the enormous cost of preparing sufficient quantities of data for input to such systems. While the proprietors of the first commercial systems were expanding their coverage, it was difficult for potential pirates to compete, since they had no immediate access to the sources which were being used on a continuing basis to augment the systems. Further protection was provided by the enormous sums required to finance the hardware and software necessary for the efficient operation of such systems. These were inherently diminishing forms of protection however. As coverage increased, so the marginal utility of the latest additions decreased. In addition the very newest material was itself being made available directly by its originators, and no longer needed to be derived from the commercial providers as intermediaries, so vastly reducing, or even eliminating, their lead-time advantage in that respect. Perhaps most potent of all, the technology continued, and indeed continues, to develop at an incremental rate, driving down cost and at the same time driving up speed, reliability, capacity, and efficiency. Cost-effectiveness has improved to such an extent that there is now very little technological barrier to competition with established providers. Indeed the balance has tended to shift in favour of the newcomer, since the established provider is saddled with older systems and methods, suitable for a bygone age[33], which are both financially and culturally difficult to change.

A further facet of these changes in the context of the law of intellectual property is that the material is gathered together in a totally different form. In medieval times, it was revolutionary to gather judgments together and to publish them

32 Illustrated at a trivial level by the greater ease of detecting 'typos' on paper than on screen (automatic spell checkers are still not sufficiently well-developed to be able to cope adequately with mis-spellings which happen to be homonyms).

33 Speed of development is so fast that this may be a very short chronological period.

in the form of a year book. After the invention of printing, books achieved their recognisable modern form, and the physical and intellectual attributes of human beings determined their most convenient size and form. It became common to aggregate judgments in individual volumes, and often to publish them in a continuing series. Although some slight adjustment was made by the advent of looseleaf publishing, it had little impact in the field of law reporting. The development of the computer, and its use in this context, did make a difference. The use of a monitor to display text transformed the utilities of size and form completely. It became much less necessary to divide the law into smaller units, at least for reasons dependent upon the attributes of human beings. Their influence was replaced by technological and commercial factors. It became a question of the optimum unit for computer handling,[34] and the commercial desirability of particular pricing strategies. This change of form has significant implications for the definition of a 'work' and of its boundaries, since material is commonly continuously aggregated to an established database, whereas in the past physical considerations would have led to the periodic publication of a new volumes to replace, or supplement, the old.

Yet another change was dictated by the newer searching strategies associated with material held in storage on a computer. In the older system searching had to be organised by means of elaborate indexing and classification systems,[35] assisted by an apparatus of telegraphic abstracts and headnotes for individual cases; indexes for volumes and series; and digests for the whole panoply of legal materials.[36] This system also dictated the form of practitioners' works that obtains to this day, in which the text is little more than a narrative index to its footnotes. Modern systems are less dependent upon such intellectual foundations, and tend to rely as a substitute upon word occurrence, and co-occurrence, as a surrogate for meaning. Relevant cases are revealed not by scouring digests and indexes for words representing concepts, but by scanning vast concordances for strings of characters.[37] So in such systems the organisation of the information has been arranged in a totally new way, challenging the application of intellectual property rules posited upon more traditional means of preserving and presenting legal information. This challenge

34 At first this imposed a constraint upon the size of aggregations for convenient handling.

35 West's key number system was at the very zenith of this technique.

36 The most prominent domestic example being the *English and Empire Digest*.

37 In the future alternative systems may well be developed depending upon altogether different principles, including such techniques as citation vector matching and artificial intelligence.

is all the greater since much of the motivation for the change from indexing to word occurrence was to transfer the intellectual effort, and the responsibility, for detecting relevant information from the provider to the user. In other words the information is to be provided in as bland and as neutral a form as possible, eliminating elements of classification, organisation and arrangement in the presentation of the material. This further undermines any possible claim for originality or creativity in these elements of the compilations so used. Yet another motive for the creation of electronic legal databases was the desire to achieve more comprehensive coverage of the primary sources than was easily possible when they were distributed between different volumes, published by different publishers, and indexed according to different principles. To avoid errors of omission, it was desirable for the collection to be as full as possible,[38] so the further element of selection was minimised as a factor in this context.

Copyright

As indicated above it is possible to consider the position either from the point of view of copyright in individual judgments, or from that of copyright in a compilation including such judgments. These will be taken separately, distinguishing where necessary between the judgments, and reports of the judgments.[39] A further section will consider relevant differences between compilations of judgments in volumes, and in unsegmented databases. Because of dissatisfaction with the scope of protection, especially on the continent of Europe, member states of the European Union have been obliged to amend their law in certain respects,[40] both in relation to copyright *stricto sensu* which will be considered in the final part of this section, and by introducing a new database right, which will consititute the subject matter of the final part of this chapter.

38 Indeed most of the competition between the commercial database suppliers was devoted to exceeding the coverage of the others.

39 Laddie, Prescott and Vitoria *The Modern Law of Copyright and Designs* (3rd edn, 2000) para 36.46 distinguishes further in the case of sound recorded judgments between copyright in the sound recordings, and copyright in the transcript of those sound recordings.

40 EU Directive 96/9 on the legal protection of databases [1996] OJ L77/20 (implementation date 1 January 1998).

Individual judgments

Under the older law it was uncertain whether or not in England copyright in reported judgments inhered in the Crown, in the reporter, in the publisher, or in the judges who delivered them. As noted above, in the US no copyright attaches to judgments,[41]

> '...no reporter has or can have any copyright in the written opinions delivered by this court; and the judges thereof cannot confer on any reporter any such right.'

which are regarded as being in the public domain:[42]

> 'Judges...can themselves have No..proprietorship, as against the public at large, in the fruits of their judicial labours....The whole work done by the judges constitutes the authentic exposition and interpretation of the law, which binding every citizen, is free for publication to all....'

In England the case for copyright in individual judgments residing in the Crown depended either upon the prerogative, or upon the judges acting under the direction and control of the Crown so as to vest copyright in the Crown under the provisions of the Copyright Act 1956, s 39(1). Neither basis was wholly convincing. As noted above the Licensing Acts seemed to adopt a different approach to statutes, the archetype for Crown copyright, and to judgments, and in any event, after they had lapsed, a return to a purely prerogative claim for Crown copyright in judgments, not endorsed by the classic expositors of Crown prerogative,[43] nor by the relevant Treasury Minute,[44] seems an eligible target for Diplock LJ's stinging rebuke[45] that 'it is 350 years and a civil war too late for the Queen's Courts to broaden the prerogative.' So far as the argument based on CA 1956, s 39(1) was concerned the difficulty lay with the condition of the judges acting under the control and direction of the Crown. This provision was clearly designed for the ordinary situation of employment, and it was well-established that judges held office by

41 *Wheaton v Peters* 33 US 591 (1834) 668.

42 *Banks v Manchester* 128 US 244 (1888) 253.

43 Chitty *Prerogatives of the Crown* (1820) p 239 where some such reference might have been expected had the prerogative extended so far; see also Blackstone *Commentaries on the Laws of England* (1765) Ch 27.

44 31 August 1887.

45 *British Broadcasting Corporation v Johns* [1965] 1 Ch 32, CA at 79.

royal appointment, and not by contract.[46] Any such suggestion of direction and control would run counter to the whole culture of judicial independence.

The case for copyright in such judgments residing in the reporter could be supported by reference to the decision of the House of Lords in *Walter v Lane*[47] where it was held that the reporter of the speeches of Lord Rosebery was entitled to assert copyright against a third party pirate publisher. This might be taken to suggest that the reporter, at least of an oral judgment, would be entitled to copyright in that judgment. The weakness of this argument is that the decision in *Walter v Lane* was based upon the provisions of the Copyright Act 1842 which significantly omitted any condition of 'originality', an omission which has been repaired in the modern legislation which does contain such a condition.[48] It may also be significant that the original speaker was not a party to the litigation. A further difficulty is that any such ascription might cause difficulty by way of anomaly between those, now few, judgments delivered orally and ex tempore, and those either read from a previously written text, or simply handed down in that form.

The case for the publisher is to some extent supported by the numerous cases in which publishers were successful in litigation against pirates.[49] In very few, if any, of these cases however was there any serious argument against copyright in the publisher, nor was there usually any need to proceed beyond copyright in the compilation of judgments. *Saunders v Smith* did raise the point, since part of the defence was that no objection had been raised to the publication of the first volume of Smith's work, which contained just one or two cases from the plaintiff's volumes, and it became relevant to know whether copyright infringement had thereby been waived, which it certainly would have been if copyright inhered in each individual judgment, but probably would not have been if it had inhered only in the volume as a whole.[50] It was not however necessary to decide the point since the defence succeeded on wider grounds. It remains the case however that in all of these cases where the publisher prevailed the copyright seems to have been asserted by assignment from the author, or for the compilation, so there is no strong precedential support for copyright

46 *Terrell v Secretary of State for the Colonies* [1953] 2 QB 482, QBD per Lord Goddard CJ at 499. Similar indications can be drawn from s 3 of the Act of Settlement 1700, and from payment being made from the Consolidated Fund.

47 [1900] AC 539, HL.

48 Currently in the Copyright, Designs and Patents Act 1988, s 1(1)(a).

49 Most of the cases mentioned in fn 12 above fall into such a category.

50 Since the amount taken would not have been sufficiently substantial.

being any more held by the publisher in this case of judgments than in that of any other literary work.

The case for the judge having copyright is simply that he provided the original creative input, and that on ordinary principles he would acquire copyright in the work so produced. Some support may be derived from dicta in the earliest cases[51] which often seem to trace the publisher's right to an assignment from the judge who delivered the judgment. There is also some isolated support from the behaviour of modern judges, one of whom is reputed to have demanded payment before allowing his judgments to be printed,[52] and others who are reputed to have struck out a recitation of Crown Copyright on transcripts of their judgments supplied to them to correct.[53] The difficulty with this argument is that there is plenty of judicial support for the proposition that the law should be accessible to the public,[54] and against any suppression.[55] Lord Diplock indeed affirmed in *Home Office v Harman*[56] that 'justice is to be administered in open court where anyone present may listen to and *report* what was said'. There is a generally resounding abstinence from any judicial claim to copyright, and the Whitford Committee stated[57] that it knew of no such claim ever having been made.

The final possibility is that in England, as in the US,[58] judgments fall outside the ambit of copyright altogether, and are in the public domain. The case for this rests on the practice of copyright in individual judgments not being enforced, on the policy that the law should be accessible to all, and on the

51 See cases mentioned in fns 8 and 12 above.

52 See Taggart 'Copyright in Judgments' (1984) 10 Syd LR 319, at 327 n 66.

53 This is more equivocal as it is just as consistent with, and indeed more likely to express, a view that the judgment is in the public domain than that copyright remains with the judge.

54 Eg *Merkur Island Shipping v Laughton* [1983] 1 All ER 334, CA per Lord Donaldson MR at 351, a sentiment explicitly endorsed by Lord Diplock speaking on appeal for a unanimous House of Lords [1983] 2 AC 570, HL at 612.

55 See *Scott v Scott* [1913] AC 417, HL at 448 'to say that all subsequent publication [of proceedings in court] can be forbidden...is...an unwarrantable interference with the rights of the subject. It is not that a court should refrain from exercising its power in such a way. It is that the Court does not possess such a power.'

56 [1983] 1 AC 280, HL at 303, emphasis supplied.

57 *Copyright and Designs Law* Cmnd 6732 (1977) para 588.

58 For the position in the US, see Patterson and Joyce 'Monopolising the Law: The Scope of Copyright Protection for Law Reports and Statutory Compilations' 36 UCLALR 719 (1989); Biscardi 'The Historical Development of the Law concerning Judicial Report Publication' 85 Law Library J 531 (1993)

complete absence of any need for any incentive to the judges to pronounce and publish their decisions. However the argument has never been presented, much less succeeded in any leading English case, and although putting the case for it, the Whitford committee deliberately diluted its full support for such a policy.[59]

The matter has now been affected by the provisions of the Copyright, Designs and Patents Act 1988. It will be recalled that under the Copyright Act 1956, s 39(1) Crown copyright was made to inhere in works made under the direction or control of the Crown. This was sometimes criticised as being too wide, and in CDPA 1988, s 163 the phrase was changed to a work made by 'Her Majesty or by an officer or servant of the Crown in the course of his duties.' Although in many cases this would operate to restrict the ambit of Crown copyright, it does seem to be a phrase more apt to relate to judges delivering judgments in the course of their judicial business.[60] It is also necessary to take into account the somewhat enigmatic provision of CDPA 1988, s 43(2):

> Copyright is not infringed by anything done for the purposes of reporting such[[61]] proceedings; but this shall not be construed as authorising the copying of a work which is itself a published report of the proceedings.

The first phrase of this provision seems to allow copying the words used by a judge in delivering his judgment for the purposes of reporting it, whether his judgment at delivery is Crown copyright, or not. This seems not to be contradicted by the proviso which relates not to the copying of judgments,[62] but to the copying of reports of judgments. Judges do not report their judgments by delivering them. It should also be noted that the CDPA 1988 defines 'publication'[63] to include

59 Para 591.

60 This view was supported by Cornish *Intellectual Property* (2nd edn, 1989) para 13-039 (the 4th edition (1999) para 13-106 is rather more equivocal) and Monotti 'Nature and basis of Crown Copyright in Official Publications' [1992] EIPR 305, but rejected by Laddie, Prescott and Vitoria *The Modern Law of Copyright and Designs* (3rd edn, 2000) paras 36.40-36.49 on the basis that the term 'officer' is to be construed congruently with that of servant, and who remark on the total absence of any declared intention to change the law in this sense, although that may be explained on the basis that the government of the day seems likely to have been advised that Crown copyright already existed for judgments: see *Crown Copyright in the Information Age* Cm 3819 (1998) Annex A.

61 Parliamentary or judicial.

62 It is submitted that in this context 'judgments' is a sufficiently accurate synonym of 'proceedings'.

63 And related expressions.

making a work available to the public by means of an electronic retrieval system. The result seems to be that it is an infringement of copyright to copy an electronic report of a judgment, and such a copy needs to be made in order for such a report to be displayed to a user. It is left unclear what or whose copyright is being infringed. In the case of an individual report made available by the Court itself, it might well be Crown copyright which would be infringed. In the normal case of an electronic report made available by a third party it is less clear, since it is hard to see how copying an individual judgment infringes the copyright in the complete compilation made available by the third party, since it would hardly be a substantial part of it, and the only other copyright which would exist is Crown copyright, which the third party would not, without some further basis for such a power, be able to waive. Yet, as noted above, the whole underpinning for the development of electronic legal information retrieval systems by commercial publishers is that users pay a fee to use the systems in the sense of locating, displaying, and indeed downloading, the judgments which they contain.

Compilations

Although, as noted above, there was plenty of early case law indicating that compilations came within the protection of the law of copyright, it was not until 1911 that the Copyright Act explicitly recognised the fact by inclusion of a compilation as a form of literary work.[64] This explicit recognition was continued in the 1956 legislation, but to the consternation of the industry the term was initially omitted from the first draft of the 1988 legislation, and was replaced only after the consultation stage. It was however still left undefined, unlike most key terms of the Act.

In the US a compilation is defined in the Copyright Act 1976 as:[65]

64 In 1948 the Berne Convention was amended by the addition of Art 2(5) to require its members to protect 'collections of literary or artistic works such as encyclopedias and anthologies which, by reason of the selection and arrangements of their contents, constitute intellectual creations.' Since 1996 members of the World Trade Organisation have also been bound by the 'Agreement on Trade Related aspects of Intellectual Property Rights' (TRIPS) which includes Art 10(2) providing that 'Compilations of data and other material, whether in machine readable or other form, which by reason of the selection or arrangement of their contents constitute creations shall be protected as such.'

65 17 USC 101.

'a work formed by the collection and assembling of preexisting materials or of data that are selected, coordinated or arranged in such a way that the resulting work as a whole constitutes an original work of authorship.'

Special rules for compilations are also set out:[66]

'(a) The subject matter of copyright as specified by section 102 includes compilations and derivative works, but protection for a work employing preexisting material in which copyright subsists does not extend to any part of the work in which such material has been used unlawfully.

(b) The copyright in a compilation or derivative work extends only to the material contributed by the author of such work, as distinguished from the preexisting material employed in the work, and does not imply any exclusive right in the preexisting material. The copyright in such work is independent of, and does not affect or enlarge the scope, duration, ownership or subsistence of, any copyright protection in the preexisting material.'

In England the legislation was[67] more sparse. Copyright extended to original literary works,[68] and a literary work was defined to include a compilation.[69] The CDPA 1988 made explicit provision for computer-generated works, the author of which was taken to be the person making the arrangement necessary for its creation.[70] It followed from these provisions that a compilation qualified for copyright protection only if it was 'original' and a 'work'. Neither of these terms is defined in the statute, and it must be assumed that the previous common law interpretation continues to apply.[71] It should be noted that there was no suggestion that the subject-matter of the elements compiled together needed itself to be susceptible of copyright protection, so it would have been

66 17 USC 103 Subject Matter of Copyright: Compilations and Derivative Works.

67 The past tense is used on account of the amendments to the CDPA 1998 as a result of the Database Directive to be discussed below.

68 Copyright, Designs and Patents Act 1988, s 1.

69 CDPA 1988, s 3(1)(a).

70 CDPA 1988, s 9(3). This was a novel provision in the CDPA 1988, and it is understandable, although unfortunate, that the precise relationship between authorship, making, generation and creation was not further elaborated. It also fits rather clumsily with s 11 vesting copyright in works made by employees in their employers in the absence of contrary agreement.

71 A view supported by the unique construction provisions of s 172, although, as will be seen, there is some doubt about this in the case of the requirement of originality as a result of the development of the new database right.

no sufficient objection to the ascription of copyright in a compilation of judgments that none of the judgments itself attracted copyright protection.

The Whitford Committee whose report prepared the way for the passage of the 1988 legislation had little to say about compilations, contenting itself with the observation that:[72]

> 'copyright case law since before the beginning of this century has made it abundantly clear that ...a wide variety of compilations are in fact protected, such as directories, tables, football coupons, business literature and lists of all kinds. We take the view that adequate copyright protection already exists for tables and lists in the compilation of which sufficient skill and/or labour has been exercised and that no special action is called for.'

The law had been closely considered by the House of Lords in *Ladbroke Ltd v William Hill Ltd*[73] in relation to a compilation of bets on a fixed odds football coupon. It was generally accepted that the requirement for originality merely meant that the work should originate from the claimant, not that it should be original in the sense of being creative.[74] It was also accepted that the originality, even in this limited sense, must relate to expression, and not to the underlying ideas, although it is not quite so clear that this is consistent with other parts of their Lordships' reasoning.[75] It must also relate to the work as a whole, which should not be dissected into disparate parts for the purpose,[76] although occasionally a work may consist of separate compilations.[77] The final strand was that originality in this sense was[78] 'a matter of degree depending on the amount of skill, judgment or labour' involved.

72 Para 870.

73 [1964] 1 All ER 465, HL.

74 Applying the dicta of Peterson J in *University of London Press Ltd v University Tutorial Press Ltd* [1916] 2 Ch 601, Ch at 608.

75 In refusing to limit their consideration to the expression of the combination, but in considering also the work and skill involved in determining what to combine.

76 Lord Reid [1964] 1 All ER 465 at 469C; Lord Pearce at 479I. This may appear to be obvious in the case of a compilation, which may wholly consist of items to which no copyright attaches, but there are sometimes different levels of abstraction at which partition may be suggested.

77 As in *Leslie v Young & Sons* [1894] AC 335, HL where a selection of tours which was protected by copyright was bound up in a penny book with a selection of timetables which were not so protected.

78 Lord Reid [1964] 1 All ER 465 at 469I. At 471A he seems to have acted upon the slightly differently phrased list, taken from the speech of Lord Atkinson in *Macmillan & Co v Cooper* (1923) LR 51 Ind App 109, PC 'knowledge, labour, judgment or literary skill or taste'.

So far as infringement was concerned the House of Lords adopted a two-stage test; first, to determine whether copyright attached to the copied work, and second, to determine whether what had been copied amounted to a substantial part of the copied work. It was further accepted that in this context 'substantial' was to be considered in terms of quality rather than quantity.[79] Further important clarification was given to this issue in the very recent decision of the House of Lords in *Newspaper Licensing Agency Ltd v Marks and Spencer plc* where the matter is linked to the reason for ascribing copyright to the particular category of work:[80]

> 'But what quality is one looking for? That question, as it seems to me, must be answered by reference to the reason why the work is given copyright protection. In literary copyright, for example, copyright is conferred (irrespective of literary merit) upon an original literary work. It follows that the quality relevant for the purposes of substantiality is the literary originality of that which has been copied.'

Although that case was concerned with a claim for a typographical arrangement it was on its facts concerned with compilations, since the claim was an attempt to restrain the defendants from copying and distributing compiled press cuttings relating to the defendants, culled from newspapers and magazines which were themselves compilations.

This decision clearly suggests that copyright in a compilation will in England be infringed only if a substantial part of what qualifies the compilation for protection as an original work has been taken. In the case of many compilations this will amount to aspects of the selection or arrangement of the items constituting it. If, however, like compilations of law reports, the main reason for protecting the compilation is no more than the effort and expense of producing it, it may be thought that quality sinks back into some consideration of quantity.

Some help in understanding the basis for protecting compilations may be derived from assessment of the few cases in which protection has been denied. The very fact that they are so few itself suggests that qualification for protection is very easily satisfied. One of the earliest such cases was *Leslie v Young &*

79 Lord Pearce [1964] 1 All ER 465 at 481C.

80 [2001] 3 All ER 977, HL per Lord Hoffmann at 983h, with whose speech all of the other members of the House explicitly agreed.

Sons[81] where the defendant had done no more than copy a local subset of timetables from a rival publication, the latter having been derived, with minor variation, from more comprehensive timetables, in respect of which no claim was made. It seems that the work of identifying, and modifying, such items was regarded as too trivial to justify protection. A slightly different example was once again provided by the House of Lords in *Cramp & Sons Ltd v Frank Smythson Ltd*[82] where the appellant had in compiling a diary copied seven out of the eight tables included as additional information from the respondent's diary. Here too it was held that the task of selection had been too trivial to attract protection.

In the US the law developed upon very similar lines, although there were changes of emphasis even within the same circuit,[83] before the Supreme Court of the US considered the matter anew in the seminal case of *Feist Publications Inc v Rural Telephone Co Inc.*[84] That case was concerned with very simple facts,[85] the unlicensed[86] copying of a white pages telephone directory. It was conceded that the directory as a whole[87] was protected by copyright, but denied that any of the parts taken were themselves susceptible of such protection, since they consisted of no more than bare factual information, such as the name of the subscriber, his telephone number and location.[88] The Supreme Court construed the statutory copyright provisions from 1790 up to the 1976

81 [1894] AC 335, HL.

82 [1944] AC 329, HL. It was conceded that no claim could be made for the arrangement, as opposed to the selection, of the tables which were of commonplace information of the sort usually inserted into such diaries.

83 Cp in the 2nd Circuit *Jeweler's Circular Publishing Co v Keystone Publishing Co* 281 F 83 (1922) with *Eckes v Card Prices Update* 736 F 2d 859 (1984); and in the 9th *Leon v Pacific Telephone & Telegraph Co* 91 F 2d 484 (1937) with *Worth v Selchow & Righter Co* 827 F 2d 569 (1989).

84 499 US 340 (1991).

85 About the only complication was that the plaintiff was under a statutory obligation to publish the names of all of its subscribers in its directory under the terms of its licence to provide a telephone service, and could thus be alleged not to have selected the names.

86 An explicit licence had been refused.

87 Including a classified yellow pages part, and introductory notes and information. The commercial basis for the dispute was that Rural derived a return for selling advertisements in its yellow pages, and Feist which published a directory relating to a much wider area of which Rural's was merely a part, was also seeking to sell yellow page advertisements, often in competition with Rural.

88 Usually at the level of the town. Feist, in many cases, added street addresses, but Rural seems to have claimed no creativity in its decision to omit this information from its own pages.

revision to require 'originality'.[89] It regarded the authorities as requiring a minimum of creativity, in the sense of an intellectual contribution from the author, and to amount to infringement only if a substantial part of that intellectual contribution were appropriated. In relation to factual compilations this gave rise only to 'thin' protection in the sense that the underlying facts could be taken from a compilation, so long only as there was no copying of the intellectual contribution, typically in the selection or arrangement of the facts in the compilation.

The Court was emphatic in its rejection of 'industrious collection' or 'sweat of the brow' as a sufficient condition for the ascription of copyright. It felt that if this were allowed the underlying facts would not be capable of being copied without infringement.[90] It should be remembered at this point that in the US it is absolutely clear that a report of the verbatim words of a judgment is no more susceptible of copyright as such than is a note of a man's name, address and telephone number. This argument is not completely convincing. While it may be true that to allow copyright to an industrious collection of facts would prevent copying a substantial part of that compilation, it is much less clear that it would prevent copying individual facts, either because that they are an insubstantial part of the complete collection, or because publishing the data base conveys an implied licence to copy individual facts, or more generally because such a use of the information is within the fair use exception.

A consequence of the decision in *Feist*, that only copying the creative elements of selection, co-ordination and arrangement is capable of amounting to infringement, is that this in itself creates a danger that the creative elements are no more than ideas, and as such themselves incapable of protection, especially in the US. This argument surfaced in *CCC Information Services Inc v Maclean Hunter Market Reports Inc*[91] in relation to the copying of used car valuations, and caused the court some difficulty, which it resolved by noting that if taken to extremes this view combined with the approach in *Feist* would have far too drastic an effect on copyright for compilations, which the federal legislation, implementing the Constitution, expressly recognises. It cannot be pretended

89 Which it determined to be implicit in the statutory phrases relating to 'authors' and 'writings' even though not used explicitly before 1976, relying upon its earlier decisions in *The Trade Mark Cases* 100 US 82 (1879) and *Burrow-Giles Lithographic Co v Sarony* 111 US 53 (1884).

90 It drew attention to 17 USC § 102(b) which excludes from copyright 'idea, procedure, process, system, method of operation, concept, principle, or discovery' (though somewhat embarrassingly not 'facts').

91 44 F 3d 61 (2nd Cir, 1994).

however that the intellectual foundations for this interpretation seem particularly robust.[92]

Electronic databases

As noted in the second section above, modern information retrieval systems employing information in electronic form challenge many of the assumptions upon which the law of copyright in relation to factual works has been based. In particular, the materials are not sub-divided into volumes; are not held, or even presented, in a particular arrangement; and certainly in the case of law reports can be represented as not having been selected so far as the system seeks to be as comprehensive as possible.

The contrast between the cost of creating such a system, and the cost of reproducing the data it contains is vast. It is ironic that much of the cost relates to the arrangement of the data in the sense of preparing it for the operation of the relevant system. Thus a comprehensive system of collection of data, of checking, of normalising, of tagging, and of inter-linking will have to be developed, to dovetail into an efficient set of programs for manipulating the data both from the point of view of maintenance and supplementation by the supplier, and also for ease of use by the customer. Yet all of this takes place behind the scenes, and when the data as presented by the system is copied it strains language to say that such a system has been reproduced, rather than used.[93]

It remains to be seen how the courts have adapted the modern approach to the protection of compilations to those held on computers, and to date most of the decisions have been found in the US in the wake of the decision in *Feist*, some of them in the area of computerised law reports.

92 See Ginsburg 'Copyright, Common Law and sui generis Protection of Databases in the United States and Abroad' 66 U of Cincinnati LR 151 (1997) at 154.

93 Which Laddie J claimed to be the essence of infringement of copyright in literary works in *Autospin (Oil Seals) Ltd v Beehive Spinning* [1995] RPC 683, Ch at 700 (original emphasis): 'It is not enough to say that the defendant has 'used' the plaintiff's work. He must have *reproduced* it.' A similar sentiment was expressed by the Supreme Court in *Feist* at 349, and quoting Justice Brennan for the view that to allow such use was 'the essence of copyright'.

The most appropriate starting point is with the pre-*Feist* decision of the Eighth Circuit in *West Publishing Co v Mead Data Central Inc.*[94] In that litigation West, the proprietors of Westlaw, obtained an injunction to prevent Mead, the proprietors of Lexis, from inserting into the body of the case law reports of decisions of the Federal courts, 'star' pagination referring to the page numbers of the hard copy versions of the reports published by the West Publishing Company. It was held that to do so would infringe West's copyright in its published volumes, because it would amount to an appropriation of West's arrangement of its volumes, which was entitled to copyright as involving sufficient skill and effort to surpass the threshold requirement of originality to justify protection. However implausible and unconvincing such a decision,[95] it represented the latest statement of the law at the time of the decision in *Feist*. It was thus to be expected that in the aftermath of the ruling in *Feist* a challenge would be mounted to quite so minimalist a view. The first decision came in *Oasis Publishing Co Inc v West Publishing Co*[96] in relation to the inclusion of West's page numbering from the *Southern Reporter* in a CD-Rom to be published by Oasis. The Minnesota District Court was so strongly of the view that *Feist* had made no difference that it went so far as to enter summary judgment in West's favour. It took the view that the decision in the *Mead* case had not depended on a 'sweat of the brow' argument, and that the very low standard of originality espoused in *Feist* had been surpassed. This proved not to be the last, or most persuasive, word, and the issue came before the Second Circuit in *Matthew Bender & Co Inc v West Publishing Co*[97] in relation to 'star' pagination on a Bender CD-Rom to cases in the New York Supplement published by West. This time the court held that the allocation of page numbers[98] fell short of the minimal standard of creativity required under *Feist*. It rejected the argument that this was an indirect means of copying the arrangement of the West volume on the basis that this had already been conceded by West which recognised the incorporation of the first page number of a case in the West volume as a fair use. By applying exactly the same technique

94 616 F Supp 1571 (D Minn, 1985) affd 799 F 2d 1219 (8th Cir, 1986).

95 For criticism of the reasoning see Tapper 'An Aspect of Copyright in Data Bases' 14 N Kentucky LR 169 (1987); Patterson and Joyce 'Monopolising the Law: The Scope of Copyright Protection for Law Reports and Statutory Compilations' 36 UCLA LR 719 (1989).

96 924 F Supp 918 (D Minn, 1996).

97 158 F 3d 693 (2nd Cir, 1998).

98 This is, in fact, accomplished completely automatically by the operation of the program driving the printing process.

to these numbers, as opposed to the internal pagination, it would also be possible to reconstruct the arrangement of the West volume. The Court went on to reject West's argument for the further more wide-ranging reason that the mere fact that by an intervening operation an apparently different arrangement could be converted to the arrangement alleged to have been reproduced would not be sufficient to amount to infringement.

Database Directive

Although, as indicated above, commercial databases attracted considerable support under English law,[99] they were less well protected on the continent of Europe.[100] Given the further attention to the issue generated in the US by commentary on the decision in *Feist*, and the perceived commercial significance of databases, the European Union reconsidered its stance. The result was the passage and implementation in the member states of the European Union of further provisions in a form dictated by a new Database Directive, the very first recital of which made such concerns explicit:

> '(1) Databases are at present not sufficiently protected in all Member States by existing legislation; such protection, where it exists, has different attributes.'

It was perceived that such differences would both disadvantage the member states by comparison with the US by inhibiting investment,[101] and that they distorted the internal market for information which was perceived as being of growing, and crucial, importance for future prosperity.[102]

The broad scheme of the directive was to distinguish between copyright protection for any originality in selection or arrangement of databases, and a

99 Many felt that they attracted too much, see Thorne 'The Infringement of Database Compilations: A Case for Reform?' [1991] EIPR 331.

100 See for example, *Inkassoprogramm* Fed Sup Ct 9 May 1985 (Germany); *Van Dale v Romme* HR 4 January 1991 (Netherlands).

101 Even after *Feist*, the precise impact of which could not be foreseen with certainty.

102 Although, or perhaps because, the lion's share, about two-thirds, of cross-jurisdictional database exploitation was enjoyed by the UK where protection was greatest.

new *sui generis* extraction right,[103] to protect the contents of such a database.[104] For the purposes of the directive a database is defined to mean:[105]

> 'A collection of independent works, data or other materials arranged in a systematic or methodical way and individually accessible by electronic means.'

The threshold for protection is stated as follows:[106]

> '...databases which, by reason of the selection or arrangement of their contents, constititute the author's own intellectual creation shall be protected as such by copyright. No other criteria shall be applied to determine their eligibility for that protection.'

It is uncertain how far this has changed the criterion in England. The second sentence might be construed to exclude the mere expenditure of time, effort or expense, but the explanatory recital[107] mentions only the exclusion of aesthetic or qualitative criteria, thus indicating more a desire to cut down the sometimes excessive continental European criteria, rather than one to expand the minimal English one. It is also arguable that since the use of this phrase[108] in the software directive[109] was not thought to affect the standard of originality adopted in England, it will not do so in this context either. It should also be noted that any change is largely prospective, and rights in databases existing before the publication of the directive[110] are preserved.[111]

It was however necessary to amend the relevant provisions of the Copyright, Designs and Patents Act 1988 in accordance with the terms of the Directive[112] by excluding databases from the category of compilations as literary works in s 3(1)(a), and creating them as a separate category as s 3(1)(d). Such databases were then defined, but in slightly different terms from those used in the Directive, as a new s 3A:

103 The subject of the next part.
104 Which are explicitly excluded from protection under the copyright provisions: Art 3.2.
105 Article 1.2.
106 Article 3.1.
107 Recital 16.
108 'Author's own intellectual creation'.
109 91/250 on the legal protection of computer programs [1991] OJ L 122/42.
110 11 March 1996.
111 Article 14.2.
112 Copyright and Rights in Databases Regulations 1997, SI 1997 No 3032, Part II.

> '(1) In this Part 'database' means a collection of independent works, data or other materials, which –
> (a) are arranged in a systematic or methodical way, and
> (b) are individually accessible by electronic or other means.
>
> (2) For the purposes of this Part a literary work consisting of a database is original if, and only if, by reason of the selection or arrangement of the contents of the database the database constitutes the author's own intellectual creation.'

This definition raises problems in relation to such new concepts as 'independent works', 'arranged in a systematic or methodical way', 'individually accessible', and 'selection or arrangement of the contents of the database'. It seems that the requirement that the works should be independent was introduced, at least in part, at the instance of the film industry to exclude films from being regarded as a database of individual frames. It is however far from clear whether runs of fluctuations in a given share price in a day's trading would be independent, nor whether in the case of law reports, the report of a higher court overruling the decision of a lower would be regarded as independent. Then again, while it might be clear that to arrange law reports according to the date of decision might be systematic, what if they are arranged simply in order of receipt by the compiler? In the case of some data a random order might be deliberately chosen, would that be systematic or methodical? Individual accessibility raises the issue of whose access is concerned. It would be possible to create a database which could be retrieved by say, title or date, but which could be displayed or downloaded only in full-text. In such a case the system could secure individual access to the relevant elements, but the user of the system could not. Most obscure, and potentially contentious, of all is the criterion of selection and arrangement. If this is to be construed literally it would seem that all databases would satisfy the test, since the compiler has to decide for himself what items to include and which to leave out. These decisions are made at many different levels. In the case of judgments, there is first a decision as to dates and jurisdictions of the courts to be included, and then such matters as whether to include reports of judgments which have been formally overruled, or reference to which has for some reason been barred, and further which parts of the reports are to be included, for example dissenting judgments, or arguments of counsel. Here too arrangement is problematic since in modern electronic systems the user can often determine the form of display,[113] but the arrangement, if it can so be described, inside the computer

113 As West's somewhat fanciful suggestions mentioned above about the possibility of achieving a display of an electronic database in hard volume form bear witness.

is dictated entirely by the storage and retrieval system in conjunction with the operating system, and is both totally obscure to the user, and of little interest to a pirate who would almost certainly be using different systems, even if he desired to achieve an identical result.[114] As yet there has been no authoritative judicial resolution of these deep uncertainties.

Database right

The approach of the European community to these problems was somewhat paradoxical, in that it sought to distinguish sharply between harmonised copyright protection only for the intellectual content of compilations, and not for their, perhaps purely factual, contents. At the same time it was apparent that to leave,[115] or to make,[116] the contents freely available for appropriation would not achieve the object of providing an incentive for investment, nor secure a competitive edge over the US.[117] It was at first[118] decided to square this circle by developing the special rules adopted in some Scandinavian jurisdictions[119] to protect certain factual compilations by, in effect, a variety of unfair competition law. As a result of lobbying by database compilers however,[120] this idea was rejected in favour of the creation of a new *sui generis*, database right[121] restricting the right to extract and re-utilise the contents of a compilation of material, whether or not it qualified for copyright protection.

It is important to note that the new form of protection is supplementary to copyright protection, and not only to new databases qualifying under the amended terms of the legislation as a result of the domestic implementation of

114 Such a view is reinforced by recital 21 which distinguishes between the systematic arrangement and physical storage of materials.

115 In the case of many continental systems.

116 In the case of the English, and Irish, systems.

117 At the time of the first formulation of the proposals for the database directive it was explained that the US had about two thirds of the European database market: Explanatory Statement to the Council's Initial Proposal OJ C 156/03 (1992) at 9.

118 See the European Union's first proposal for a Council Directive on the Legal Protection of Databases, COM (92) 24 final–SYN393, Art 1 (1992).

119 See Karnell 'The Nordic Catalogue Rule' in Dommering and Hugenholtz (eds) *Protecting Works of Fact* 67-72 (1991).

120 This lobbying also succeeded in ridding the proposal of its original scheme for compulsory licensing by monopoly suppliers, and in confining the fair dealing exception to very narrow limits.

121 It is called a *sui generis* right in the Directive, but a database right in the English regulations.

the directive, but also to those older databases which qualified under the previous law.[122] In England then, old 'sweat of the brow' databases, even if they would under the new criterion[123] no longer be regarded as original literary works, would attract both the old rights which applied to them under the old copyright regime for the full copyright term, and the new database right, which, as will be seen, may last even longer in the case of compilations of judgments.

The principal criterion for protection, apart from jurisdictional origin, is stated in the directive to be one where the maker can show 'that there has been qualitatively and/or quantitatively a substantial investment in either the obtaining, verification or presentation of the contents'.[124] This is rather more tersely expressed in the English regulations as 'a substantial investment in obtaining, verifying or presenting the contents of a database'.[125] The definition of 'substantial' indicates that it can relate to quantity or quality, or to a combination of the two.[126] This still leaves the matter very obscure, and in particular whether or not the judgment is to be related to the resources of the compiler, or to be judged more objectively. 'Presenting' is also somewhat vague in its connotation, and in particular in the case of work made available electronically, leaves unclear quite how much of the computing substructure counts as a contribution to presentation.[127]

The principal contents of the right are to prevent 'extraction' or 're-utilisation'. Both the directive[128] and the regulations[129] define 'extraction' in more or less the same form[130] as meaning 'the permanent or temporary transfer of those contents to another medium by any means or in any form'. A slightly different

122 Provided that its, or one of its, makers was sufficiently connected to the European Economic Area (EEA): see reg 13(3), referring to reg 18.

123 Supposing it to have become more stringent.

124 Article 7.1.

125 Regulation 13(1).

126 'Investment' is itself defined to include investment in human and technical, as well as financial, resources which saves the concept of quality from complete absurdity in this context.

127 This point was mentioned as a difficulty by Laddie J in *British Horseracing Board v William Hill Organisation* [2001] RPC 31, Ch, at para 37.

128 Article 7.2(a).

129 Regulation 12(1).

130 The directive uses the phrase 'all or any part of the contents' while the regulations refer simply to 'those contents' referring back to 'any contents'.

approach is adopted to the definition of 're-utilisation' which in the directive is defined to mean: [131]

> ...any form of making available to the public all or a substantial part of the contents of a database by the distribution of copies, by renting, by on-line or other forms of transmission.

Regulation 12(1) is less explicit, and simply states that 're-utilisation', in relation to the contents of a database means making those contents available to the public by any means. It is worth noting that this definition of re-utilisation seems to concentrate on competing use, and that merely to use the data in connection with a different service offered to the public would not be so prevented. Thus it would seem that if law reports were substantially used in the preparation of legal advice there would not be a re-utilisation of them, [132] but it might be different if they were repackaged, perhaps by being presented in an abridgement, or in a manual for a particular legal topic. It is possible however that the initial display of the data would constitute extraction, as being a temporary transfer of the contents to a different medium. [133]

Both the directive and the regulations are clear that insubstantial extraction and reuse by a lawful user of a publicly available database is permissible, [134] though with the caveats that such use is not to prejudice the normal exploitation of the database, nor unreasonably to prejudice its maker's legitimate interests, [135] and that repeated or systematic extraction or re-utilisation of even insubstantial parts might thereby become substantial extraction or re-utilisation. [136] This appears to be designed to prevent collusive action to secure the contents of a database by extracting and re-utilising small complementary parts. Needless to say the verbiage, especially of the directive, is redolent with undefined and vague terms.

131 Article 7.2(b).
132 But see the broad approach of Laddie J to this issue in *British Horseracing Board v William Hill Organisation* [2001] RPC 31, Ch, below fn 154.
133 See recital 44. Presumably the transfer is from computer storage to visual display. The recital begins with the word 'when', which may suggest that this is not invariably the case, but the matter is obscure.
134 Article 8.1; reg 19(1).
135 Article 8.2; this provision appears not to be reproduced in the regulations.
136 Article 7.5; reg 16(2).

The period of protection is 15 years, to run from the time of completing the database.[137] This provision is interesting since it contemplates what must be the rather rare case of a database which is not maintained after first being made available. If, like most, it is maintained by deletion of old and the addition of new material, then questions will arise as to whether the investment in such activities is sufficient to satisfy the stated condition:[138]

> 'Any substantial change to the contents of a database, including a substantial change resulting from the accumulation of successive additions, deletions or alterations, which would result in the database being considered to be a substantial new investment shall qualify the database resulting from that investment for its own term of protection.'

This is a problematic provision which does not easily accommodate the typical case law database which is in continuous existence, and is never completed. The provision seems much more suited to the older system where databases were regularly replaced by new volumes, with substantial amounts of the data being taken over from one edition to the next.[139] Certainly if 'substantial' is here taken in an absolute, or perhaps even if in only a relative, sense, it would seem that a large case law database would never lose database right, which would be renewed from one year to the next. If that is the case, then, despite the protestation, in recital 45 to the directive, that this right does not extend copyright to facts, its effect is not far short of a massive extension of copyright protection for the contents of such databases. This problem is exacerbated by the extremely restricted ambit of a fair dealing defence to infringement of database right.[140]

It should be noted that database right is designed to fall outside the traditional national treatment applied to copyright, but as a *sui generis* right to be applied reciprocally, and to protect foreign makers only to the extent that the foreign jurisdiction offers comparable protection.[141] It seems that this provision was aimed at the US, and it has had the effect of raising the issue to much greater

137 Article 10.1; reg 17(1). Or a similar period from the time when a database is made publicly available, Art 10.2; reg 17(2). For databases completed after 1 January 1983, Art 14.5 and reg 30 allow 15 years' database right to run from the implementation date.

138 Article 10.3; reg 17(3).

139 As in a non-legal context in *Blacklock v Pearson* [1913] 2 Ch 376, CA.

140 Article 9; reg 20, Sch 1.

141 Recital 56, Art 11.

prominence in that jurisdiction.[142] It is certainly true that this form of the extension of protection has met a much more critical response from American scholars[143] than from European,[144] perhaps because of greater time to consider the impact of its provisions, and perhaps because of the greater strength there of constitutional protection for freedom of speech, and for innovation based upon technological advance.[145]

The first substantial judical examination of database right,[146] in England,[147] was undertaken, in that capacity, by Laddie J in *British Horseracing Board v William Hill Organisation.*[148] Once again the issue arose in a sporting setting, here the use by the defendants of some of the information provided by the former.[149] As a preliminary matter it was held that database right was conceptually distinct from copyright, and to be assessed independently. It was further accepted that the focus for consideration was to be the formulation adopted in the directive, rather than that in its expressions in the English regulations, on the basis that the regulations were to be construed according to the directive. This is itself a somewhat surprising constitutional stance. It seems hardly to have been disputed that the information here constituted a

142 A number of different bills, usually entitled Collections of Information Antipiracy bills, have been introduced in the US since the Database Directive, and the US supported a new WIPO Treaty to the same effect, but these efforts attracted considerable criticism, with the result that the bills have not yet been passed, and the draft treaty was abandoned in 1996 for further consideration.

143 See eg Ginsburg 'Copyright, Common Law and sui generis Protection of Databases in the United States and Abroad' 66 U of Cincinnati LR 151 (1997); Reichman and Samuelson 'Intellectual Property Rights in Data?' 50 Vand LR 51 (1997); Hunsucker 'The European Database Directive: Regional Stepping Stone to an International Model?' 7 Ford IP Media and Ent LJ 697 (1997). Two separate websites were created solely to contain discussion of database protection proposals in the US and in WIPO.

144 But see Cornish 'The European Community Directive on Database Protection' 21 Col-VLA JL and Arts 1 (1996).

145 See eg *Mazer v Stein* 347 US 201 (1954).

146 Copyright infringement was also claimed, but not pressed.

147 It was also considered on 30 January by the Court of Appeal in the Netherlands in *Holdingmaatschappij de Telegraf v Nederlandse Omroep Stichtung* and on 3 May 2001 by the Court of Appeal in Sweden in *Fixtures Marketing Ltd v AB Svenska Spel*, apparently to a different effect, and for this reason the English Court of Appeal on 31 July 2001 referred the case to the European Court of Justice pursuant to Art 234 of the Treaty of Rome.

148 [2001] RPC 31, Ch.

149 They were indeed entitled to use the information for their conventional activities, but were not licensed to use it in connection with betting services offered over the Internet.

database in the sense of being a collection of information, nor even that sufficient intellectual effort had gone into its creation for it to qualify for copyright protection as an original literary work, although in the context of database right the more relevant question was whether there had been a sufficiently substantial investment in its creation. Here Laddie J regarded the threshold as set low,[150] but once again there was little dispute that on the facts of the case it had been surpassed. More interestingly he accepted that the investment must be in the creation of the database,[151] and should disregard the preliminary work in creating what the database was to contain, although in a case where one party both creates and gathers the data together he felt that there might be difficulty. He noted that here investment in verification was particularly substantial.

Perhaps the most fundamental point was whether the new right protected the items comprising the compilation, or the items as compiled, described in argument, and borrowed by the judgment, as the 'database-ness' of the items. Thus it was argued that since to qualify as a database the items needed to be systematically arranged and to be individually accessible, so any infringement must extract or re-utilise those elements. If the items were protected simply as individual items it was argued that the protection would be indistinguishable from an extension of copyright to those items, which might well otherwise not qualify for protection by copyright. Laddie J rejected this argument upon the basis that the qualification for protection and the definition of infringement need not coincide. He held that the argument:[152]

> 'runs together two entirely distinct concepts, namely the features of form which have to exist before a database will be recognised as existing and the features of content or investment which are protected once a database is held to exist. Thus a database consists of a collection of data brought together in a systematic or methodical way so as to be

150 Apparently relying upon the example of insufficient investment indicated in recital 19, but it is hard to see that very much can be derived about the precise height of a barrier from one example of something falling below it.

151 The directive itself mentions obtaining, verifying and presenting data.

152 [2001] RPC 31 at para 47. Laddie J's reasoning at this point is wholly consistent with his rejection in para 78 of an attempt to evade the consequences of an injunction in terms of using the names of runners in races designated by course and time, by using instead identification of runners by number instead of name, and sequential numbering instead of time, which he held would amount merely to a rearrangement of the very data extracted and reutilised, and would not as such fall outside the prohibition which under database right applied to any extraction and re-utilisation of that data, and not merely to its arrangement.

> individually accessible by electronic or other means....But the fact that it has to take this form before database right can apply to it does not mean that the database right protects that form.'

He supported this argument by reference to copyright law, perhaps unwisely since to use such an illustration both contradicted his premise that database right is quite different from copyright, and the argument seems to amount to the exact opposite of the view subsequently expressed by the House of Lords in *Newspaper Licensing Agency Ltd v Marks and Spencer plc* .[153] First, he also relied upon those articles and recitals stressing the function of the directive to protect investment, concluding that the object went beyond the preventing of use to create a competing product, thus taking a broad view of the re-utilisation right.[154] Second, he further pointed out that substantial investment in verification was protected, thus suggesting that database right could arise in respect of items which were no different in form from the unverified source. Third, he argued that compilations held on a computer had no intrinsic arrangement or form, and unless his view were taken, such compilations would be freely extractable, capable of rearrangement, and in that form re-utilisable, which he considered quite alien to the object of the directive. His final argument was simply that the directive forbade the extraction and re-utilisation of part of a database, and it would be absurd to argue that the items it contained were not part of a database.

None of these strands of the argument is immune from criticism. The first seems to attach little importance to the need in the case of re-utilisation to show that the part has been 'made available to the public'; the second ignores the possibility that this refers only to verification of individual items, as in the directory cases; the third assumes that the directive is well-adapted and drafted in this respect to deal with databases held on computer, which it can be argued is not the case; and the last can be countered with the argument that the provisions were deliberately drafted more elaborately than this expression of them encapsulates, and that it would be equally absurd to ignore such drafting in order to promote a more simplistic interpretation.

More specific objections were made to the application of the concepts of 'extraction' and 're-utilisation' in this context. In relation to 'extraction' it was argued that in order to extract something from something else, it had to be

153 See above p 94.

154 It is true that while restricted to making the taken contents available to the public, it allows *any form* of so doing.

taken away, while in this sort of case nothing is taken away. Laddie J was surely right to reject this argument,[155] since the whole motivation of the directive was to prevent exactly such extraction, and the contrast with copyright cannot be so sharp as this argument supposes. Even if infringement of copyright is not theft, it does not follow that unauthorised extraction of data must be. A second argument, peculiar to the facts of this case, was that there was no extraction from the plaintiff's database, because the data had in fact been derived from a third party, who, if anyone, had extracted data from the plaintiff's database. Here Laddie J held[156] that indirect extraction was just as much extraction as direct extraction. This may go too far if taken as a universal and absolute rule, and further reflection in the light of different ranges of circumstances would be desirable.

In the case of re-utilisation the argument was that since the directive required the part that was taken to be made available to the public, it was fatal that much of this data had already been made available to the public by the time that the defendant made it available. Laddie J decided on this point[157] that there was nothing in the directive to require that the part made available should previously have been unknown to the public. In other words the focus should be on the nature of the defendant's acts, rather than on their result. It was immaterial to whether or not the defendant had made the matters available to the public, that others had already done so. Once again this seems little more than a further aspect of the answer to the first extraction argument. Just because information can be taken without its possessor being deprived of it, so it can be made available to the public, by any number of holders. To make information available to the public is, in short, to publicise it. This highlights one of the features of the directive which has excited persuasive criticism,[158] which is that the database right seems, unlike copyright, not in any way to recognise entry of the factual items with which it is concerned into the public domain. Combined with the vestigial extent of the fair dealing defence this has aroused considerable apprehension in the academic and scientific communities.

Issues also arose as to the substantiality of the data taken. The directive refers to 'a substantial part, evaluated qualitatively and/or quantitatively',[159] while

155 [2001] RPC 31 at para 56.
156 [2001] RPC 31 at para 57.
157 [2001] RPC 31 at para 59.
158 See Reichman and Samuelson 'Intellectual Property Rights in Data?' 50 Vand LR 51 (1997), at 84.
159 Article 7.1; reg 12(1).

the regulations simply define 'substantial' to mean 'substantial in terms of quantity or quality or a combination of both'. Laddie J regarded it as mistaken to consider quality and quantity separately, and while agreeing that the substantiality referred to the part of the database from, or of, which the extraction, or re-utilisation, took place, also felt that the purpose of the taker was of assistance in determining these questions.[160] In the case of this database, although only a minute fraction of the total number of items in the target database had been taken, he regarded the principal purpose of the database as being to culminate and find expression in the publication of the very parts taken by the defendant, namely those giving as authoritative a list as possible of the runners in a particular day's racing. The argument looked particularly at the return on the investment in the database which largely came from these elements, but many parts of the database were not of primarily commercial significance.[161] In such a case where the commercial part of a database is itself relatively insubstantial, it would hardly seem enough that it has been even wholly copied in order to render it a substantial taking, although that is where this judgment seems to be leading. The judgment is nevertheless quite clear in rejecting a rigid separation between quality and quantity, considering first one and then the other. Both are normally to be considered in conjunction with each other.

Another issue of some interest in this context was whether in the case of a continuously updated database of this sort, and a database of judgments would be of the same sort, it could be said that there was one database, or a succession of different databases. The argument was particularly acute in this sort of case where it could easily happen that if the database were to be regarded as being renewed at short intervals, say each day, that only an insubstantial amount would be taken from each one, and that thereby Art 7.5 assimilating a repeated and systematic taking of insubstantial parts to the taking of a substantial part would not bite since although the taking might be systematic and repeated, it would not be from the same database, but from different ones. Laddie J rejected this argument also,[162] holding that in the case of such a continuing database it would be impractical to distinguish between different separate temporal databases. He took the view that this meant that the term of protection was being constantly renewed for the newer material, but that if extraction and re-utilisation were confined to material more than 15 years old,[163] then no

160 [2001] RPC 31 at para 53.
161 For example the parts devoted to the distinctive colours of each different owner.
162 [2001] RPC 31 at para 72.
163 The period of protection, see Art 10.1; reg 17(1).

infringement of database right would have taken place. As noted above, this seems impossible to square with the terminology of the directive, or its recitals, or the regulations. It may well be the case that this would lead to a rational result, but it is not the most obvious, or perhaps even a possible, reading of the relevant provisions.[164]

He did not find it necessary to consider in detail whether or not the extraction or re-utilisation conflicted with the legitimate exploitation of the database by its compiler, since he took the view that the answer was that it obviously did, but he fired a warning shot in expressing the view that such a phrase is impossible to define with precision.[165]

It seems quite likely that, if the European Court of Justice approves the approach of Laddie J, proprietary databases of judgments held on computer will be protected by database right. The main reason for doubt relates to the determination whether such compilations will be regarded as being arranged in a systematic or methodical way. The consequences of so deciding will however remain obscure pending the determination of such questions as what will be regarded as a substantial part of such a database, and what sorts of use will count as re-utilisation. It is also possible that some parts at least of Laddie J's decision will not be upheld, and it will then be necessary to reconsider the position in relation to any such holding.

Conclusions

It cannot be pretended that recent developments in this area of the law of intellectual property have resulted in a simple, clear and rational scheme for the protection of databases, whether of the law, or anything else. The current mixture of protections offered to different entities, on different principles, extending to different periods in the past, and enduring for different periods in the future, and offering different rights protected by different remedies is particularly unlikely to imbue potential investors with complete confidence in their ability to calculate the probable return on any such investment.

It should be noted also that the law of intellectual property does not stand alone. As mentioned above, technological means of protection may supersede

164 Even Laddie J seemed to recognise the weakness of his holding on this point by his protestation that it did not make Art 10(3) meaningless.

165 [2001] RPC 31 at para 75.

the protection it offers with more certain ways of controlling the use of information. But technology alone is not enough. It also needs some measure of legal support. The Database Directive is accordingly careful to supplement rather than to supplant other legal means of protecting databases:

> 'This Directive shall be without prejudice to provisions concerning in particular copyright, rights related to copyright or any other rights or obligations subsisting in the data, works or other materials incorporated into a database, patent rights, trade marks, design rights, the protection of national treasures, laws on restrictive practices and unfair competition, trade secrets, security, confidentiality, data protection and privacy, access to public documents, and the law of contract.'

In many of the cases considered above considerations of competition law were prominent. The European Union has always emphasised the law relating to competition, and its overlay with intellectual property was the subject of the expansive decision in *RTE and ITP v EC Commission ('Magill')*.[166] It is not here possible to explore the arcane mystery of the difference between the existence and exploitation of the power to withhold information from potential competitors.[167] Nor to speculate on what view a court might take of the competitive position in relation to legal publishing. It is perhaps sufficient to note that so far English law has not shown itself eager to develop a more far-reaching concept of misappropriation, and still less to hypostatise a property right upon such a foundation.[168] It should also be noted that although the majority[169] of the Supreme Court of the US was prepared to move in such a direction in *International News Service v Associated Press*,[170] its development, even in the US, has been impaired by influential criticism,[171] and cramped by the doctrine of pre-emption by the law of intellectual property, and especially by copyright.[172] The position in the British Commonwealth was even less receptive to the doctrine, and in *Victoria Park Racing v Australia*[173] Dixon J in

166 [1995] FSR 530, ECJ.

167 *Volvo AB v Veng* [1988] ECR 6211, ECJ.

168 *Phillips Electronics NV v Ingman* [1999] FSR 112, Pat.

169 Justices Brandeis and Holmes were however in the minority.

170 284 US 215 (1918).

171 Learned Hand J in *Chenet Bros v Doris Silk Corp* 35 F 2d 279 (2nd Cir, 1929).

172 See 17 USC § 301(a).

173 58 CLR 479 (1937) HCA at 509: an opinion echoed in Australia by Deane J in *Moorgate Tobacco v Phillip Morris* [1985] RPC 219, HCA at 236; and in England by Lord Diplock in *Erven Warnink Besloten Vennootschap v Townend (J) & Sons (Hull)* [1979] AC 731.

the High Court of Australia took the dissenting line of Justice Brandeis in the *INS* case and the conceptual basis of the pre-emption doctrine in declaring that the creation of new intellectual property rights was more the province of the legislature than of the judges.[174] In England, the Law Commission recognised the absence of any such comprehensive remedy, although it also deplored it as a 'glaring inadequacy'.[175] Not all commentators take the same dyspeptic view of the current absence of a general remedy.[176]

It should also be pointed out that the directive refers to the existence of contractual remedies. Since access to the most extensive databases of the law has always been granted by contractual licence, it might be thought that re-use could itself be governed by such means. The problem here, as always, is that such contractual protection can be effective only so far as the personal obligation of the defendant is likely to be effective, and the parasitic means of visiting contractual breaches upon non-parties, are far from comprehensive. So if a man of straw downloads a legal database and makes it freely available on the Internet, the proprietor of the database is little better off than if he had no contractual rights in respect of the initial breach.

174 See especially Justice Brandeis at pp 264-267.

175 Law Com No 110 *Breach of Confidence* Cmnd 8388 (1981) para 5.5.

176 See eg Kaufmann *Passing Off and Misappropriation* (1986); Spence 'Passing Off and the Misappropriation of Valuable Intangibles' 112 LQR 472 (1996).

Notes

Bibliography

Bannon: Copyright in reasons for judgment and law reporting 56 ALJ 59 (1982)

Baron: Back to the Future: Learning from the Past in the Database Debate 62 Ohio St LJ 879 (2001)

Biscardi: The Historical Development of the Law concerning Judicial Report Publication 85 Law Library J 531 (1993)

Boyarski: (1999) 21 Cardozo LR 871

Cerina: [1995] 2 EIPR D-41

Chalton: Database Right: Stronger Than It Looks? [2001] 23 EIPR 296

Denicola: Copyright in Collections of Facts: A Theory for the Protection of Nonfiction Literary Works 81 Col LR 516 (1981)

Dmitrieva: State Ownership of Copyright in Primary Law Materials 23 Hast Comm. & Ent LJ 81 (2000)

Ginsburg: Copyright, Common Law and sui generis Protection of Databases in the United States and Abroad 66 U of Cincinnati LR 151 (1997)

Ginsburg: Creation and Commercial Value: Copyright Protection of Works of Information 90 Col LR 1865 (1990)

Ginsburg: No 'Sweat'? Copyright and Other Protection of Works of Information 92 Col. LR 338 (1992)

Gorman: Copyright Protection for the Collection and Representation of Facts 76 Harvard LR 1569 (1963)

Hicks: Copyright and Computer Databases: Is Traditional Compilation Law Adequate? 65 Texas LR 993 (1987)

Hunsucker: The European Database Directive: Regional Stepping Stone to an International Model? 7 Ford IP Media and Ent LJ 697 (1997)

Leith: Owning Legal Information [2000] 22 EIPR 359

MacPherson CB: The Political Theory of Possessive Individualism (1962)

Monotti: Copyright Protection of Computerised Databases 3 Aust Int Prop J 135 (1992)

Monotti: Nature and Basis of Crown Copyright in Official Publications [1992] EIPR 305

Patterson and Joyce: Monopolising the Law: The Scope of Copyright Protection for Law Reports and Statutory Compilations 36 UCLA LR 719 (1989)

Patterson LR: Copyright in Historical Perspective (1968)

Reichman and Samuelson: Intellectual Property Rights in Data? 50 Vand LR 51 (1997)

Snow: Who Owns Copyright in Law Reports? 64 CPR 2nd 49 (1982)
Taggart: Copyright in Written Reasons for Judgment (1984) 10 Sydney LR 319
Tapper: An Aspect of Copyright in Data Bases 14 N Kentucky LR 169 (1987)
Tapper: Genius and Janus: Information Technology and the Law 11 Monash ULR 75 (1985)
Thorne: The Infringement of Database Compilations: A Case for Reform? [1991] EIPR 331.
Tussey: Owning the Law: Intellectual Property Rights in Primary Law 9 Fordham Int Prop Med & Ent LJ 173 (1998)
von Nessen: Law Reporting: Another Case for Deregulation 48 Mod LR 412 (1985)
York: Note Warren Publishing Co v Microdos Data Corpn: Continuing the Stable Uncertainty of Copyright in Factual Compilations (1999) 74 Notre Dame LR 565

Article 10 ECHR and freedom of expression: what has it added to the common law?

Desmond Browne

Article 10 and the common law

In July 1973, when the House of Lords gave its decision in *A-G v Times Newspapers Ltd*[1], the UK had been a signatory to the European Convention for the Protection of Human Rights and Fundamental Freedoms for over 20 years. Yet nowhere in the argument of counsel, nor in the judgments of the Court of Appeal.[2] (which had discharged the injunction granted to the Attorney) or of the House of Lords (which restored it), is there any reference to be found to Art 10. When Lord Denning MR, in the course of argument, asked the Attorney-General Sir Peter Rawlinson QC whether he was saying that if a real risk of prejudicing the proceedings was established, any other consideration was subordinate to it, the Attorney appears not to have hesitated before answering yes.[3] In the House of Lords Brian Neill for the *Sunday Times* urged that a court, holding the balance, will give most weight to freedom of speech [4], but this was an argument which was not to succeed until the decision of the European Court of Human Rights some six years later.[5]

The decision of the Strasbourg court in the thalidomide litigation was an historic first use of Art 10 to extend the ambit of freedom of expression in the

1 [1974] AC 273.
2 [1973] QB 710.
3 [1973] QB 710 at 731D.
4 [1974] AC 273 at 285G-H.
5 *The Sunday Times v UK (*1979*)* 2 EHRR 245.

teeth of orders of the English Court. However, despite this reverse and others subsequently[6], English judges at the highest levels have not hesitated to express the belief that where freedom of expression is concerned, there is no inconsistency between English law and Art 10. In *A-G v Guardian Newspapers (No 2)*[7], Lord Goff commented that the consistency was 'scarcely surprising, since we may pride ourselves on the fact that freedom of speech has existed in this country as long as, if not longer than, it has existed in any other country in the world.' In *Derbyshire CC v Times Newspapers*[8], Lord Keith echoed Lord Goff's words in the course of a decision by the House refusing elected governmental organs the right to sue for defamation. Significantly, the House did this by applying the common law, and did not find 'any need to rely upon the European Convention'[9].

However, while Lord Goff and Lord Keith plainly felt confident that 'there was no difference in principle' between English law in the field of freedom of speech and Art 10, there is a pressing question as to whether there has been, and maybe still is, a difference in practice. In *Ashworth Hospital Authority v MGN Ltd*,[10] Lord Phillips MR acknowledged that 'the decisions of the European Court demonstrate that the freedom of the press has in the past carried greater weight in Strasbourg than it has in the courts of this country.' It is a nice question whether this is likely to change as English judges, applying the Human Rights Act 1998, grapple with the increasingly familiar European doctrines of pressing social need and proportionality. The purpose of this article is to examine the use to which Art 10 has been put in the past to reform the English law of freedom of expression (in particular, the law of defamation), and then to consider how the Strasbourg case law can be most usefully deployed in an English court.

The slow emergence of Article 10

When the Human Rights Act 1998 came into force on 2 October 2000, it was nearly half a century since the UK had ratified the Convention on 8 March

6 *Observer & Guardian v UK (1992)* 14 EHRR 153, *Goodwin v UK (1996)* 22 EHRR 123.
7 [1990] 1 AC 109 at 283F.
8 [1993] AC 534 at 551F.
9 [1993] AC 534 at 551F.
10 [2001] 1 WLR 515, [97] at 536h-537A.

1951. The UK was the first country to accede to the Convention [11], but it did so with marked reluctance. In a letter to Hugh Dalton in August 1950, Mr Attlee's Lord Chancellor, Lord Jowitt, spoke of 'our European friends' jeopardising 'our whole system of law', and denounced the Convention as 'some half-baked scheme to be administered by some unknown court'. In a cabinet paper he deplored 'an appeal to a secret court, composed of persons of legal training possessing the unfettered right to expound the meaning of 17 Articles', which elsewhere he described as 'so vague and woolly that it may mean almost anything.' [12]

One particularly percipient fear which Lord Jowitt expressed to his Cabinet colleagues was that 'we shall have to bring in legislation, applying the conditions of the Convention to our domestic law' [13]. Such proved to be the fear of 'the unknown court' that when ratification took place, the right of individual petition to the Commission or the Court of Human Rights was withheld. It was not until January 1966 that Harold Wilson's Government decided to sanction British cases going to Strasbourg, and then the decision was taken without it even being discussed in Cabinet. [14]

It is hard to resist the conclusion that Lord Jowitt's antipathy to the Convention was no more than a reflection of that shared by those on the Bench and at the Bar. It is a striking aspect of *Broome v Cassell* [15] that when in February 1972 no less than seven Law Lords sat to consider the anomalous civil law remedy of punitive damages, only one of their number made even a passing reference to the European Convention. Lord Kilbrandon pointed out:

> '...one must be watchful against holding the profit motive to be sufficient to justify punitive damages: to do so would be seriously to hamper what must be regarded, *at least since the European Convention was ratified*, as a constitutional right to free speech.' [Emphasis added.][16]

11 Sir William Wade QC 'Human Rights and the Judiciary' (1998, JSB Annual Lecture) p 2.

12 Passages quoted from Lord Jowitt are taken from the highly illuminating AW Brian Simpson *Human Rights and the End of Empire* (OUP, 2001).

13 Sir William Wade QC 'Human Rights and the Judiciary' (1998, JSB Annual Lecture) p 2.

14 Lord Lester 'The Roman Candle' (Counsel, October 2000) 25.

15 [1972] AC 1027.

16 [1972] AC 1027 at 1133A.

Article 10 only really began to make its effect felt in English courts at the end of the 1970s. As late as March 1975 the Faulks Committee (whose members included Lord Keith and David Hirst QC) recommended the continuance of the law of criminal libel without any reference to the European Convention. [17] Nor was the Convention raised when Wien J decided in April 1976 to grant Sir James Goldsmith leave under Law of Libel Amendment Act 1888, s 8 to prosecute *Private Eye* for criminal libel.[18] The Judge considered that the public interest required criminal proceedings, but performed no analysis of either social need or proportionality.

A very different approach in relation to criminal libel was adopted by Lord Diplock in April 1979 in his speech in *Gleaves v Deakin* [19] , when he pointed out that the requirement that the accused should have to prove that publication was for the public benefit was 'to turn Art 10 of the Convention on its head.' He suggested a reform (which is still not part of our law) whereby the consent of the Attorney-General should be required for the institution of criminal libel proceedings, and that consent should be refused unless he were satisfied that a prosecution was necessary on any of the grounds specified in Art 10(2).

Later in the same month as the speeches were delivered in *Gleaves v Deakin*, the European Court gave judgment in *Sunday Times v UK (No1)*. It may be that the English legal profession regarded the impact of the decision as confined to the law of contempt of court, but in *Blackshaw v Lord* [20] in February 1983 the Court of Appeal ruled against the existence of a qualified privilege for fair information on a matter of public interest, without a single reference to either Art 10 or any Strasbourg case law.

Even when Strasbourg case law was deployed (as it was over four full days of argument before the House in *Derbyshire County Council v Times Newspapers* in December 1992), its effect was much blunted. Lord Keith and his brethren arrived at their decision directly by means of the common law, whereas the Court of Appeal had taken the Art 10 route.[21] It is curious, given that the House considered 'the chilling effect' of libel law on freedom of speech, that it should have confined that consideration to the threat of actions by local councils, and not considered the substantially identical effect produced by the potential

17 *Report of the Committee on Defamation:* Cmnd 5909: March 1975.
18 *Goldsmith v Pressdram Ltd* [1977] 1 QB 83.
19 [1980] AC 477 at 483E-F.
20 [1984] QB 1.
21 [1992] QB 770.

for actions by individual councillors. Indeed, the Court of Appeal actually prayed in aid the availability of such actions as affording some protection to the local authority [22].

Deployment of Article 10 as means of preventing excessive awards by juries of damages for defamation

The first marked effect of Art 10 in reforming defamation practice came a month after the *Derbyshire County Council* judgment; in *Rantzen v MGN* [23] a Court of Appeal presided over by Brian Neill tackled the longstanding problem of excessive awards of libel damages and introduced new guidelines for juries in an effort to ensure that in future awards of damages conformed with the requirement of proportionality. The plaintiff, the television presenter Esther Rantzen, had been awarded £250,000 compensatory damages by a jury after failed pleas of justification and fair comment relating to a libel alleging that she had condoned child abuse and acted inconsistently with her position as founder of the charity Childline. On appeal, the Defendants invoked the newly enacted Courts and Legal Services Act 1990, s 8 and invited the Court of Appeal to substitute its own award. Holding that the jury's award was not proportionate to the damage suffered, the Court reduced the award to £110,000.

On behalf of the appellants, Charles Gray QC invoked Art 10 in terms that have since become familiar. He contended [24] that the amount of damages, although notionally compensation, in reality operated as a penalty subjecting the newspaper to a violation of their right to freedom of expression, which (a) was not 'prescribed by law', (b) was not 'necessary in a democratic society' for the legitimate aim of protecting the plaintiff's reputation, and (c) was not proportionate to that legitimate aim. The reliance on Art 10 introduced a new element into the debate on levels of damages for libel, since previously appellate courts had been very reluctant to interfere with awards of damages by juries. In the words of Brian Neill, 'the barrier to be surmounted was a high one.'

In giving the judgment of the Court, Brian Neill tackled head-on the submission that the Convention was not part of English domestic law and

22 See, eg, Ralph Gibson LJ [1992] QB 770 at 827C-D.
23 [1994] QB 670.
24 [1994] QB 670 at 674A-C.

therefore the courts had no power to enforce Convention rights directly. 'Where freedom of expression is at stake,' he said, 'recent authorities lend support for the proposition that Art 10 has a wider role and can properly be regarded as an articulation of some of the principles underlying the common law'. [25] He then proceeded to consider how the word 'excessive' in CLSA 1990, s 8(1) was to be interpreted, and (as if anticipating Human Rights Act 1998, s 2(1)(a) and s 3(1)) he concluded that the power to intervene must be interpreted in such a way as to give proper weight both to the guidance given by the House of Lords and by the European Court of Human Rights. He went on:

> '... it seems to us that the grant of an almost limitless discretion to a jury fails to provide a satisfactory measurement for deciding what is "necessary in a democratic society" or "justified by a pressing social need". We consider therefore that the common law if properly understood requires the courts to subject large awards of damages to a more searching scrutiny than has been customary in the past. It follows that what has been regarded as the barrier against intervention should be lowered. The question becomes: "Could a reasonable jury have thought that this award was necessary to compensate the plaintiff and to re-establish his reputation ?" ' [26]

In the latter part of his judgment, Brian Neill turned to consider whether the absence of guidelines to the jury as to quantum offended the principle in Art 10(2) that restrictions on the exercise of freedom of expression should be prescribed by law, and therefore be 'formulated with sufficient precision to enable the citizen to regulate his conduct'. [27] The Court rejected the submission that juries should be referred to awards made in actions involving serious personal injuries, but considered that to prohibit reference to awards made by the Court of Appeal under CLSA 1990, s 8 would fall foul of the need for restrictions on freedom of expression to be prescribed by law. Brian Neill considered that 'the decisions of the Court of Appeal could be relied upon as establishing the prescribed norm'. [28] As it happens, the tariff envisaged has not evolved, possibly because of a paucity of appellate decisions. The Court of Appeal has also discouraged counsel from indulging in so-called 'battles of comparables'.[29]

25 [1994] QB 670 at 691C-D.

26 [1994] QB 670 at 692G-H.

27 *Sunday Times v UK* (1979) 2 EHRR 245, 271.

28 [1994] QB 670 at 694C-D.

29 *Kiam v MGN Ltd* [2002] 3 WLR 1036, [55] 1053H-1054C.

The new approach of the Court of Appeal in *Rantzen* (involving a reminder to juries to consider the purchasing power of any award which they might make) satisfied the European Court of the compatibility of English law with the Convention in *Tolstoy-Miloslavsky v UK*[30], decided in July 1995. The *Tolstoy* case was the aftermath to the notorious award of £1.5m damages by a jury to Lord Aldington in November 1989. In accordance with the practice after the Court of Appeal decision in *Sutcliffe v Pressdram Ltd*[31], the trial judge directed the jury to consider the cost of a house or a row of houses, adding: 'most of us have a pretty good idea how much houses are worth.' The European Court rejected the contention that the award was not prescribed by law, but unanimously held that the size of the award was a violation of Art 10. Referring to the intervention by the Court of Appeal in *Rantzen*, the European Court stated:

> 'The Court cannot but endorse the.... observations by the Court of Appeal to the effect that the scope of judicial control, at the trial and on appeal, at the time of the applicant's case, did not offer adequate and effective safeguards against a disproportionately large award.'[32]

Six months after the decision in *Rantzen*, the new guidance proved insufficient to restrain a jury from awarding the singer Elton John £75,000 compensatory and £275,000 exemplary damages for an article in the *Sunday Mirror* suggesting that he was a bulimic on a bizarre diet of chewing but not swallowing his food. This was not the only award of substantial six-figure damages[33] in the period between *Rantzen* and *John v MGN Ltd*[34] being heard in the Court of Appeal in November 1995. On the latter appeal, Brian Neill sat with Sir Thomas Bingham MR and Hirst LJ, and the awards were reduced to £25,000 compensatory and £50,000 exemplary respectively on the footing that the libel 'though false, offensive and distressing, did not attack [the plaintiff's] personal integrity or damage his reputation as an artist.'[35]

Partly because of the continuing high level of awards, and partly because the corpus of awards by the Court of Appeal under CLSA 1990, s 8 had not

30 (1995) 20 EHRR 442.

31 [1991] 1 QB 153, see Lord Donaldson MR at 178G-179C.

32 (1995) 20 EHRR 442, at [50] 473.

33 The football manager, Graham Souness, was awarded £750,000 (settled for £100,000), and in *Walker v Sheahan* in July 1994 there were awards totalling £1.5m, again settled on appeal.

34 [1997] QB 586.

35 [1997] QB 586 at 621C-D.

developed, the Court was persuaded that the question of guidelines to the jury deserved reconsideration, notwithstanding the short period since the ruling in *Rantzen*. Two innovations were to follow:

(1) Firstly, the Court ruled that the time had come when judges and counsel should be free to draw the attention of juries to comparisons with awards for pain and suffering in personal injury cases. The Court considered that it was 'offensive to public opinion, and rightly so, that a defamation plaintiff should recover damages for injury to reputation greater, perhaps by a significant factor, than if that same plaintiff had been rendered a helpless cripple or an insensate vegetable'. [36]
(2) The second innovation was to permit counsel and the judge to suggest appropriate brackets to the jury for damages. The Court emphasised that the jury must still be directed to make up their own mind, and if they 'make an award outside the upper or lower bounds of any bracket indicated and such award is the subject of appeal real weight must be given to the possibility that their judgment is to be preferred to that of the judge.' [37]

Although exemplary (or punitive) damages do not exist in Scots law, and neither French or German law recognise them as such [38], it was not contended that an award of such damages on top of compensation in itself fell foul of Art 10. The Court stated:

> '... principle requires that an award of exemplary damages should never exceed the minimum sum necessary to meet the public purpose underlying such damages, that of punishing the defendant, showing that tort does not pay and deterring others.' [39]

The Court reached their conclusions independently of the Convention, stating that they 'would reach them even if the Convention did not exist.' They simply regarded Art 10 as reinforcing and buttressing the conclusions resulting from the application of the common law.

36 [1997] QB 586 at 614H.

37 [1997] QB 586 at 616B-C. In *Kiam v MGN Ltd* [2002] 3 WLR 1036, the Court of Appeal applied this principle, when refusing by a majority of 2 to 1 to interfere with a jury's award of £105,000 damages, when the trial judge had suggested a bracket of £40,000 to £80,000.

38 See fn 17, p 216, *Gatley, Libel and Slander* (9th edn, 1998).

39 [1997] QB 586 at 619F.

The European approach of evaluating the competing rights and interests of the parties in the light of the concrete facts of each individual case

The Human Rights Act 1998, s 6(1) now makes it 'unlawful for a public authority (which by virtue of s 6(3)(a) includes a court or tribunal) to act in a way which is incompatible with a Convention right'. Section 2(1) requires a court determining a question which has arisen in connection with a Convention right to take into account the Strasbourg case law, in so far as it is relevant. Legislation must also 'so far as it is possible to do so... be read and given effect in a way which is compatible with the Convention rights': see s 3(1).

HRA 1998, s 12 makes provision for cases where the grant of relief might affect the exercise of the Convention right to freedom of expression, and directs the court to have 'particular regard to the importance of the Convention right to freedom of expression': see s 12(4). Lord Lester and David Pannick have pointed out that both alarm about the application of the HRA 1998 and journalistic satisfaction with the section are misguided: 'all that can be said for s 12 is that it does no positive harm to the principle of the HRA 1998...'. [40]

The statutory provisions of the HRA 1998 may well prove harder for an English court to apply than at first appears, for the simple reason that the European approach is *not* to consider principles of domestic law in the abstract, but to examine the facts of each individual case. Having identified the alleged interference with free expression, the Court then goes on to examine whether *on the facts of the particular case*, that interference is proportionate to the achievement of the legitimate aim pursued (eg the protection of reputation, or the maintenance of the authority or impartiality of the judiciary).

In his speech in *Reynolds v Times Newspapers* [41] Lord Steyn reflected on the manner in which the Strasbourg court 'in cases of competing rights and

40 Lester & Pannick *The Human Rights Act 1998 – An Introduction* (1999) para 2.12, 46-7.

41 [2001] AC 127 at 210H-211B. The appeal took full account of what Lord Steyn (at 206H) called 'the new legal landscape', and effectively proceeded as though the HRA 1998 were in force: 'it was common ground that in considering the issues before the House, and the development of English law, the House can and should act on the reality that the Human Rights Act 1998 will soon be in force': see 207H-208A.

interests requires a balancing exercise in the light of the concrete facts of each case'. As in German law, the Court insists on the individual evaluation of each case on its own facts, rather than setting up categories or rules, which involve 'the attendant sacrifice of individual justice in particular cases'. Lord Cooke agreed, pointing out that the ECHR jurisprudence showed that the Court proceeded by carrying out 'a careful examination of all the circumstances of a particular case before a decision is reached as to whether freedom of expression is to be treated as the dominant right.' [42]

In *Loutchansky v Times Newspapers Ltd (No 1)*[43] Brooke LJ adopted the fact-based approach, when holding that knowledge acquired by the publisher *after* publication was irrelevant to a defence of *Reynolds* qualified privilege. He cited from the judgment in *Sunday Times v UK (No 1)*[44] to the effect that 'the court has to be satisfied that the interference was necessary having regard to the facts and circumstances prevailing in the specific case before it'.

In contrast, in *Ashdown v Telegraph Group* [45] Sir Andrew Morritt V-C at first instance rejected the submission that scrutiny of the facts of a particular case might show that the defences provided in intellectual property legislation needed to be supplemented. Otherwise, he feared, intellectual property litigation might burgeon out of control. The Vice-Chancellor did not consider that it followed that 'because Art 10 is engaged, the facts of each case have to be considered to determine whether the restriction imposed by the law of copyright goes further than what is necessary in a democratic society'. The Court of Appeal considered Sir Andrew's floodgates argument exaggerated, and reached the conclusion that 'rare circumstances can arise where the right of freedom of expression will come into conflict with the protection afforded by Copyright Act 1988, notwithstanding the express provisions to be found in the Act'. [46] It was therefore 'necessary for the Court to look closely at the facts of individual cases.'

42 [2001] AC 127 at 223E-F.
43 [2002] QB 321, [46], 338C-D.
44 (1979) 2 EHRR 245, [65] 280.
45 [2001] Ch 685 at 693.
46 [2001] 3 WLR 1368, [45] 1382E.

European approach concerned with facts of individual cases, not reform of principles of domestic law

It follows from the fact-centred approach of the European Court that it is not concerned to lay down a uniform legal code for signatory states, nor to reform their domestic law. A striking example of the relatively limited use to which the European case law can be put is shown by the Court of Appeal decision in *Berezovsky v Forbes Inc (No 2)*.[47] This was a case of the relatively frequent sort in which the claimant contends that the words mean he was guilty of a criminal offence (in this case, murder), while the defendant merely seeks to justify reasonable grounds for suspicion. The contents page of *Forbes* had contained the words: 'Murder. Boris Berezovsky could teach the guys in Sicily a thing or two', and in an editorial the magazine claimed that behind him 'lies a trail of corpses ... Russians have good reasons to be afraid of Berezovsky... the new crime bosses use KGB-trained assassins ...'.

At first instance the defendants contended that the wording of the article was mere exaggeration, and that they were entitled to justify a meaning less grave than that which ordinarily would have been within the range of possible natural and ordinary meanings. They argued that following the HRA 1998 an article written ethically and honestly was to be judged, not by making nice distinctions of pleaded meaning, but according to a broad judgment whether, having regard to those true facts and fair comments which the article contained, it was necessary in a democratic society to restrict the journal's freedom of expression by making its publisher liable for its inaccuracies. [48]

Founding their argument on the decisions of the European Court in *Bladet Tromso v Norway* [49] (the seal hunting case) and *Bergens Tidende v Norway* [50] (the cosmetic surgery case), the defendants tried to persuade the Court to cull as sacred jurisprudential cows whose survival was incompatible with ECHR Arts 6 and 10 both:

(1) the very long-standing repetition rule recently affirmed by the Court of Appeal in *Stern v Piper* [51], and

47 (2001) EMLR 1030.

48 See (2001) EMLR 1030,[8] 1036.

49 (2000) 29 EHRR 125.

50 (2001) 31 EHRR 16.

51 [1997] QB 123. In *Chase v News Group Newspapers Ltd* [2002] EWCA Civ 1772, [50-51] the Court of Appeal modified the rule so that, depending on the terms of the

(2) the more recent rule laid down by a Court of Appeal including Brian Neill in *Shah v Standard Chartered Bank*[52] that a plea of justification of reasonable grounds for suspicion must focus on the claimant's own conduct.

In his judgment at first instance, Eady J pointed out that English law made allowance for exaggerated opinions in the defence of fair comment, and for exaggerated facts in Defamation Act 1952, s 5. Rhetorically he asked what was left, if one stripped the exaggeration out of the statement that behind Mr Berezovsky stood a trail of corpses. Expressly resisting 'any temptation to become unduly intoxicated by the heady atmosphere engendered by the HRA 1998', he raised the question 'to what extent, if any, English law failed to accommodate the policy considerations expounded in the Strasbourg jurisprudence', and decided that it did not. The Court of Appeal, though declining the temptation to rest on the laurels provided by Lord Goff and Lord Keith, dismissed the appeal.

In giving the judgment of the Court, Sedley LJ[53] reiterated that the right to free expression was not absolute, since it was conditioned by the reputations and rights of others. If for no other reason, he said, that was why the Court of Appeal had made it clear in *Douglas v Hello*[54] that HRA 1998, s 12(4) added little if anything to the legal armoury of the press:

> 'It remains therefore for national legal systems to set their own thresholds of defamation and justification, subject always to the Convention standard of proportionality and (although Art 13 is omitted from the Convention rights scheduled to the Act) the right to a legal remedy for breaches.
>
> To require a defendant, albeit a serious and reputable publisher, to be able to justify not a diminished version of a damaging assault on a claimant's reputation but the essence or substance or sting of that assault is not in our judgment a disproportionate invasion of the right of free expression ...'.

publication, a defendant may rely on strong circumstantial evidence implicating the claimant which might amount, objectively speaking, to the requisite grounds for reasonable suspicion.

52 [1999] QB 241, 261C.

53 (2001) EMLR 1030, [11] 1039.

54 [2001] 1 WLR 992.

The Court of Appeal rejected the argument that the course of Convention jurisprudence had been altered by the *Bergens Tidende* decision, where the Norwegian Supreme Court had reached what Sedley LJ described as the 'not immediately obvious finding'[55] that a defensible criticism of a plastic surgeon's standard of aftercare carried a defamatory sting of incompetence as a surgeon. In England, as he pointed out, the case would probably have come within the Defamation Act 1952, s 5, but in any event the secondary meaning would have been a question for the jury and the issue would almost certainly have come to rest with their verdict. The conservative approach of the Court of Appeal in *Berezovsky* was further demonstrated by their declining to accede to the invitation to use their power under HRA 1998, s 2 and construe Defamation Act 1952, s 5 so as to bring lesser meanings as well as discrete meanings within the adjective 'distinct' used in the section.[56]

The repetition rule has received further recent support from Simon Brown LJ in *Al Fagih v HH Saudi Research & Marketing (UK) Ltd*[57], where he makes the point that the whole law of statutory privilege presupposes the existence of the rule since, without it, such a regime would not be necessary. On the other hand, the *Al Fagih* decision was a notably liberal application of *Reynolds* qualified privilege in distinguishing between attributed and unadopted *reportage* on the one hand and non-attributed and adopted investigative journalism on the other. In this context the Court of Appeal once again reached its decision without deployment of the European case law. Even though it might have been thought of as being strong support for his ruling, Simon Brown LJ made no mention of the important decision of the European Court in *Thoma v Luxembourg*[58]. In that case, where one journalist quoted a defamatory remark made by another, the Court held that it was a disproportionate interference with his right of free expression to require him formally to distance himself from the remark he had quoted. *Thoma* makes it clear that there will be cases where the facts are such that scrupulous adherence to the repetition rule would breach Art 10, but it will not be so in every case.

Although it is perhaps still early days, on one view experience since October 2000 tends to indicate that the opportunities to use the HRA 1998 to persuade English judges to make radical reforms of English defamation law in favour of freedom of expression will be few and far between. Their decisions show them

55 [2001] 1 WLR 992, [13] 1039-1040.
56 [2001] 1 WLR 992, [15] 1040.
57 (2002) EMLR 215, [35] 231.
58 29 March 2001.

firmly of the view that historically our law has developed in a manner which satisfies Art 10, but (like Monsieur Jourdain talking prose) without their even knowing it. Thus, as Eady J pointed out in *Branson v Bower* (cited by Latham LJ in the Court of Appeal):

> 'In this jurisdiction we have a civil law of defamation which is sophisticated and highly developed and includes a range of defences for the media. It is by affording the defences of justification (which need only be substantial to succeed), fair comment, and qualified privilege that English law gives effect to the general (and in itself uninformative) proposition that it is not always reasonable for a journalist, or other defendant in libel proceedings, to have to establish the objective truth of what he has said.' [59]

In the view of Eady J (which experience shows that most English judges share), 'if one applies the English law of defamation properly, there should be no reason to think that the principles underlying the Convention are infringed.' As the *Berezovsky* case shows, some of the more extravagant pipe-dreams of the media as to the likely liberalising effect of the HRA 1998 were no more than that. If rules of English defamation law cannot, in the abstract, constitute an interference with freedom of expression, the use to which the Strasbourg case law can be put in interlocutory arguments before final judgment will inevitably be distinctly limited.

The Strasbourg case law shows this, too. In *Times Newspapers v UK* [60] the Commission rejected as manifestly ill-founded the applicant's complaint that the failure of the Court of Appeal in *Watts v Times Newspapers Ltd*[61] to afford it a defence of qualified privilege for the publication of a bona fide apology was a breach of Art 10. The Commission did not accept that TNL's freedom of expression was somehow affected by the absence of a defence of qualified privilege, pointing out that '[the court] never found that the statement was defamatory and there is no indication that TNL is slow in publishing apologies because of the absence of qualified privilege.' It went on:

> '... Art 10 of the Convention guarantees the right to freedom of expression, but also underlines that the right carries with it duties and responsibilities; in the context of civil proceedings, its aim is not to prevent persons who are alleged to have defamed third parties from

59 (2001) EMLR 800, [8] 803.
60 26 February 1997.
61 [1997] QB 650.

having to justify their actions, but rather to ensure that the State strikes a fair balance in weighing up the interests of the maker and the object of the statement.'

In *HS and DM v UK*[62] the Commission also rejected as manifestly ill-founded a complaint of an infringement of Art 10 by the defendants in the notorious *McLibel* action then proceeding. It noted that the freedom conferred by Art 10 was 'not of an absolute, unfettered nature. It does not authorise the publication of defamatory material.' McDonalds were therefore entitled to seek the determination of their civil rights to a good reputation, and, if successful, the protection of that reputation against an alleged libel. HS and DM had published their views without prior restraint, and 'if those views are subsequently found to be libellous, any ensuing sanctions would in principle be justified for the protection of the reputation and rights within the meaning of Art 10(2) of the Convention.'

The European cases show that a court asked to rule on an alleged infringement of Art 10 has first to identify the precise nature of the interference alleged, and then to consider whether *on the facts of that particular case*, the interference is proportionate to the legitimate aim pursued. In the majority of cases, the interference will include penal sanctions or 'the substantial award of damages' as was the case in *Bergens Tidende v Norway*.[63] In numerous Strasbourg cases[64] the amount of the sanction imposed has been determinative (or substantially determinative), so cases will be rare where it is possible to get Art 10 to operate in favour of the media before judgment.

A rare example of Article 10 changing the common law: *O'Shea v MGN Ltd*

In *O'Shea v MGN Ltd*[65] the claimant was the spitting image of another woman who posed for an advertisement for a pornographic website published in *The Sunday Mirror*. Her action seems to have been the first brought in an English court by a look-alike claiming to have been identified from a photograph. Because there is strict liability at common law for unintentional

62 5 May 1993.
63 (2001) 31 EHRR 430, [55] 458.
64 Contrast *Maronek v Slovakia* 19 April 2001 with *Janowski v Poland* (1999) 29 EHRR 705, [47-48] 715.
65 (2001) EMLR 943.

defamation [66], the claimant appeared to have a good case, even though (as Morland J pointed out [67]) the harshness of the principle has long been the subject of concern. That harshness was in no way relieved by the offer of amends procedure introduced by Defamation Act 1996, s 2 which does not provide a true defence, because 'the blameless publisher has not only to make and publish a correction and apology but also to offer compensation'.[68]

The defendant publisher in *O'Shea* succeeded in obtaining summary judgment from Morland J on the footing that the claimant had no real prospect of success, since it would offend Art 10 to impose liability in such circumstances. The judge took heed of 'the impossible burden it would impose on a publisher if he were required to check if the true picture of someone resembled someone else who because of the context was defamed'. [69] As he pointed out, theoretically the real Artemus Jones (in *Hulton v Jones*) could have been discovered, but not a look-alike.

Ruling that there was no pressing need for strict liability in order to protect the reputation of a look-alike, the judge was impressed by the fact, firstly, that there had been no similar claim by a look-alike in over a century and, secondly, that the tort of malicious falsehood would catch the person who deliberately published a look-alike photograph in a defamatory context.

The chilling effect and the 'public right to know'

Based on Art 10, arguments on behalf of the media since October 2000 have far too readily invoked the supposed 'public right to know', usually coupled with an invocation of 'the chilling effect', mentioned by Lord Keith in *Derbyshire County Council v Times Newspapers*.[70] As Brooke LJ emphasised in *Loutchansky v Times Newspapers (No 1)* [71], it is 'misleading' to talk of 'a public right to know' without more, and facile to do so, if there is no duty to publish.The requirement of duty is necessary, because 'the right to freedom of expression has never been absolute', either at common law or under the *ECHR* jurisprudence:

66 See *Hulton v Jones* [1910] AC 20.
67 (2001) EMLR 943, [30] 952.
68 (2001) EMLR 943, [33-34] 953.
69 (2001) EMLR 943, [43] 955.
70 [1993] AC 534, 548D-E.
71 [2002] QB 321, [44-5], 337F-H.

> 'if the public "right to know" was to be adopted, as it has not, as the sole criterion for conferring immunity from liability for damaging and untrue statements, then the courts would be turning their back on their duty to prescribe such restrictions on freedom of expression as are needed in order to achieve that public good'.

The so-called 'chilling effect' may in itself be no bad thing: thus the fear of possible libel proceedings does not only prevent 'the publication of matters which it is very desirable to make public'. It also operates in the public interest to prevent the publication of untruths. Indeed, Lord Cooke in *Reynolds* commented[72] that experience of libel litigation was apt to generate the suspicion that the tendency to chill the publication of untruths was greater than the tendency to prevent the publication of that which may be true but cannot be proved to be true. Lord Hope also warned against the oversimplification of treating the chilling effect, 'as if this in itself showed that something was wrong with it'.[73] He pointed out that 'there are situations in which this is a necessary protection for the individual'.

The dicta of Lord Cooke and Lord Hope in *Reynolds* were reiterated by the Court of Appeal in its judgment in *Loutchansky v Times Newspapers (Nos 2-5)*[74]. One of the points unsuccessfully raised on this appeal was that the limitation period for suing on articles maintained on a newspaper's website should run from the moment of original publication in hard copy, regardless of how long they remained displayed on the website. In essence, the appellants sought to use the HRA 1998 to introduce the American single-publication rule into English law and thereby overcome the long-standing principle derived from *Duke of Brunswick v Harmer*[75] that each individual publication of a libel gives rise to a separate cause of action with its own limitation period. The obstacle to this contention was the dicta of Lord Steyn, Lord Hoffman and Lord Hope in *Berezovsky v Michaels*[76], approving the rule in *Duke of Brunswick*, or at any rate showing how deeply it is embedded in English law.

In deciding the question whether the rule in *Duke of Brunswick* was in conflict with Art 10, the Court of Appeal had to weigh its chilling effect on freedom of expression and consider whether that effect went beyond what was necessary

72 [2001] AC 127, 220D-E.
73 [2001] AC 127, 235C-D.
74 [2002] 2 WLR 640, [40] 655F-G.
75 (1849) 14 QB 185.
76 [2001] 1 WLR 1004, at respectively, 1012, 1024 and 1026.

and proportionate for the protection of reputation. While accepting that the maintenance of archives had some utility, the Court concluded that it was 'a comparatively insignificant aspect of freedom of expression'.[77] Lord Phillips MR continued:

> 'Archive material is stale news and its publication cannot rank in importance with the dissemination of contemporary material. Nor do we believe that the law of defamation need inhibit the responsible maintenance of archives. Where it is known that archive material is or may be defamatory, the attachment of an appropriate notice warning against treating it as the truth will normally remove any sting from the material.'

The decision in *Loutchansky (No 2)* shows that the courts will seldom be persuaded by a merely formulaic reliance on the chilling effect of defamation law. They will consider all the circumstances of the case, as well as the impact of the relevant law on similar cases, before deciding whether the chilling effect lacks a legitimate aim which is necessary and proportionate. Thus, in the future, it may prove sensible, where the chilling effect is invoked in relation to a particular publication, to add substance to what would otherwise be bare assertion by pleading (pursuant to CPR Pt 16.1 PD) that newspapers are deterred from publishing the class of article concerned by the fear of liability. This would avoid the Court concluding (as was the case, for example, in *Times Newspapers v UK*[78]) that there was no indication that the prospect of liability made publishers slow to publish.

The chilling effect and confidentiality of journalistic sources: Contempt of Court Act 1981, s 10

The comments by Lords Cooke and Hope in *Reynolds* that the chilling effect may be no bad thing find an echo in the judgment of Lord Phillips MR in *Ashworth Hospital Authority v MGN Ltd*[79] in the context of a *Norwich Pharmacal* order for the disclosure of a journalist's source. In that case the journalist had received by fax from an intermediary pages from the computerised medical records maintained by Ashworth Hospital on the moors murderer,

77 [2002] 2 WLR 640, [74], 665A-C.
78 Commission: 26 February 1997.
79 [2001] 1 WLR 515, [99] 537, CA; [2002] 1 WLR 2033, HL.

Ian Brady. The journalist published only a fraction of what he received, and Rougier J held at the trial that the information published had already been placed by Brady himself in the public domain in support of his media campaign to be allowed to die. The judge held that what was important about the leak to the journalist was not the nature of the information, but the fact that it had happened at all. Both the Court of Appeal and the House of Lords seem to have shared this view, upholding the disclosure order on the grounds that the facts of the case fell within the exceptional circumstances acknowledged by the European Court in *Goodwin v UK*[80] where 'vital public or individual interests are at stake'.

The approach of Laws LJ to the impact of the chilling effect might at first sight be thought rather different to that of Lord Phillips MR, even though he concurred in the result. Laws LJ emphasised that the public interest in the non-disclosure of press sources was constant, and thought it 'a misreading of the principles engaged' to treat the imposition of a chilling effect in some circumstances as no bad thing.[81] He did not consider the chilling effect in any way lessened, still less abrogated, by either the fact that the information published was of no legitimate, objective public interest or that the source was a disloyal and greedy individual, prepared for money to betray his employer's confidences. In the House of Lords, Lord Woolf CJ resolved any apparent difference by pointing out that what Lord Phillips regarded as being 'no bad thing' was not the disclosure of the identity of the source, but the discouragement of the wrongful disclosure of the contents of medical records by sources. It was this conduct which exceptionally justified ordering the disclosure of documents which would reveal the identity of the source[82].

Lord Woolf regarded the situation in *Ashworth* as exceptional, as also (he said) was that in *Interbrew SA v Financial Times Ltd*[83], a case where various newspapers received anonymously doctored documents which suggested that the claimant was contemplating a takeover bid. In his judgment Sedley LJ dissented from Laws LJ's approach that it was of no consequence that the information was of no legitimate objective public interest and shared Lord Phillips' view that, where a case for overriding the privilege against disclosure

80 (1996) 22 EHRR 123, 137. The European Court held that the order for disclosure approved by the House in *X v Morgan Grampian* [1991] 1 AC 1 infringed the rights of the journalist under Article 10.

81 [2001] 1 WLR 515, [101] 537F-G.

82 [2002] 1 WLR 2033, [65] 2052F-G.

83 (2002) EMLR 446.

was made out, the consequent chilling effect may be no bad thing. In a subtle distinction, Sedley LJ considered that in the chilling effect of disclosure orders, there was an affirmative policy reason for ignoring *motive* in individual cases. In contrast, he thought that the *purpose* of the leak was likely to be highly material [84].

It is arguable that a court which sees merit in the general deterrent effect of a disclosure order *pour encourager les autres* attaches less than the proper weight to journalistic confidentiality as a critical element of freedom of expression under Art 10. In any event, as Lord Wilberforce commented in *British Steel v Granada Television* [85], it must be speculation whether if an order is made, fewer leaks will occur in the future. It is not a matter which a court can judicially value. The decision of the House in *British Steel* in November 1980 led Lord Salmon, who was the single dissentient, to introduce in the House of Lords what subsequently became Contempt of Court Act 1981, s 10. It is a striking feature of the speeches in *British Steel* and the lack of impact made by Art 10 at that time that Lord Wilberforce should have met Granada's appeal to the public's right to know by stating that the case did not 'touch upon the freedom of the press even at its periphery'. [86] This approach remains startling, even when one takes account of the fact that Granada was not asserting that it had a right to publish in the public interest, a stance which cut the ground from under Lord Salmon's feet.

Twenty years later, the Committee of Ministers of the Council of Europe reminded the public authorities of member states and their judiciary that 'the free and unhindered exercise of journalism is enshrined in the right to freedom of expression and is a fundamental prerequisite to the right of the public to be informed on matters of public concern'. It described the protection of journalists' sources of information as constituting 'a basic condition for journalistic work and freedom as well as the freedom of the media.' [87] For disclosure to be ordered, there must exist 'an overriding requirement in the public interest' and circumstances 'of a sufficiently vital and serious nature'.

The Contempt of Court Act 1981, s 10 enabled the court to order disclosure of the source of information in a publication, where it is established that it is

84 (2002) EMLR 446, [42] 468.

85 [1981] AC 1096, 1173.

86 [1981] AC 1096, 1168B-C. Lord Dilhorne at 1176F also considered that freedom of the press could not in any way be affected by the decision of the House.

87 Recommendation No R (2000) 7, adopted on 8 March 2000.

necessary 'in the interests of justice or national security or for the prevention of disorder or crime'. Initially this exception was given a limited construction: in *Secretary of State for Defence v Guardian Newspapers*[88] Lord Diplock (with whom Lord Roskill agreed) interpreted the expression 'justice' not 'in a general sense as the antonym of "injustice", but in the technical sense of the administration of justice in the course of legal proceedings in a court of law'. The phrase therefore encompassed the administration of justice both in particular legal proceedings already in existence and (in *Norwich Pharmacal* bill of discovery cases) a particular civil action which it was proposed to bring against a wrongdoer whose identity had not yet been ascertained.

Lord Diplock's construction did not extend to cases where the *Norwich Pharmacal* procedure was used to obtain discovery of a source merely in order to enforce a private law right, such as dismissal of a disloyal employee or the withdrawal of pension rights. In *British Steel* both Lord Wilberforce and Lord Fraser [89] had expressed the view that, provided there was a cause of action, an intention to seek redress was sufficient, and that redress could be by 'court action or otherwise.' In *Handmade Films v Express Newspapers plc* [90], Sir Nicholas Browne-Wilkinson refused a disclosure order relating to photographs of the singer, Madonna, taken on a film set on the ground that the plaintiffs (the film production company) had not disclosed in their evidence an intention to sue the wrongdoer.

Lord Diplock's approach to CCA 1981, s 10 prevailed for over five years until the decision of the House in *X v Morgan Grampian* [91], when Lord Bridge considered that confining 'justice' to its technical sense of 'the administration of justice in the course of legal proceedings in a court of law' was too narrow. He expressed the opinion that it was 'in the interests of justice, in the sense in which the phrase is used in s 10, that persons should be enabled to exercise important legal rights and to protect themselves from serious legal wrongs whether or not resort to legal proceedings in a court of law will be necessary to attain these objectives.' Although the House in *Morgan Grampian* believed themselves to be acting in conformity with Art 10 (for example, Lord Templeman expressly stated that disclosure was 'necessary in the sense in which that word has been interpreted by the European Court of Human

88 [1985] AC 339, 350B-C, F-G.
89 [1981] AC 1096, 1174D-E, 1200E-F.
90 (1986) FSR 463, 470.
91 [1991] 1 AC 1, 43.

Rights'[92]), in March 1996 the European Court in *Goodwin v UK*[93] held by a majority of 11 votes to 7 that the disclosure order had violated the journalist's rights under Art 10. In the Court's view, there was not 'a reasonable relationship of proportionality between the legitimate aim pursued by the disclosure order and the means deployed to achieve that aim'.

The European Court emphasised that the considerations to be taken into account when conducting a review under Art 10(2) tipped the balance of competing interests in favour of the interest of a democratic society in securing a free press. The interests of the plaintiff company in eliminating, by proceedings against the source, the residual threat of damage through dissemination of the confidential information otherwise than by the press, in obtaining compensation and in unmasking a disloyal employee or collaborator, were, even if considered cumulatively, not regarded by the Court as sufficient to outweigh the vital public interest in the protection of the journalist's source.

The Court only considered the divergence of view between Lord Diplock and Lord Bridge in the context of an unsuccessful contention by the applicant that the latter's construction of CA 1981, s 10 left the law insufficiently foreseeable to satisfy the condition in Art 10(2) that it be prescribed by law.[94] There was no adverse comment from the Court concerning Lord Bridge's construction, though it may be open to question whether the majority would have agreed with Lord Phillips' comment in *Ashworth Hospital Authority v MGN Ltd*[95] that the interpretation of Lord Bridge accords more happily with the scheme of Art 10 than that of Lord Diplock.

In *Camelot Group v Centaur Communications*[96] ,the first case on journalists' sources to come before the Court of Appeal after *Goodwin v UK*, Schiemann LJ described the differing conclusions reached on the same facts by the House of Lords and the European Court as 'a no more surprising legal phenomenon' than the Court of Appeal concluding that particular conduct amounted to negligence when the court at first instance decided it was *not*. This explanation will hardly suffice, since it fails to take account of the margin of appreciation afforded to the national court by Strasbourg. Thorpe LJ advanced a different explanation, namely that in the period of six years which elapsed between the

92 [1991] 1 AC 1, 49G-H.
93 (1996) 22 EHRR 123, [45-46] 145-6.
94 (1996) 22 EHRR 123, [32-34], 140-1.
95 [2001] 1 WLR 515, [84] 533E-F.
96 [1999] QB 124, p135G.

House's decision and that of the European Court 'standards fundamental to the performance of the balancing exercise may change materially.'[97] If this hypothesis is right, then, in the words of *Arlidge, Eady and Smith*[98], 'the influence of the Convention itself may have tipped the scales rather more heavily in favour of the protection of journalists' sources.'

In *Camelot* the defendants' journalist had received the plaintiffs' draft accounts and published an article based upon them some six days before the accounts would have been made public in any event. Schiemann LJ accepted the plaintiffs' submission that in assessing whether to make an order for disclosure of the source, a relevant but not conclusive factor was that the employer might wish to identify the source to exclude him from future employment.[99] He also acknowledged that 'the effect of disclosing the identity of one source who has leaked unimportant material can have a chilling effect on the willingness of other sources to disclose material which is important'. His solution was that 'the well informed source is always going to have to take a view as to what is going to be the court's reaction to his disclosure in the circumstances of his case'.[100] It is hard to disagree with the comment of *Arlidge, Eady and Smith*[101] that it is not obvious that the European Court would have come to the same conclusion as the Court of Appeal on the facts in *Camelot*. In particular, the uncertainties involved in leaving the source (well informed or otherwise) to assess for himself the likely reaction of the court are hardly likely to commend themselves to the European Court. As they say: 'the source of the difficulty may be that some English judges are not yet giving sufficient weight to the presumption in favour of the non-disclosure at the outset of the balancing exercise.'

Article 10 and the public right of access to information

The definition of freedom of expression in Art 10 expressly includes the freedom 'to receive and impart information and ideas without interference by public authority'. In a striking example of the right to impart information,

97 [1999] QB 124, 139A.
98 *Arlidge, Eady & Smith, Contempt* (2nd edn, 1999) para 9-141, 546.
99 [1999] QB 124, 134F.
100 [1999] QB 124, 138D-E. Thorpe LJ at 139C also thought that a potential source would be wise to inform himself how the courts apply CCA 1981, s 10.
101 [1999] QB 124, para 9-156-7, 550.

Elias J held in R *(Hirst) v Home Secretary* [102] that prison policy which denied serving prisoners the right to contact the media by phone was unlawful in so far as it denied a prisoner the right to comment on matters of legitimate public interest relating to prisons and prisoners.

As the European Court said in *Sunday Times v UK* [103], publicity 'serves as a brake on speculative and unenlightened discussion', and it is a truism that the press cannot perform its critical role of exposing abuses in administration and miscarriages of justice of which it is denied knowledge [104]. In *R v Shayler*[105], Lord Bingham restated the rationale of freedom of expression in the context of modern democratic government of the people by the people for the people:

> 'But there can be no government by the people if they are ignorant of the issues to be resolved, the arguments for and against different solutions and the facts underlying those arguments. The business of government is not an activity about which only those professionally engaged are entitled to receive information and express opinions. It is, or should be, a participatory process. But there can be no assurance that government is carried out for the people unless the facts are made known, the issues publicly ventilated.'

Whatever conclusions might be drawn from generalised statements such as those of Lord Bingham, it is clear from Strasbourg cases such as *Leander v Sweden* [106] (where the applicant sought information on file suggesting he was a security risk) that Art 10 does not in such cases 'confer on the individual a right of access to a register containing information on his personal position, nor does it embody an obligation on the government to impart such information to the individual'.[107] Simon Brown LJ emphasised this approach in *R (Persey) v Environment Secretary* [108], where the Divisional Court refused judicial review of the decision to hold the foot and mouth inquiry in private. The applicants

102 [2002] 1 WLR 2929.
103 (1979) 2 EHRR 245, [66] 282.
104 See *R v Home Secretary, ex p Simms* [2000] 2 AC 115, especially the classic passage from Lord Steyn at 126.
105 [2002] UKHL 11, [21].
106 (1987) 9 EHRR 433, [74] 456.
107 The same approach was adopted by the ECHR in *Gaskin v UK* (1989) 12 EHRR 35, where the applicant was refused access to the case file prepared on him when he was in care.
108 [2002] 3 WLR 704, [51-2] 730B-E.

had naturally relied strongly on the dicta of Kennedy LJ in *R (Wagstaff) v Health Secretary*[109] (the Shipman inquiry case), who had said:

> 'Where, as here, an inquiry purports to be a public inquiry, as opposed to an internal domestic inquiry, there is now in law what really amounts to a presumption that it will proceed in public unless there are persuasive reasons for taking some other course.'

In *Persey* Simon Brown LJ took a more restrictive view of Art 10's remit, detecting in the application an impermissible attempt to enforce the setting up by government of a quite different form of inquiry to what which had been commissioned, namely an open public inquiry such as that carried out by Lord Phillips into BSE. Freedom of expression was one thing, he said, access to information quite another. He went on:

> 'It is not a corollary of the right to freedom of expression that public authorities can be required to put in place additional opportunities for its exercise. Art 10 imposes no positive obligation on government to provide, in addition to existing means of communication, an open forum to achieve the yet wider dissemination of views. Article 10 prohibits interference with freedom of expression: it does not require its facilitation.'[110]

It is a curious feature of the Strasbourg case law that on occasions Art 8 has proved successful in gaining access to information where Art 10 has failed. Thus, in *Guerra v Italy*[111] the Court rejected the argument that the ignorance in which the Italian Government had kept those living downwind of a toxic chemical plant of the risks of pollution and accident infringed Art 10. On the other hand, the claim succeeded under Art 8, since the Court held that respect for private and family life carries with it a right to information, where access to that information is relevant to the enjoyment of the right. The information sought by the applicants was essential to enable them to assess the risks which they and their families might run if they continued to live in the area of the plant.

Article 8 was also invoked in *McGinley & Egan v UK*[112], where the claim by former servicemen who had been exposed to nuclear tests failed on the facts,

109 [2001] 1 WLR 292, 320F.
110 [2002] 3 WLR 704, [53], 730H.
111 (1998) 26 EHRR 357.
112 (1998) 27 EHRR 1.

but the Court nevertheless ruled that where a government engaged in hazardous activities, respect for private and family life required that an effective and accessible procedure be established which enabled those affected to seek all relevant and appropriate information. Thus a right which one might have expected to flow from Art 10 has been born of Art 8, a situation which has made Sir Stephen Sedley acidly wonder why the framers of Art 10 bothered to insert the words 'freedom... to receive... information and ideas without interference by public authority' at all.[113] Once again, Art 10 has proved not to have the reach that its libertarian supporters would wish.

113 Sir Stephen Sedley 'Information as a Human Right' ch 14, p 245 in *Essays in Honour of Sir David Williams* (OUP, 2000) .

Defamation: some recent developments and non-developments

David Eady

The background

By the end of the 1980s the law of defamation in England and Wales was under regular attack. It was criticised as being inimical to freedom of communication, and especially as creating a hostile environment for the free flow of information between the media and their viewing, listening and reading public. Editors and media tycoons had become increasingly conscious of the potential of Art 10 of the European Convention on Human Rights for expanding the reach of coverage – for their several purposes[1]. Not only was there scope for investigative journalists to reveal in greater depth where responsibility might lie for misdeeds and wrongdoing in public life or in business, but there was also the possibility of exploring a wider terrain for 'human interest' stories and thus for intrusions into personal privacy. Not surprisingly, in their lobbying campaigns it tended to be the former that was given greater emphasis than the latter. Both prospects, however, offered tantalising vistas of market penetration in a competitive world.

Yet joy was by no means unconfined. Inevitably, there was a certain ambivalence towards the impact that the Convention was likely to have upon the media. Article 10(2) itself makes specific reference to the need to protect reputation, and thus for there to be such limitations upon freedom of speech as were proportionate and necessary in a democratic society. Furthermore, it contained a sweeping-up phrase about the protection of other 'rights'; this too rang

1 Especially since the decision on contempt in *Sunday Times v UK* (1979) 2 EHRR 245.

warning bells. In the context, it could well be taken to embrace the 'right to respect for private and family life' protected under Art 8. Although it had not been originally conceived as affording protection against media intrusion, when drafted in the aftermath of the Second World War[2], it was becoming apparent that this article might have implications for tabloid journalism. This apprehension led to strong warnings over the threat to investigative journalism if too much weight was to given to personal privacy – especially in representations to the Calcutt Committee on Privacy[3]. The ambivalence was well illustrated by the evidence given in person by the late Mr Robert Maxwell, then presiding over the Mirror Group (but also, in those days, one of the most proficient wielders of the libel writ). He spoke movingly of the need to protect investigative journalism in its fight against crime and corruption – and of how a law of privacy would lead to 'many a rogue going undetected'.

Apart from matters of substantive law, the practice and procedure in the field of defamation attracted much obloquy for what was perceived as its complexity, obscurity and arcane rules. It was true that there seemed to be almost endless potential for interlocutory wrangling – leading to expense and apparent delay in the resolution of the 'real issues' between the parties. In fact, however, the early disposal of troublesome side issues would often remove obstacles in the way of a negotiated settlement. Yet to those observers whose previous experience lay primarily in the area of (say) personal injury litigation, or in the disposal of commercial or building disputes, it seemed frustrating that libel actions failed to conform to the familiar pattern of pursuing the straightest route to trial or arbitration. The thinking seemed to be that, if only the lawyers would stop all this unproductive squabbling about particulars of justification, disclosure of documents, or the different layers of meaning to be found within the libellous words, then their clients would be able to move quickly forward to the end of the rainbow and obtain the verdict of a jury. There was frequent resort to unflattering analogies for these preliminary processes – usually associated with a minuet or some more distant dance form, such as the sarabande.

2 See eg *Marckx v Belgium* (1979) 2 EHRR 330. It had, in the words of Sir G Fitzmaurice, been directed primarily against '... the whole gamut of fascist and communist inquisitorial practices'.

3 The Committee on Privacy and Related Matters was set up in 1989 by Mr Douglas Hurd, when Home Secretary, following concerns about press intrusions in a number of well-publicised cases. The report was published in June 1990: (1990) Cm 1102. (Meanwhile, Mr David Mellor MP when a junior Home Office minister had been unwise enough, during the course of its deliberations, to speak on television about the press 'drinking at the last-chance saloon'. This he was never permitted to forget and he soon fell victim himself to tabloid intrusions into privacy.)

It was against this background that the then Lord Chancellor, Lord Mackay of Clashfern, invited Brian Neill in the summer of 1990 to chair an investigation into defamation practice with a view to suggesting improvements. The mechanism proposed was that of a sub-committee of the Supreme Court Procedure Committee, of which he had been chairman since 1986. In fact, as it turned out, the members were invited on an ad hoc basis[4]. Brian Neill at once sought clarification of the terms of reference because it soon became obvious that any effective overhaul would require examination of the substantive law as well as matters of procedure. The response was that the enquiry could be as wide-ranging as he thought necessary, subject only to two qualifications. First, there was to be no challenge to the scope for jury trial, which was regarded as so fundamental that it did not need the specialist assessment of lawyers as to the effectiveness of its role. It was perceived as being a matter for everyone. Indeed, it is sometimes described as the 'constitutional' tribunal for libel actions[5] – although in the intervening period there have been considerable inroads, largely judicial, into its unfettered discretion in the award of damages[6]. Secondly, the possibility of legal aid funding for defamation was also put out of bounds. This form of assistance has never, of course, been available to anyone, whether bringing such proceedings or defending them[7]. (More recently, defamation has naturally proved to be fertile territory for conditional fee agreements.)

The recommendations of the committee were presented to the Lord Chancellor a year afterwards, in July 1991. Some were rejected altogether[8], while others

4 Brian Neill was assisted by three specialist practitioners (two barristers and a solicitor) and a professor of journalism.

5 See eg *Cassell v Broome* [1972] AC 1027, 1065-1066 (Lord Hailsham).

6 Most notably perhaps in *Rantzen v Mirror Group (1986) Ltd* [1994] QB 670 and *John v MGN Ltd* [1997] QB 568 (to both of which key decisions, as it happens, Brian Neill was a party). There are also the statutory inroads contained in the Defamation Act 1996, ss 3(10) and 8(5) providing expressly for hearings without a jury in the specified circumstances (ie in relation to 'offer of amends' and 'summary disposal', respectively).

7 There is no guarantee of legal assistance under the Convention in relation to civil proceedings, and the Commission has accepted that it is not unreasonable to give a low priority for the funding of parties to libel actions: see *X v FRG*, App No 3925/69, 32 CD 56, *Steel & Morris v UK*, App No 21325/93 (1993) 18 EHRR CD 172, *McVicar v UK*, App No 46311/99, 7 May 2002.

8 Such as the one to abolish the so-called rule in *Scott v Sampson* (1882) 8 QBD 491. The concern was expressed by Mr Paul Boateng MP, in the discussions in the House of Commons on the Defamation Bill, that it could prove to be 'a muckraker's charter': Hansard, HC, Vol 280, col 133 (21 May 1996). It appears that one supporter

found their way eventually into the Rules of the Supreme Court (subsequently reflected in corresponding provisions of the CPR)[9] or into the Defamation Act 1996[10]. The content of the report is useful in providing a summary of most of the pressing issues of the day, and of the arguments thrown up in the course of the consultations carried out among interested parties. Curiously, however, the limitation set upon the terms of reference did mean that the topic then causing the greatest public concern, and receiving the most media discussion, could not be addressed – namely, the jury's role in the award of libel damages. Such awards were often perceived as excessive and sometimes punitive in all but name. The modern approach to compensation was eventually worked out a few years afterwards, as a matter of judicial evolution, and under the spur of human rights jurisprudence.

It is perhaps worth tracing through not only the development of the law on this topic but also what has happened in relation to three other important issues identified in the report. These were all causing concern at that time on the part of media lawyers, but none of them was addressed in the 1996 Act. I propose to consider to what extent such concerns have been allayed in the intervening years and whether any of them still requires to be resolved.

A special common law privilege for the media?

One of the perennial issues was that of qualified privilege for media publications. The traditional approach of the common law in England and

of the clause was Tony Weir, who has observed that '... to claim for damage to a reputation you do not deserve is like a thief claiming for loss of his swag': *Casebook on Tort* (9th edn) p 537. As matters turned out, the rule was eventually holed below the water-line in the Court of Appeal's decision in *Burstein v Times Newspapers Ltd* [2001] 1 WLR 579. Other important proposals that were not taken up included those for the abolition of criminal libel and of the closely related concept of punitive or 'exemplary' damages (discussed below).

9 One example, the provision for obtaining a judge's ruling at an early stage on whether the words complained of were capable of bearing a certain meaning or meanings, proved immediately popular (see now CPR Part 53, Practice Direction, para 4.1); hitherto, such decisions could only be taken by the trial judge. Another was the obligation placed on claimants to plead by way of detailed response to particulars of justification (discussed further below).

10 These include the reduction of the limitation period for defamation and malicious falsehood to one year (from three and six years, respectively); the introduction of a new 'offer of amends' defence; and the extension of statutory privilege for media reports of events or statements of public interest both here and abroad.

Wales has been that there could be no privilege in respect of publications to the world at large unless it could be shown *both* that the subject-matter was of legitimate public interest *and* that the publisher had a duty ('social, legal or moral') to make the specific communication[11]. Only when these conditions were fulfilled, was it accepted as being *in the public interest* that such information should be published. The debate was driven partly by the influence of the First Amendment to the United States Constitution and the case of *New York Times v Sullivan*[12] – with its so-called 'public figure' defence. There was also the hope that the growing influence of the European Convention might lead to a 'shift in the balance'[13] between the priorities given to protection of reputation, on the one hand, and to freedom of information on the other. This is largely a matter of public or social policy, and it could either be tackled judicially or through the legislature.

The government of the day rejected suggestions for widening media privilege along these lines when the Defamation Bill was debated in the Lords. The reasons given corresponded largely to those set out in the Neill Report:[14]

> 'Standards of care and accuracy in the press are, in our view, not such as to give any confidence that a "Sullivan" defence would be treated responsibly. It would mean, in effect, that newspapers could publish more or less what they liked, provided they were honest, if their subject happened to be within the definition of a "public figure". We think this would lead to great injustice. Furthermore, it would be quite contrary to the tradition of our common law that citizens are not divided into different classes. What matters is the subject-matter of the publication and how it is treated, rather than who happens to be the subject of the allegations.
>
> In our view the media are adequately protected by the defences of justification and fair comment at the moment, and it is salutary that these defences are available to them only if they have got their facts substantially correct'.

11 See eg *Adam v Ward* (1915) 31 TLR 299 and *Blackshaw v Lord* [1984] 1 QB 1.

12 (1964) 376 US 254.

13 Just as there had been such an adjustment, in the context of the law of contempt, as between the two competing priorities of fair trial and freedom of communication: see eg the remarks of Lloyd LJ in *A-G v Newspaper Publishing plc* [1988] Ch 333, 382.

14 At p 164. See the comments of Lord Inglewood, for the government, in House of Lords Debates, 8 March 1996, at col 607. Cf the similar remarks of Cantley J in *London Artists v Littler* [1968] 1 WLR 607, 615 in the context of the possible defence of 'fair information on a matter of public interest'.

It might be thought that there would have been thereafter, for a time at least, a degree of judicial restraint about suggestions that the balance should be redressed despite the express refusal of the legislature to do so. Lord Lowry in *C v Director of Public Prosecutions* had recently attempted to highlight (albeit in a criminal context) the need for caution in judicial law-making[15]:

> '(1) if the solution is doubtful, the judges should beware of imposing their own remedy; (2) caution should prevail if Parliament has rejected opportunities of clearing up a known difficulty or has legislated while leaving the difficulty untouched; (3) disputed matters of social policy are less suitable areas for judicial intervention than purely legal problems; (4) fundamental legal doctrines should not lightly be set aside; (5) judges should not make change unless they can achieve finality and certainty'.

The introduction of a *Sullivan* defence by the judicial route could arguably be said to fall foul of all these guidelines. On the other hand, this restrictive approach was likely to recede into the distance as the judges came to exercise greater influence upon the law in those areas to which the Convention has relevance and where the European Court jurisprudence points in a clear direction. In such a context, Lord Lowry's self-denying ordinance would be unlikely to hold sway for long. At all events, little time was lost after the Parliament's rejection of a broad (or 'generic') qualified privilege defence for the media before the opportunity presented itself for another battering ram to be brought to bear. In *Reynolds v Times Newspapers Ltd*[16] it was argued that the time had come to recognise judicially that greater protection should be afforded to media coverage of important political issues and events – whether within this jurisdiction or elsewhere.

In the Court of Appeal[17], one factor prayed in aid on behalf of *The Sunday Times* was that Brian Neill himself appeared to have had something of a change of heart on the subject since the date of his 1991 Report. A passage was cited from the Goodman lecture he had given in 1994. The relevant words had been uttered in the context of the famous remark of Brandeis J that 'Sunlight is the most powerful of all disinfectants'. Brian Neill had been addressing the consequences of the (then recent) decisions of the House of Lords and the

15 [1996] 1 AC 1, 28.

16 [2001] 2 AC 127.

17 [1998] 3 All ER 961, 999. Lord Lester of Herne Hill QC had made a similar point in the Parliamentary Debate, on 8 March 1996, at col 600-601.

Court of Appeal in *Derbyshire County Council v Times Newspapers Ltd*[18], to the effect that a local (or national) government body could not itself bring defamation proceedings in respect of criticisms made of it but, on the other hand, it would be open to any individual upon whom such criticisms also reflected to bring an action in his or her own name. He was considering the observation of Brennan J in *New York Times v Sullivan* that the opportunity for such individual claims would undermine the primary rule; the 'chilling effect'[19] would still inhibit journalists. They could still find themselves in court – there would simply have been a reduction in the range of possible claimants. Brian Neill too had observed that it is not altogether clear how one can distinguish satisfactorily between an elected body and those who compose it or govern its affairs. Yet the lecture also included the following significant words:

> '... it seems to me that one must first establish that the information is of a nature that the public has a *right* to know it; it may then be possible to say that those in possession of the information have a duty or at least a right to communicate it ... Furthermore, it is essential to distinguish between the facts which the public 'ought to know' and facts which it might be interested in knowing'.

Much depends, as Brian Neill was implicitly accepting, on the facts of the individual case. In some circumstances, the facts relating to the individual government employee might well be such that there would be a duty to communicate them to the public – and correspondingly a right on the part of the public to be informed of them. In others they would not. The case of *Blackshaw v Lord*[20] provides a good example. No one would seriously doubt that the apparent loss of £52m of public monies was more than just a matter *of* public interest; it would clearly be a matter on which the public would have the 'right to know' the facts. It by no means follows, however, that privilege should also attach to the publication of the journalist's speculation or musings as to which individual civil servant might be responsible – to the effect that it 'must be Blackshaw' – even if some readers might be interested in learning of them. In other words, it would not be *in* the public interest for such material to be made generally available.

18 [1993] AC 534, HL, [1992] QB 770, CA.

19 This popular phrase is often used in the debate over the restrictions imposed by the law of defamation, contempt or confidence: see eg *Derbyshire County Council v Times Newspapers Ltd* [1993] AC 534, 548 (Lord Keith); *Goodwin v UK* (1996) 22 EHRR 123, 142-143.

20 [1984] 1 QB 1.

In these circumstances, Brian Neill's comments in the lecture do not necessarily indicate any change of heart from the views expressed in the report; nor indeed do they appear to support any blanket extension of qualified privilege to 'political speech' for the purpose of recognising wider limits of acceptable criticism in that context[21].

There is no obvious answer offered in the human rights jurisprudence for the striking of the balance between the interests of those who wish to defend their reputations and the protection required for the journalists who wish to attack them. It is provided in Art 10(2) that there is an exception to the right of freedom of information to take account of the need to protect inter alia the right to reputation – but only to the extent necessary in a democratic society (ie where there is a 'pressing social need'). It has been made clear that this does not give rise to choosing between two conflicting principles but rather to '... a principle of freedom of expression that is subject to a number of exceptions which must be narrowly interpreted'[22]. For this reason, one has to be careful about metaphorical allusions to 'striking balances'; this may give the impression that there *are* two principles of comparable priority. Moreover, it is recognised that the notion of a signatory state's margin of appreciation will vary according to the Convention right being addressed, and that there may be greater scope for variation in (say) the context of 'public morals' than in that of free speech[23]. There remains, however, considerable room for debate as to how far there is, either in general terms or on the facts of any given case, a pressing social need for the law to give priority to the protection of reputation.

There is obvious force in the arguments that the right to communicate true factual information should prevail in most cases and that the opportunity to express opinions on accurate factual material should equally be given high priority. Correspondingly, in this jurisdiction we have long provided for the defences of justification and fair comment, respectively. There have been minor inroads over the years upon the unqualified right to tell the truth, for example in the context of confidential information and in the application of the provisions of the Rehabilitation of Offenders Act 1974[24]. There may yet be others to come, as the implications for journalism of the right to privacy are carefully

21 See the discussion in the Court of Appeal's judgment in *Reynolds v Times Newspapers Ltd* [1998] 3 All ER 961, 999-1001.

22 *Sunday Times v UK* (1979) 2 EHRR 245, 281.

23 See eg Clayton & Tomlinson *The Law of Human Rights* (OUP, 2000) paras 15-202, 15-205.

24 ROA 1974, s 8(5).

worked out in the light of Art 8. What is important about the pressure for a *Sullivan* type of defence is that it would operate independently of the truth of the allegations sought to be protected. In general terms, the journalist would have a defence in relation to charges made, however serious, about people falling within certain defined classes – or perhaps relating to certain specified areas of human activity (such as, for example, politics). The protection would arise *irrespective* of truth or falsity; it could only be defeated if the complainant were able to prove negligence or bad faith (depending on the version of the defence adopted).

What is not often articulated is why it is perceived to be in the public interest that journalists should communicate inaccurate or false information, or why the public has a legitimate interest in receiving such material[25]. It could hardly be disputed that, *all things being equal*, it is desirable that the public should be protected against being fed false information. One might almost suggest that it is necessary in a democratic society that this should happen, and especially perhaps where the government is the source of the misleading material. The difficulty is, however, that there are certain circumstances, albeit not necessarily easy to define, which may require from time to time that *some* risk of misleading the public has to be countenanced[26]. What is critical is for the particular democratic society to debate and to decide, through its courts or legislature, what those circumstances might be. There will always to some extent be a 'chilling effect' brought about by the need to check one's facts, but that will also bring to bear a discipline which, according to one legitimate viewpoint, may in itself be serving the public interest.

25 In *Constitutional Law* (2nd edn), for example, I Loveland simply asserts (at 545-6) that the Court of Appeal's refusal in *Blackshaw v Lord* to recognise that the electorate had any legitimate interest in receiving the (false) information about the individual civil servant provides a most compelling illustration of the 'antediluvian state of the common law's human rights jurisprudence'. By contrast, in *McCartan Turkington Breen v Times Newspapers Ltd* [2001] 2 AC 277, 301D, Lord Cooke commented, more thoughtfully, that '*Blackshaw*'s case ... was far from a plain case of circumstantial qualified privilege'.

26 See eg *Blackshaw v Lord* [1984] 1 QB 1, 27 (per Stephenson LJ). The court was there positing situations of emergency, where the public interest might require that the available material be brought into the open *despite* the lack of an opportunity for proper checks to be carried out. It is noteworthy that one of the factors mentioned by Lord Nicholls in *Reynolds v Times Newspapers*, in his catalogue of non-exhaustive tests for determining the existence of a social or moral duty, was whether the publication could be said to be justified by considerations of urgency: [2001] 2 AC 127, 205. If so, this will clearly have a bearing on the extent to which it is reasonable for checks on accuracy to be carried out.

The matter of principle seemed largely to have been resolved by the decision of the House of Lords (divided three to two) in *Reynolds*. It was made clear that there would always be a need to judge issues of 'social or moral duty' sensitively in the light of prevailing attitudes, and general guidelines were identified to assist courts in their task. The majority recognised, however, that the traditional duty/interest approach should continue to be followed – involving, presumably, the application of objective criteria. As Lord Cooke of Thorndon later observed,[27] 'It seems to me that *Reynolds'* case was less a breakthrough than a reminder of the width of the basic common law principles as to privilege, although undoubtedly it is much more encouraging of their invocation than previous English decisions'. In particular, there was to be no specific exception in the political context to the 'duty' requirement. Moreover, Lord Hobhouse of Woodborough made the following important observation[28]:

> 'There is no human right to disseminate information that is not true. No public interest is served by publishing or communicating misinformation. The working of a democratic society depends on the members of that society being informed, not misinformed. Misleading people and the purveying as facts statements which are not true is destructive of the democratic society and should form no part of such a society. There is no duty to publish what is not true: there is no interest in being misinformed'.

This decision of judicial policy bears, in general terms, a degree of similarity to the approach taken in Canada, where there has been an awareness of the risks of stripping those who go into public life of all recourse to the courts for redressing injury to reputation[29]. It has there been held that the law of defamation was not unduly restrictive of freedom of speech or inconsistent with the protection afforded to 'freedom of the press and other media of communication' by the Canadian Charter of Rights and Fundamental Freedoms. So too in England, it has been recognised as by and large consistent with the demands of Art 10[30].

27 In *McCartan Turkington Breen* [2001] 2 AC 277 at 301G-H.

28 [2001] 2 AC 127, 238.

29 See eg *Globe & Mail v Boland* (1960) 22 DLR (2d) 277; *Hill v Church of Scientology* (1995) 126 DLR (4th) 174, Supreme Court of Canada.

30 See the well-known remarks to that effect of Lord Keith in *Derbyshire County Council* ([1993] AC 534 at 551F-G) and of Lord Goff in *A-G v Guardian Newspapers Ltd (No 2)* [1990] 1 AC 109, 248A. A decade later, however, after the coming into effect of the Human Rights Act 1998, the Court of Appeal expressed itself unwilling to 'rest on the laurels' of those statements, albeit of high authority: *Berezovsky v Forbes Inc*

It was hoped that after *Reynolds* a body of case law would emerge, so as to enable journalists and their advisers to determine with reasonable clarity, in advance of publication, whether any proposed article was likely to pass muster according to Lord Nicholls' non-exhaustive tests – thus gradually thawing the 'chill'. Inevitably, there would be an interim period while the guidelines were applied case by case. This element of uncertainty, and its concomitant frost, were major factors in the decision of the New Zealand Court of Appeal in June 2000 not to adopt the *Reynolds* approach in that jurisdiction.[31]

At the time of writing, and as the practical implications of *Reynolds* are still being worked through, a new element of flux (and thus of further uncertainty) may perhaps be detected. The Court of Appeal in the more recent decision of *Loutchansky v Times Newspapers Ltd*[32] might be construed as pointing a way round the established duty/interest criterion by acknowledging that:

> 'There will undoubtedly be occasions when one newspaper would decide to publish and quite properly so, yet a second newspaper, no less properly, would delay or abstain from publication. Not all journalists can be or should be expected to reach an identical view in every case. Responsible journalism will in certain circumstances permit equally of publication or of non-publication'.

This comes close to introducing a subjective test of duty (and thus of public interest too) or departing from the notion of duty altogether in favour of that which is 'responsible'. Yet their Lordships in *Reynolds* had surely not intended that 'responsible journalism' should become in itself a touchstone – rather that it should be one issue to be explored by the court en route to deciding, on the particular facts, the critical question of duty/public interest. This seems to be confirmed in Lord Cooke's own distillation in *McCartan*[33] of 'the main principle for which the *Reynolds* case stands'; namely that the 'classical interest–duty test' is adaptable to a great variety of circumstances.

[2001] EWCA Civ 1251, 31 July 2001 CA, per Sedley LJ. Where necessary, judges must be prepared 'to cull sacred jurisprudential cows' (as happened with the capping of libel damages).

31 *Lange v Atkinson* [2000] NZCA 95.

32 [2002] 1 All ER 652 (at para 49).

33 [2001] 2 AC 277 at 300.

The burden of proof – and other minor irritants

It has for some time been the received wisdom in academic circles that one of the fundamental problems with the law of defamation is the burden of proof[34]. It is thought to be, quite simply, the wrong way round. If only the obvious need for this reform were recognised, much injustice would easily be removed and the interests of a democratic society well served. Journalists would be free of their shackles; much skulduggery would be exposed which now has to remain uncovered because of the inhibitions imposed on freedom of speech by this outdated rule. It is, supposedly, a leftover from a bygone age, when the rich and famous sought to control the press in their own interests. It is necessary to consider perhaps whether this line of thinking is right as a matter of principle and whether, if it is, such a reform would make very much difference in practice to the way in which journalists conduct themselves.

First, the point of principle. It may have seemed curious that this apparent panacea was omitted from the recommendations of Brian Neill's committee. The report certainly records that a number of comments had been received in favour of such a measure. The response was expressed in the briefest terms[35], on the basis that '... it is normally the [claimant] who is the "accused", and who should therefore be presumed innocent'. The matter will perhaps, for present purposes, bear closer scrutiny. This passage brings out, however, the point that when people speak of the burden of proof in this context they generally have in mind that relating to the defence of justification. This is, of course, only one aspect of a more complex issue. Judges who sum up in libel actions are used to explaining how the burden of proof shifts from one side to the other in such proceedings. This is because jurors need to be mindful, throughout their assessment of the evidence, of the issue to which their consideration is at the moment directed.

It will not do to draw analogies too readily with other legal wrongs by suggesting, for example, that journalists should be presumed innocent in respect of their

34 For relatively recent espousal of this theory, see Barendt, Lustgarten, Norrie and Stephenson *Libel and the Media* (OUP, 1997) 195-196, and Tony Weir *Tort Law* (OUP, 2002) 168.

35 At pp 72-73. The Committee's comment was cited by Lord Mackay, the then Lord Chancellor, on 2 April 1996 when speaking against an amendment to the Defamation Bill proposed by Lord Lester, the purpose of which was to reverse the burden of proof. The amendment was then withdrawn (Lord Williams of Mostyn having also spoken against it): House of Lords Debates, col 239-243. See also *McVicar v UK*, App No 46311/99, 7 May 2002.

published articles as are those accused of crimes or other torts such as negligence. The nature of the wrong may be quite different in each case. It is in the nature of defamation that the defendant will be accusing or attacking the claimant by publishing allegations tending to lower him or her in the eyes of fellow citizens. Just as in the case of assault or battery[36] the burden will lie on the claimant to prove that the relevant 'attack' has taken place – and that it was the defendant's responsibility. It will then be for the defendant to raise such matters as may, according to law, throw a different light on the conduct in question. It may be, in the assault case, an explanation on the basis of accident or self-defence or, in the libel context, a defence of qualified or absolute privilege, consent, justification or fair comment.

In some libel cases the words complained of may be utterly trivial, or at least seem so to the casual onlooker, but in others the allegations may be of the utmost gravity. If a person is accused of serious child abuse, perhaps when exploiting a position of trust in relation to those in local authority care, the charge obviously equates to an accusation of criminal activity meriting a very long custodial penalty. Personal reputations can be terminally damaged, overnight, when accusations of this gravity appear in the media. There is also the daunting problem, for people still of an age to work, that employment prospects will almost certainly have vanished as effectively as if there had actually been a conviction. This is simply one example of the awesome power of the press. Such consequences will have been brought about without any trial, or effective opportunity to refute what has been said. Emotive allegations of this kind can also put personal security and physical safety in jeopardy, as was demonstrated by the consequences in August 2000 of a Sunday tabloid's campaign to 'name and shame' a large number of individuals it deemed to be paedophiles. People were abused and threatened, and several victims were forced to leave their homes. Some were reported to have committed suicide. It so happened that a number of those attacked were innocent – a factor which may not matter greatly when one is addressing dispassionately the general undesirability of 'mob rule'. Nonetheless, it is a chastening thought in the present context. Does the public interest require that the media should have added to the armoury of their powers a presumption that their allegations, however serious, are true?

36 Cf the analogy drawn by Sir John Donaldson MR in *A-G v Newspaper Publishing plc* [1988] Ch 333, 370-372.

The person concerned could in practice never hope to regain his or her good name except through libel litigation. The Press Complaints Commission[37] could offer no practical assistance in such circumstances, because it is not in a position to resolve contested issues of fact, save in the case of straightforward errors.

Yet no one without substantial capital resources could hope to undertake the cost of such litigation – save perhaps nowadays by means of a conditional fee arrangement (though there is no *right* of access to justice by that route). There would never have been any chance of legal aid for defamation, although it may be available to support a claim for malicious (or 'injurious') falsehood[38]. (This may be thought something of an anomaly. The first drawback of trying to establish the latter cause of action is that the claimant would have to show bad faith on the part of those who wrote or published the story; negligence or incompetence would not suffice. Secondly, the complainant would also have to assume the burden of proving what was said to be false. In any event, the tort of malicious falsehood is not directed to the restoration of reputation, as such, but to providing compensation for financial loss.[39])

Apart from the self-evident interests of the media defendants, it may be difficult to detect any public interest imperative pointing to a reversal of the burden of proof in relation to the defence of justification. It would be yet one further hurdle for the hapless individual to surmount in seeking vindication. One must ask the question: 'Do the interests of the media owners, or of the (*ex hypothesi* negligent) journalists, constitute in themselves a sufficient public interest to justify taking such a course?' It is perhaps worth recalling the words of Sir John Donaldson MR in *Francome v Mirror Group Newspapers Ltd*[40] when assessing this inter-relationship. He naturally paid tribute to the 'invaluable' role of the media in exposing crime, anti-social behaviour and hypocrisy, as well to their campaigning for reform and propagating the views of minorities. He went on, however, to observe that they '... are peculiarly vulnerable to the error of confusing the public interest with their own interest'.

37 A self-regulatory body operating as successor to the Press Council with effect from 1 January 1991, after having been hastily constituted by the newspaper industry in the light of recommendations of the Calcutt Committee some six months earlier (see fn 3 above).

38 See eg *Joyce v Sengupta* [1993] 1 WLR 337, CA.

39 [1993] 1 WLR 337 at 348 (per Sir Donald Nicholls V-C); see also *Lonrho plc v Fayed (No 5)* [1993] 1 WLR 1489 at 1495, 1504, 1509.

40 [1984] 1 WLR 892, 898.

Is this comment now to be dismissed as evincing no more than an outdated judicial prejudice against the press? Was he doing no more than paying lip-service to their fundamental role in a democratic society?

A good deal has been said since those words were uttered, not only in the European Court of Human Rights[41] but also in the higher courts of England and Wales[42], to emphasise just how fundamental a role and status the media must be accorded in a modern society. Nevertheless, the question implicit in Sir John's remarks surely remains a legitimate one to ask – even though the answer may now differ, in some cases, from that which would have been given 20 years ago. Making due allowance for their enhanced status, it cannot surely be contended that the media do not have interests of their own to protect, especially when brought before the courts in costly litigation, or that they are in some way incapable of acting from self-interest.

Much of what has been said about the importance of press freedom in recent years has focussed particularly on the protection of journalists' sources or upon the value of court reporting in the context of open justice. It is necessary to bear in mind, in the present context, that the right to protect one's reputation (and indeed to an extent one's privacy) is also enshrined in the European Convention. There is thus an obligation on us all to make effective provision (albeit reasonable and proportionate) towards achieving that objective. It must therefore be necessary to afford (even if not to fund) access to the courts for the purpose of having this 'civil right' to reputation determined '... at a fair and public hearing within a reasonable time by an independent and impartial tribunal established by law'. It is true that Art 6(2) only refers expressly to a presumption of innocence in the context of a person who is 'charged with a criminal offence'. Yet it is difficult to see, even in a civil context, how a person charged by the media with (say) child abuse could expect a 'fair' hearing from

41 See eg *Lingens v Austria* (1986) 8 EHRR 407; *Sunday Times v UK (No 2)* (1991) 14 EHRR 229; *Castells v Spain* (1992) 14 EHRR 445; *Thorgeirson v Iceland* (1992) 14 EHRR 843; *Oberschlick v Austria* (1995) 19 EHRR 389; *Prager & Oberschlick v Austria* (1996) 21 EHRR 1; *Goodwin v UK* (1996) 22 EHRR 123; *Bladet Tromsø v Norway* (2000) EHRR 125.

42 To name but a few, see *A-G v Guardian Newspapers Ltd (No 2)* [1990] 1 AC 109, 183F (per Sir John Donaldson MR himself); *Hector v A-G of Antigua* [1990] 2 AC 312, 318 (per Lord Bridge); *A-G v Guardian Newspapers Ltd (No 3)* [1992] 1 WLR 874, [1992] 3 All ER 38, QBD; *Chief Constable of Leicestershire v Garavelli* [1997] EMLR 543, QBD; *Hodgson v Imperial Tobacco Ltd* [1998] 1 WLR 1056, [1998] 2 All ER 673, CA; *Reynolds v Times Newspapers Ltd* [2001] 2 AC 127, HL.

an 'impartial tribunal' if he is required to prove his innocence – and guilt is presumed by that very tribunal.

Moreover, it is clear in other contexts that the European jurisprudence tends not to be unduly hung up on whether 'criminal' or 'civil' labels are traditionally attached by domestic law[43]. Greater importance is attached to substance. More specifically, 'trial by newspaper', which may well carry with it some of the punitive consequences often attaching to a criminal conviction (affecting for example one's freedom to work), is something clearly recognised by the Strasbourg Court to be in itself undesirable[44]:

> 'Again it cannot be excluded that the public's becoming accustomed to the regular spectacle of pseudo-trials in the news media might in the long run have nefarious consequences for the acceptance of the courts as the proper forum for the settlement of legal disputes'.

If a person is, to all intents and purposes, to be found guilty of a criminal offence it is surely desirable that this process should take place before a judicial tribunal. Nor is it obvious why, if such a hearing happens to take place in proceedings traditionally treated as 'civil' in character, the person so accused should be put at a disadvantage (for example, as to burden of proof) merely because there has already been a 'trial by newspaper' resulting in the publication of its defamatory 'verdict'.

In so far as the present rule as to burden of proof does in itself constitute a restriction on freedom of communication, it may be characterised for these reasons as one that is 'necessary in a democratic society'[45]. Those reasons may perhaps be conveniently be summarised by the two short propositions already cited from the Neill Report, the validity of which has not subsequently been undermined. (They are obviously closely related to the policy debate, already considered, as to whether journalists should have a special defence of privilege.) First, it is the complainant, as the 'accused', who should be presumed innocent. Second, it is salutary that a defence should *normally* only be available to a defendant who has got his facts substantially correct.

43 See eg *Benham v UK* (1996) 22 EHRR 293; *Steel v UK* (1999) 28 EHRR 603.

44 *Sunday Times v UK* (1979) 2 EHRR 245, at para 63.

45 Nor does this view appear to be inconsistent with any of the Convention jurisprudence, which certainly draws a distinction between allegations of fact and value judgments and seems to accept that in the former case domestic law may require the facts to be demonstrated: see eg *Lingens v Austria* (1986) 8 EHRR 407 and *Prager & Oberschlick v Austria* (1996) 21 EHRR 1.

So much for the debate on principle which, although of interest to theorists, is in one sense largely beside the point. In practical terms, reversal of the burden of proof would yield little advantage to media defendants. It is surely an exceptional case in which the jurors, having heard the conflicting evidence from witnesses or weighed up the arguments as to what inferences should be drawn from documents, will say to themselves that the matter is so evenly balanced that the issue can only be decided in the claimant's favour on the basis of what the judge told them about the burden of proof. If the claimant has gone into the witness box in the usual way, and stated on oath that the defamatory allegation is untrue, the defendants will in practice have to persuade the jurors by cross-examination, contrary evidence, or a combination of the two, that his evidence should be rejected. In the majority of cases, the 12 individuals will by the end of the trial simply prefer one set of witnesses (or arguments) to the other. It will make little difference where the burden of proof lay at the outset.

It is to be noted, finally, that the balance of advantage as to the defence of justification has by no means remained static over the intervening years. There are at least two respects in which the balance has shifted significantly in favour of defendants. First, it has now become the regular practice at a relatively early stage in the action for claimants to plead a response to particulars of justification. Traditionally, one did not plead to particulars of any kind. Specifically, in defamation actions, a claimant could keep his powder dry, even being permitted to remain mute in the face of an apparently overwhelming raft of particulars detailing his misconduct. There was no obligation to 'confess and avoid' or to narrow the issues by making admissions. It was simply presumed that issue would be joined on every factual allegation raised by the defendant. As more detailed and complex pleas of justification became increasingly common, it was apparent that this secretive approach was not serving the interests of the parties or of the administration of justice more widely. Nothing was being done to confine the issues, whether for the purposes of document disclosure, gathering evidence or trial preparations generally. The situation tended to favour claimants with infinite wealth, who needed to do nothing by way of limiting the defendants' expenditure of time and money in putting together a defence which might well have to range widely over many years of the claimant's business career[46].

46 In 1990 notable examples were to be found in libel actions brought by Robert Maxwell and Armand Hammer, in the wake of unauthorised biographical coverage that did not meet with the subjects' approval.

One solution was fairly obvious and easy to implement. It was observed by the Neill Committee that it was surprisingly rare at the time to find a reply served in relation to a plea of justification, and it was recommended that this should become the normal practice[47]. Reference was made to the decision of the Court of Appeal a year earlier in *Morrell v International Thompson Publishing Ltd*[48] where, effectively, the way had been shown by reference to existing but little used powers. It was there said (by Brian Neill):

> 'The power to order a party to serve a statement of case, even in a libel action, is in my judgment quite clear. I think it is important that one should emphasise that, if it is necessary for the proper administration of justice, the Court can require the issues in an action to be defined by further pleadings. Thus the Court has the power to order parties to set out exactly what their case is. But the Court would have to look with great care at each individual case to make certain that any order which was made did not affect the [claimant] adversely so as to weaken the position which he enjoyed in regard to the burden of proof, which, where justification is pleaded, rests fairly and squarely on the defendant'.

It has indeed now become the norm in such actions for a claimant to identify his response to the plea of justification, and the rules have been adapted accordingly[49]. There is normally no need to make any application to the court to achieve this.

The second significant change of practice was brought about by the Court of Appeal's decision in *McDonald's Corpn v Steel*[50]. It is now clear from the judgment of Brian Neill in that case that, when determining the propriety of entering a plea of justification, it is not necessary to expect a defendant to have

47 See pp 88-89.

48 18 July 1990, unreported.

49 See the former RSC Ord 18, r 8(1)(b) and (c) and Ord 82, r 3(2A), and now the provisions of CPR Part 52, Practice Direction, para 2.8. (It is true that there has been something of a counter-tendency since the introduction of the CPR, which gives greater emphasis to the content of witness statements rather than to particularised pleadings. Inevitably, the effect in some cases is unhappily to delay the point at which the parties find out the detailed case they have to meet.)

50 [1995] 3 All ER 615, 623. Several years later, following the two and a half year trial, the Court of Appeal reaffirmed in the same case (31 March 1999, unreported) the general principle that the burden of proof remains on the defendant. See also *Grobbelaar v News Group Newspapers Ltd* [2002] UKHL 40, at para 73, per Lord Scott.

had to hand at the time 'clear and sufficient evidence'[51] to support the plea. It will suffice if there are reasonable grounds to suppose that sufficient evidence *will* be available at trial. Otherwise an unrealistic burden would be placed on defendants who intend to support their case from the disclosure of documents or the content of witness statements (served by either side). This is obviously of great potential benefit to investigative journalists in helping to reduce the 'chilling effect'.

The lottery of compensatory damages: how the Convention was brought to bear

Except in the comparatively rare cases in which a claim for exemplary damages is left to the jury[52], it is customary to explain that the purpose of libel damages is essentially threefold: (i) to compensate for hurt feelings and distress, (ii) to compensate for injury to reputation, and (iii) to serve as an outward and visible sign of vindication. There were always examples of jury awards that caused eyebrows to be raised, and were difficult to understand, but the real boom began in the summer of 1987. First, there was the award of £450,000 to one Martin Packard who had sued in respect of allegations made in the Greek newspaper *Eleftherotypia* of which only about 40 copies had been published in this jurisdiction. Shortly afterwards came the now infamous Jeffrey Archer victory of July 1987, when he recovered £500,000 against the *Daily Star* newspaper (albeit, as things turned out, only temporarily).

The main criticisms thereafter were that there appeared to be no consistency or predictability. Libel litigation seemed to be a 'lottery'[53]. It was also obvious that people were recovering in some cases, for temporary hurt to their feelings and perhaps loss of *amour propre*, amounts that bore no relation to the sums recovered by personal injury victims who were permanently damaged and unable to fend for themselves or their families. This caused resentment and a

51 A phrase sanctioned by Lord Denning MR in *Associated Leisure v Associated Newspapers Ltd* [1970] 2 QB 450, 456.

52 For a convenient summary of the daunting hurdles to be overcome, see eg the passage from *Duncan & Neill on Defamation* (2nd edn, 1983) adopted in *Riches v News Group Newspapers Ltd* [1986] QB 256, CA. This is further discussed below.

53 The expression used by Rose LJ in *Gorman v Mudd* (15 October 1992, unreported), CA, after he observed that 'It was not even open to the judge ... to invite the jury to consider whether an award in one, two, three, four, five or six figures might be appropriate'.

widespread feeling of injustice. The comment was often made that jurors were losing any real sense of the value of the money they were handing out. There was a perception that, despite clear guidance from judges that they were to compensate and not to punish, jurors were taking the opportunity to penalise newspaper proprietors for what was perceived to be irresponsible behaviour – and yet out of all proportion to any injury suffered by the individual claimants. Indeed, it was suggested that they were seeking in some cases to make up for the absence in this jurisdiction of a law of privacy. In other instances, there was apparently no rational explanation at all.

To what extent these arguments were valid remains a matter of speculation – because of the long-established rule that the deliberations of jurors are not to be enquired into, even for the purposes of bona fide research into the administration of justice[54]. Nevertheless, even without such impermissible enquiries, it was easy to conclude that there was no pattern to the awards and that in some cases the figures awarded, ostensibly for compensation, were wholly disproportionate to even the most generous assessment of distress or damage to reputation. Even if Parliament was not prepared to intervene, it was becoming obvious that the goals of predictability and proportionality, already well established in human rights jurisprudence[55], might provide the means of at least confining the perceived injustices.

There were various possibilities. It was often said that judges should give more guidance – as though there were some right answer available to the professionals but not to the uninitiated. The difficulty about such an approach is that the whole point of jury trial in this field was supposed to be that the jurors themselves had something to offer by way of common sense and everyday experience. If judges really knew the right answer – or at least the correct bracket – why not let them decide the award as they have now done for a long time in (say) personal injury cases?

One of the most experienced judges in the field at the time was Sir Michael Davies, having been judge in charge of the jury list for some years. He readily gave guidance to juries, in general terms, about the value of money and the

54 *Ellis v Deheer* [1922] 2 KB 113, 121 (per Atkin LJ); *R v Thompson* [1962] 1 All ER 65, 66 (per Lord Parker CJ). See also the Contempt of Court Act 1981, s 8.

55 It was observed in *Goodwin v UK* (1996) 22 EHRR 123, 140 that '... the relevant national law must be formulated with sufficient precision to enable the persons concerned – if need be with appropriate legal advice – to foresee, to a degree that is reasonable in the circumstances, the consequences which a given action may entail'.

need to bear in mind what any sum awarded could purchase by way of consumer goods or investment. On the other hand, he argued tellingly that there were genuine difficulties of principle in the idea of judges simply pronouncing *ex cathedra* that the 'right' bracket in the case in hand was £5,000 to £10,000 or £75,000 to £100,000. He queried, if the jury were to settle upon a figure outside the chosen bracket, whether there would not be an automatic route to an appeal on the basis that the jurors had failed to obey the judge's directions and thus behaved unlawfully. Alternatively, if they *did* follow the guidance and stuck dutifully to the bracket, could it not be said that they had failed to exercise the function for which they were there in the first place and were just acting as a 'rubber stamp' – in other words, that the judge was usurping their role by substituting his own discretion?[56]

Others favoured handing over to judges altogether the task of assessing general damages. The analogy was drawn with sentencing in criminal cases. If the judge could find the 'right' sentence following a jury's conviction of a criminal offence, or offences, then why not also entrust the quantification of damages to the same body of persons? There are real practical difficulties about any such solution. The judge might easily not be able fully to understand the basis of the jury's conclusion; alternatively might fundamentally disagree with it. In either case, the judge could find it difficult, if not impossible, to reflect its verdict fairly. It may well happen in a criminal case too, of course, but the judge can at least consult either personal experience or a tariff, set in guideline cases, in order to identify the appropriate range of possible sentences for the offence in question. By contrast, defamatory allegations vary enormously in their nature and also by reference to such matters as scale of publication and the degree to which anyone might reasonably be expected to take them seriously.

If the defence is one of justification, the jurors have the responsibility of determining whether the libel published was 'substantially true'. In the case of (say) a fairly lengthy or complex article, it would be difficult for the judge to ascertain to what extent the jury actually found the allegations false and whether

56 This line of reasoning had been approved in the Court of Appeal by Russell LJ in *Sutcliffe v Pressdram Ltd* [1991] 1 QB 153, 190, although it was found unconvincing by the differently constituted Court in *John v MGN Ltd* (per Bingham MR [1997] QB 568 at 615C-G). This was largely because it is always for the jurors to make up their own minds; if they depart from the judge's suggested bracket, real weight has to be given to the possibility that their judgment is to be preferred ([1997] QB 568 at 616B).

the plea of justification had been held partially established. (This is by no means an uncommon situation in contested cases. After all, if the issue is straightforward, the parties are correspondingly more likely to settle.) In such a situation, it would be the judge's duty to honour, so far as possible, the jury verdict and to implement it. In trials where there is a whole range of possible interpretations of the meanings of the article, and of the evidence itself, this places the judge at risk of misreading the situation – so far as the jury's view of the case is concerned. The danger then is that the judge will appear, quite unintentionally, to be differing from the jury and subverting its decision. In some cases, one could imagine gasps from the jury box as the judge announced a decision that failed adequately to reflect their reading of the parties or the evidence.

The judge could no doubt fix the overall sum of damages in the light of a personal appraisal of these matters from the evidence (as happens when a sentencing judge has to assess the gravity of an assault, for example, or of its effect upon the victim). Yet if it is to be the judicial interpretation of these manifold issues that is in the end to count, for the purposes of vindication, compensation and aggravation, this substantially diminishes the role of the jury and surely also the justification for jury trial. It would give rise to an undesirable tension between the two roles; this in turn could only be damaging to the process of justice.

Another less radical possibility was to discard the rule that there should be no comparison with personal injury awards[57]. In this field there are conventional tariffs and well established upper limits. Such cross-references might therefore assist jurors to keep a sense of proportion and bring greater consistency. Since they would be likely to have only an imperfect awareness of such tariffs (if any), it would be appropriate sometimes to offer them selected examples of recent awards for some kinds of injury. A reform along these lines could also have the incidental effect of at least 'capping' libel awards. It is perfectly true that the function of libel damages is quite different from that of personal injury awards. On the other hand, this does not necessarily mean that there should be no comparison at all – even for the purpose of reminding oneself as

57 See eg the remarks of Lord Hailsham in *Broome v Cassell* [1972] AC 1027, 1071, citing Windeyer J in *Uren v John Fairfax & Sons Pty Ltd* (1967) 111 CLR 118, 150. See also *Sutcliffe v Pressdram Ltd* [1991] 1 QB 153, CA.

to the value of money or of keeping a sense of proportion[58]. As Diplock LJ had commented in *McCarey v Associated Newspapers (No 2)*[59]:

> 'I do not believe that the law today is more jealous of a man's reputation than of his life or limb. That is the scale of values of the duel. Of course, the injuries in the two kinds of case are very different, but each has as its main consequences pain or grief, annoyance or unhappiness, to the plaintiff'.

Rather than providing a direct means of comparison, which would be inevitably artificial, reference to the tariffs prevailing currently in such cases could at least be used to fix a ceiling. It could be left to the jury then to arrive at a figure somewhere on the scale of gravity. To assist jurors in carrying out such an exercise, they would need to be given some other examples of defamatory allegations – especially perhaps some that would seem to them obviously more serious than the case in hand. There would otherwise be the risk of focussing too narrowly on the particular complaint in the case before them and awarding 'too much'. Room needs to be left at the top of the scale to accommodate the appropriate levels of award to compensate for charges of (say) murder, rape or serious child abuse.

This was broadly the means by which the objective was eventually achieved by the Court of Appeal in *John v MGN Ltd*[60], where a serious (and apparently largely successful[61]) attempt was made to bring a limit to libel awards and to achieve a measure of consistency.

In *Rantzen v Mirror Group (1986) Ltd* close attention had been given (in March 1993) to the disciplines imposed by the European Convention. In

58 It was confirmed by Hirst LJ in *Jones v Pollard* [1997] EMLR 233, CA, that when the Court of Appeal had finally sanctioned comparison with personal injury awards, in *John v MGN Ltd* [1997] QB 586, its purpose had indeed been to assist in maintaining a sense of proportion.

59 [1965] 2 QB 86, 109.

60 [1997] QB 586. See also the decision to similar effect of the High Court of Australia in *Carson v John Fairfax* (1993) 113 ALR 577.

61 In early 2000, there was a case in Newcastle (*Garfoot v Walker*) in which a jury awarded a claimant nearly half a million pounds for a false allegation of rape – despite being warned by the judge that the ceiling in defamation had by then effectively become £150,000. Since *Heil v Rankin* [2001] QB 277, it seems to be recognised that the ceiling has become £200,000: see eg *Campbell v Newsgroup Newspapers* [2002] EWCA Civ 1143 and *Lillie and Reed v Newcastle City Council* [2002] EWHC 1600, QB, 30 July 2002.

some signatory states jury trial plays no part in the judicial process[62]. It is very different in nature from trial by judge alone. In particular, it is necessary to reconcile its essential characteristics with the values reflected in Arts 6 and 7; not least because lay persons decide the issues in the light only of such legal guidance as they have been given by the judge, tailored to the particular case, and without having to reveal their reasoning. The matter seems to have been approached in European jurisprudence on the basis that it is possible to achieve consistency with Convention values by proceeding on the assumption that the jury will have applied the reasoning and principles presented to them in the summing-up[63]. This could hardly apply to jury awards of libel damages as traditionally approached, since little or no guidance was given. Until the early 1990s, judges would customarily advise simply that the jurors should 'keep their feet on the ground'. O'Connor J, for example, used to say, 'You decide the right sum. What do I mean by the "right sum"? It means not too much, and not too little'[64].

Despite all this, the Court of Appeal in *Rantzen* had rejected the proposition that it was necessary, at that time, to go so far as to permit reference to levels of personal injury awards. Reference was naturally made to the memorable words of Diplock LJ and to the concerns expressed in the High Court of Australia[65] that appellate courts should not be indifferent to the need to ensure that there is a 'rational relationship' between the scale of values applied to the two classes of case. Nevertheless, the authority of Lord Hailsham's comments in *Cassell v*

62 See eg N Vidmar *World Jury Systems* (OUP, 2002).

63 The right to a fair hearing would ordinarily entail (a) that the tribunal is free from bias and (b) that reasons will be given for significant decisions reached: see eg *Hadjianastassiou v Greece* 16 EHRR 219. Where the decisions are made by a jury, whether in a criminal or civil case, there are obvious limitations on how any challenge for bias can be judged; moreover, reasons will not be given by a jury (although to some extent reasoning processes *may* emerge from the terms of the verdict itself, depending on the questions the jury are asked). The only practical way of addressing such concerns has been to focus on what the jury have been told either in evidence or by way of judicial directions: see *X v UK* (1973) 45 CD 1; *X v UK*, 3 DR 10 and also *X v UK* (1978) App No 7542/76, 2 Digest 688. See too now *Gregory v UK* (1997) 25 EHRR 577 and *Sander v UK* (2001) 31 EHRR 1003.

64 Although perhaps banal, the statement does at least serve to remind one of the starting point for any consideration of the issue. 'Any legal process should yield a successful [claimant] appropriate compensation which is neither too much nor too little': per Bingham MR giving the judgment of the Court in *John v MGN Ltd* [1997] QB 586 at 611D.

65 By Mason CJ and Deane J, dissenting, in *Coyne v Citizen Finance Ltd* (1991) 172 CLR 211.

Broome still held sway. The element of vindication in libel damages especially proved a stumbling block, because there was no comparable component in personal injury cases; the validity of any analogy was thus undermined. Brian Neill explained:

> 'We see the force of the criticism of the present practice whereby a [claimant] in an action for libel may recover a much larger sum by way of damages for an injury to his reputation, which may prove transient in its effect, than the damages awarded for pain and suffering to the victim of an industrial accident who has lost an eye or the use of one or more of his limbs. We have come to the conclusion, however, that there is no satisfactory way in which the conventional awards in actions for damages for personal injuries can be used to provide guidance for an award in an action for defamation'.

The Court considered itself 'bound' at that stage to reject the proposal, and it was hoped that in time some standards might be established, through a corpus of appellate decisions, as to the level of 'proper' awards in such cases[66]. Meanwhile, the Court had to content itself with stating that juries should be invited to consider the purchasing power of any figure they might have in mind and encouraged to ensure that it was 'proportionate' to any damage suffered[67]. Further echoes of the European jurisprudence are to be found in the test, also propounded in *Rantzen*, that any sum awarded should be 'necessary' for the purpose of compensation and vindication.

One reason why the personal injury argument was allowed to be re-opened in *John*, only two and a half years later, was that in the interim the European Court had decided the important case of *Tolstoy Miloslavsky v UK*[68] specifically with reference to English libel awards. In that well-known case, it was ultimately

66 The Court felt to some extent liberated by the terms of the Courts and Legal Services Act 1990, s 8 which gave the Court of Appeal, for the first time, a power to substitute a figure for damages where a jury award was considered 'excessive', rather than having to order a retrial. This power was construed in a manner that was deemed consistent with the values of Art 10 of the Convention. In the circumstances, the original award of £250,000 was set aside and the figure of £110,000 was substituted. Appeals on libel damages are relatively few in number, however, and the gradual approach contemplated would surely have taken years to have any impact.

67 The difficulty of giving only general guidance and coded messages was illustrated when a judge told the jury not to award 'Mickey Mouse' damages. They did not understand whether this was advising them not to make too small an award or one that was too large.

68 (1995) 20 EHRR 442.

held that the jury's award of £1.5m compensatory damages had amounted to a violation of the defendant's rights under Art 10. This was partly a matter of the disproportionate scale of the award and partly because English law at the time provided no adequate or effective safeguards against such excesses. This therefore gave the Court of Appeal the opportunity to make yet bolder inroads into the conventional approach:

> 'It is in our view offensive to public opinion, and rightly so, that a defamation [claimant] should recover damages for injury to reputation greater, perhaps by a significant factor, than if that same [claimant] had been rendered a helpless cripple or an insensate vegetable'.

In finally permitting comparisons with personal injury damages, the Court emphasised that the change would buttress the 'constitutional role of the libel jury' by rendering such proceedings more rational and so more acceptable to public opinion. For so long as this role remains, it is difficult to imagine what more could be done to overcome misgivings about compensatory awards. Exemplary damages are, however, quite another matter.

Exemplary damages: why add to the aggravation?

Clearly, the outstanding question of exemplary/punitive damages is not confined to defamation. The principles laid down in *Rookes v Barnard*[69] apply much more widely. But it is in the context of jury cases, both defamation and police actions, that the anomaly and the difficulties of application are thrown into relief. Furthermore, the reasons for awarding them will generally differ quite considerably from tort to tort; so too the policy grounds for retaining the concept. High-handed conduct on the part of public officials might need to be met by a remedy that would not necessarily have any relevance to newspapers making profits from publishing libels; also, in the latter case freedom of expression will usually be an important consideration, whereas in the former it will not. It may be appropriate to ask, 10 years on, whether the recommendation of the Neill Committee for abolition, at least in the libel context, might not be looked at afresh[70].

69 [1964] AC 1129, HL.

70 The issue was also addressed by the Law Commission in its Consultation Paper No 132 (1993).

The problems are fairly obvious. The concept requires a punitive element to be grafted on to a case that is primarily about compensation. The tribunal has therefore to keep the two notions quite separate but to bring each into play in the course of its deliberations at the appropriate stages and, more importantly, *not* to do so at inappropriate stages. For example, a jury has to ignore the means of the parties for the purposes of determining compensatory damages, but is bound to take them into account at the stage (if reached) of deciding what penalty is required in addition. So too the mental gymnasts will have to remember to apply the normal civil standard of proof for most issues in the case, including those relating to compensation, but to bring something approaching the criminal standard to bear before inflicting a penalty[71].

Although in some respects punitive damages resemble the imposition of a fine, there are obvious differences. Not only do the jurors fix the penalty, rather than the judge, but also any sums recovered go to the individual claimant rather than to the Crown. When this practice is sought to be justified, even more cerebral agility is required to understand the basis for it. It has obviously caused some concern on the part of jurors in the past, since the jury in *Riches v News Group Newspapers*[72] sent a note in the midst of their deliberations to ask whether it might be possible to award the punitive element to someone other than the individual officers concerned (for example, a charity).

Here, incidentally, there is a difference between claims against police forces, for torts such as false imprisonment or malicious prosecution (also regularly tried by juries), and those brought against media groups for defamation. As was pointed out in *Thompson v Metropolitan Police Comr*[73], a factor justifying the award of exemplary damages in the latter class of litigation is the need to prevent a newspaper proprietor from profiting from a libel through increased circulation. Almost invariably, however, the element of unjust enrichment plays no part in the police cases. While it might just be possible, therefore, to explain such a windfall to the claimant in a libel action, on the footing that it

71 The Court of Appeal drew back from prescribing the criminal standard in *John v MGN Ltd* [1997] QB 586 at 619A-C, despite endorsing the words of Widgery J in *Manson v Associated Newspapers Ltd* [1965] 1 WLR 1038, 1044-1045. It appears that he had told the jury that the relevant inferences could only be drawn if they were 'quite inescapable' and, moreover, that they should not draw an inference adverse to the publisher unless they were *sure* that it was the only one to be drawn (emphasis added).

72 [1986] QB 256.

73 [1997] 2 All ER 762, 773, CA (Lord Woolf MR, Auld LJ and Sir Brian Neill).

was his or her reputation that was being exploited, no such rationale is available in relation to false imprisonment or wrongful arrest.

Another sophisticated exercise required of the jurors (applying to aggravated as well as to punitive damages) is that they are expected to focus only on the lowest common denominator in assessing the conduct deemed worthy of punishment[74]. Where there are several defendants in a libel action, one sum has to be awarded as between all of them. It is thus necessary to identify the worst element of punishable conduct for which all can be held responsible, and to make the 'fine' fit that element taken in isolation from what other individuals may have perpetrated. Accordingly, if the editor or printer of a newspaper is joined in the action, but had no direct part in the libel – or at least in the relevant misconduct – then it may well be that no punitive damages could be awarded at all. Such a party (unlike an employing proprietor) could not be held responsible on principles of vicarious liability for the conduct of (say) staff reporters. Yet further agility is required when one seeks to reconcile what seems to be the rule[75] that the lowest common denominator does *not* apply when it comes to assessing the defendants' means. (The rationale is obvious if somewhat lacking in intellectual rigour.)

It is generally supposed that an award of punitive damages should be regarded as out of the ordinary. They should only be awarded in a libel case where two criteria have been fulfilled. The court must be satisfied that the allegations were known to be false *and* that the defendant was motivated by the calculation that he would profit in some way from committing the wrong. As Lord Hailsham observed in *Cassell v Broome*, one object of making punitive awards is to demonstrate that 'tort does not pay'. Furthermore, such damages should only be awarded in circumstances where the court concludes that the conduct meriting punishment (*ex hypothesi*) will not be adequately penalised by the award of compensatory damages alone.

While it is true that actual awards are numerically rare[76], the fact remains that it is by no means uncommon to see a claim for such damages pleaded – most frequently perhaps on the footing that the defendants have supposedly been 'reckless' as to the truth or falsity of the defamatory allegations sued upon. The

74 *Cassell v Broome* [1972] AC 1027, 1063 (Lord Hailsham), 1090 (Lord Reid).

75 See *Thompson v Metropolitan Police Comr* [1997] 2 All ER 762 at 776.

76 One of the very few to recover exemplary damages from a jury in defamation proceedings was Robert Maxwell: *Maxwell v Pressdram Ltd* [1987] 1 WLR 298 (not perhaps the best illustration of a 'pressing social need').

effect of this, it may be thought, is inevitably to run counter to the benefits otherwise flowing from the Court of Appeal's decision on compensatory damages in *John v MGN Ltd.* That case has to some extent had the effect of removing the lottery element attaching to such damages and thus made awards easier to predict, at least within broad bands. Correspondingly, disputes are easier to settle in the light of that knowledge. By contrast, so long as punitive damages are available as a weapon, the tactician is enabled to re-introduce a degree of uncertainty and so 'up the ante' in negotiations. In Convention terms, it provides another stick with which to beat journalists and, indirectly, to exert a 'chilling effect' on their freedom of expression.

One of the main arguments advanced for the retention of punitive damages is that newspapers behave badly and will go on doing so unless there is the power to hit the proprietors hard and 'where it hurts'. This is an argument that undoubtedly has had its attractions in the past, and factors of that kind may well go a long way to explaining some of the high awards granted by juries in the days before *John v MGN Ltd*, whether they were classified officially as 'punitive' or not. It reflects a line of thinking, however, that does not chime too well with the modern approach to the 'chilling effect' or with the policy being gradually worked out by the courts of this jurisdiction to take account of the imperatives of the European Convention. The availability of the award of punitive damages against media defendants in libel actions (especially perhaps by juries) gives rise to worries, which have become no doubt more acute in the last decade, both with regard to the rights provided for under Art 10 and those under Arts 6 and 7. Quite apart from issues of principle, it inevitably increases the complexity of libel actions. It also leads to undesirable confusion and uncertainty of resolution; this in turn increases the scope for avoidable and costly appeals. None of this matches the spirit of the times.

That is not to say, on the other hand, that legitimate concerns on the part of the public about the behaviour of some journalists should simply be put to one side. It is well recognised that 'aggravated damages' (properly considered as an element in the overall award of compensatory damages) can legitimately reflect the court's disapproval of the defendant's conduct in so far as it 'adds insult to injury'. As Lord Reid explained in *Cassell v Broome*[77]:

> '[The defendant] may have behaved in a high-handed, malicious, insulting or oppressive manner in committing the tort or he or his counsel may at the trial have aggravated the injury by what they there

77 [1972] AC 1027 at 1085.

> said. That would justify going to the top of the bracket and awarding as damages the largest sum that could fairly be regarded as compensation'.

Aggravated damages give rise to some problems of their own, but we ought at least to be able to cope with Ossa if we leave Pelion out of it. We can then surely stand a significantly better chance of doing fair and open justice for all concerned, while compensating claimants proportionately for the wrongs of journalists – however badly they may have behaved. It is clear from the speeches in *Cassell v Broome* that Lords Reid and Wilberforce[78] thought the law at least anomalous in this regard and were, apparently, also of the view that there was no countervailing public interest in its retention.

The time may well have come to adopt Brian Neill's 1991 recommendation on the subject:

> 'In our view, exemplary damages should no longer be obtainable in defamation actions and, in so far as the exercise of a defendant's freedom of communication should ever be met with criminal sanctions, this could be covered by the criminal law of libel if Parliament considers that for some reason public policy requires its retention. At least in criminal proceedings [defendants] would be protected by the traditional safeguards and subject to far less arbitrary sanctions. Our own unanimous view, however, is that exemplary damages should be dispensed with so far as defamation is concerned'.

At all events, of the four areas of contention I have addressed, this is in my opinion the only one still requiring significant reform. It cannot be achieved judicially, although the suggestion was canvassed in *John v MGN Ltd.* It would almost certainly need to be done by statute. The opportunity was not taken in the Defamation Act 1996; nor was it something recommended by the Law Commission when it addressed the issue. On the other hand, if such exponents of the common law as Lord Reid, Lord Wilberforce and Sir Brian Neill are of one view on a significant matter of reform, it may be safe to say that it is at least worth another glance.

78 [1972] AC 1027 at 1113-1121.

The bastion of freedom of expression – is it threatened by the laws of confidentiality, privacy or contempt?

Charles Gray

Fetters on free speech

The area of the law with which Brian Neill had the closest connection, during his career at the Bar, was defamation. There had been for some years a general perception that the law of defamation needed reform in order to avoid the 'chilling effect' on the right to freedom of expression [1]. Now that judges are required firmly to restrain the enthusiasm of juries in their awards of damages in libel actions [2] and the scope of the defence of privilege has been enlarged [3], English defamation law currently inhibits freedom of discussion less than once it did.

But it is not only the law of defamation which has the capacity to chill free speech. Both the law of confidentiality (now supplemented, but not displaced, by the developing law of privacy) and, to a lesser extent, the law of contempt have the potential to do so. Claimants seeking to ward off unwelcome (and often defamatory) publicity are nowadays well advised to complain of breach of confidence or invasion of their right to privacy rather than the unwieldy (and costly) law of defamation. Moreover the term 'sub judice' still has the capacity to unsettle editors [4].

1 A phrase adopted by Lord Keith in *Derbyshire v Times Newspapers Ltd* [1993] AC 534, 548.

2 *John v MGN Ltd* [1997] QB 586.

3 *Reynolds v Times Newspapers* [2001] 2 AC 127.

4 *A-G v MGN Ltd*: the *Sunday Mirror* was fined £75,000 for causing the trial of two Leeds United footballers to be aborted and the editor resigned.

A retrospective look at two milestone cases

Over a quarter of a century ago, Brian Neill QC (as he then was) represented the defendants in two celebrated cases, in the fields of contempt and confidence respectively. Each posed the question what limitations might legitimately be put upon the right to freedom of expression. In their different ways, both cases made a significant contribution to the judicial and statutory recognition of the importance, if not primacy, to be accorded to the right to freedom of expression. The two cases were the contempt proceedings related to the litigation arising out of the marketing of the drug thalidomide, reported as *A-G v Times Newspapers* [5] and the *Crossman Diaries Case* [6].

In the latter, Brian Neill represented the publishers of the Crossman diaries and the literary executors of Richard Crossman, the Labour politician and Cabinet minister. The case was significant because it marked the first occasion on which an injunction was sought, principally on public interest grounds, to restrain the publication of public or governmental, as opposed to personal or commercial, information. The argument for the Attorney-General was rejected: publication of the diaries in an unexpurgated form was allowed.

In the contempt proceedings arising out of the thalidomide scandal, Brian Neill represented the *Sunday Times*, which intended to publish articles about the thalidomide affair. Having been shown one of the proposed articles, the Attorney-General took the view that it would prejudice the civil litigation pending against the manufacturers of the drug in England, Distillers. He sought an injunction to restrain publication. In the domestic courts the newspaper lost: the House of Lords unanimously upheld the contention that an injunction should be granted to restrain publication of the articles.

But the arguments for the *Sunday Times* eventually prevailed in Strasbourg: the European Court of Human Rights decided that the English law of contempt of court, as the House of Lords had held it to be, infringed the right of the newspaper to freedom of expression under Art 10 [7]. That decision was directly instrumental in securing that the Contempt of Court Act 1981 (CCA 1981) included a number of provisions which in significant respects relaxed the fetters on freedom of expression previously imposed by the English common law of contempt.

5 [1974] AC 273.

6 *A-G v Jonathan Cape Ltd* [1976] 1 QB 752.

7 *Sunday Times v UK* (1979) 2 EHRR 245.

These two authorities can be taken as points of departure from which to examine the evolving relationship between, on the one hand, the right to freedom of expression and, on the other, the restrictions on that right imposed by the laws of contempt, confidentiality and its youthful stable companion, privacy.

Confidentiality and privacy: the Crossman Diaries Case

Over the 20 years before his premature death in 1974 Dick Crossman kept diaries recording his life as a journalist and later as a politician, both in and out of office. He joined the Cabinet in 1964 as Minister for Housing and Local Government. He continued to maintain his diary with the avowed purpose of dispelling the tradition of secrecy surrounding government in Britain. The diaries included detailed accounts of Cabinet discussions; accounts of the sometimes sharply differing views expressed in Cabinet and details of the advice given to ministers by senior civil servants.

In accordance with the conventional practice, the diaries were submitted to the Cabinet Secretary for him to approve publication. Not surprisingly, by the standards of the time, Sir Burke Trend, the Cabinet Secretary, declined to approve publication of the diaries either in whole or in part. After prolonged preliminary fencing, the Attorney-General sought an injunction restraining Jonathan Cape, the publishers of the diaries in book form, and the *Sunday Times*, who had bought the serialisation rights, from publishing the diaries in their entirety.

Seeking a cause of action

Viewed from the perspective of the 21st century, the *Crossman Diaries Case* is striking in two respects. The first is the uncertainty within the Attorney's camp how best to formulate the claim in law. At one stage in his argument the Attorney-General advanced the bold submission that, even if no cause of action was available in private law, he was entitled in his representative capacity to injunctive relief where such relief was justified in the public interest.

Other more conventional grounds were prayed in aid. It was argued that publication would breach the oath sworn by ministers on their appointment as Privy Councillors. Publication would breach the 30-year rule contained in the Public Records Act 1958. Reliance was placed on the Official Secrets Act. The convention protecting the secrecy of Cabinet discussions was or should be enforceable in law. The uncertainty provided James Comyn QC, appearing for the *Sunday Times*, with the opportunity to observe: 'The Attorney is the wrong plaintiff seeking the wrong relief in the wrong way against the wrong people'.

In the end the Attorney-General (who had the advantage that his team included the future Lords Slynn and Woolf) concluded that the law of confidentiality was the most promising legal basis for his claim to prevent publication. It was, however, fraught with difficulty. There was no evidence of any express undertaking of confidentiality given by Crossman. There was on the contrary abundant evidence that he had not sought to conceal from his Cabinet colleagues that he was keeping a diary and that it contained accounts of Cabinet meetings. It was not easy to disentangle that material which was in the public domain or anodyne from that which was truly confidential.

Paucity of authority

The second striking feature of the case is the paucity of authority which then existed as to the scope, and even as to the existence, of a right of action in confidence. Brian Neill adopted the submission which had been made on behalf of the *Sunday Times* that it was questionable whether English law recognised a right to sue for breach of confidence. Prince Albert had in 1849 prevented Mr Strange from publishing a catalogue of etchings made by Queen Victoria and himself [8]. Although in that case Knight-Bruce VC referred to 'a sordid spying into the privacy of domestic life' and commented that 'pain inflicted in point of sentiment or imagination is not always disregarded in Courts of Justice', the decision was based primarily on the proprietary rights of the Prince Consort rather than upon any equitable right of confidentiality [9].

Two years later Mr Morison obtained an injunction restraining Mr Moat from making use of a recipe for his Universal Medicine [10]. But confidence was

8 *Prince Albert v Strange* (1849) 1 De G & Sm 652. The same could be said of *Saltman Engineering v Campbell Engineering* (1948) [1963] 3 All ER 413, 65 RPC 203.

9 Brian Neill 'Privacy: a challenge for the next century' in Markesinis (ed) *Protecting Privacy* (Clarendon Press, 1999).

10 *Morison v Moat* (1851) 9 Hare 241.

but one of several grounds canvassed by way of justification for the relief granted. Lord Ashburton obtained an injunction preventing Mr Pape from making use of letters he had written to his solicitor but the decision has been said to be based on privilege [11]. In *Pollard v Photographic Co*[12] the defendant photographer was restrained from using in Christmas cards to be put on general sale to the public a photograph which had been commissioned from him by the claimant for her private use. But there again the plaintiff had claims in contract and copyright.

Over the following 100 years as a general rule those who wanted to be let alone invoked other remedies, such as trespass, defamation or nuisance. Successful claims for infringement of a personal right to confidence were rare. 'The main cases on confidentiality are significant for their lack of any uniform jurisprudential basis. The confidences were mainly commercial and arose generally in the context of contracts, such as contracts of partnership, employment, agency and sale' [13].

In 1967 the Duchess of Argyll successfully applied to restrain her ex-husband (and a newspaper) from divulging their marital secrets. The ground of that decision was that the court had an equitable jurisdiction to enforce the implied obligation of confidence arising out of marriage. It was a decision which broke new ground. But it was slender authority for the proposition that Her Majesty's Government, claiming to act in the public interest, could restrain by injunction the publication of governmental or political information.

The case which on its facts bore the closest resemblance to the *Crossman Diaries Case* was *Fraser v Evans* [14] (in which Brian Neill had appeared for the plaintiff). Fraser was a public relations consultant retained by the Greek Government. A report by him to his client describing his activities on its behalf came into the hands of a Sunday newspaper. Lord Denning MR accepted that no person is permitted to divulge to the world information which he has received in confidence. But nothing was said in *Fraser* about the quality of the information contained in the report or about any special considerations which should apply in the case of governmental information. Moreover the ground on which the Court of Appeal refused to grant an

11 *Ashburton v Pape* (1913) 2 Ch 469.
12 (1889) 40 Ch D 345.
13 Toulson *Confidentiality* (1st edn) at para 1-09.
14 [1969] 1 QB 349.

injunction was that the duty of confidence was owed to the Greek Government (which was not a party to the action) and not to Fraser personally.

As Brian Neill put it in argument in *Crossman*, the essential (and novel) question which fell to be decided was whether, apart from statute, the Attorney-General could establish that the protection sometimes given to private or commercial confidences should extend also to government information. In a judgment which ran to no more than a dozen pages Lord Widgery answered that question succinctly in favour of the publishers. Addressing the question posed by Brian Neill, and pointing out that 11 years had expired since the events first recorded in the diaries, he said:

> 'The Attorney-General must show (a) that such publication would be a breach of confidence; (b) that the public interest requires that the publication be restrained and (c) that there are no other facts of the public interest contradictory of and more compelling than that relied upon. Moreover the court, when asked to restrain such a publication, must closely examine the extent to which relief is necessary to ensure that restrictions are not imposed beyond the strict requirement of public need' [15].

The enduring significance of the decision is that it recognised for the first time the right of government to invoke a private law right to prevent the dissemination of governmental information. Lord Widgery was at pains to confine that right within narrow limits by superimposing upon the private right of confidence a requirement that the grant of relief must be shown to be strictly necessary in the public interest. Although he did not spell out those limits in his judgment, the potentially contradictory and more compelling aspects of the public interests to which Lord Widgery referred no doubt included the public interest in the exposure of wrongdoing (or iniquity as it was then called) and the public interest in free speech.

Crossman can be seen as the precursor of landmark decisions in Australia [16] and England [17], in which the limitations upon the right of government to pursue claims in confidence were defined and the relationship between such claims and the right to freedom of expression was examined.

15 [1976] 1 QB 752 at 770H-771A.

16 *Commonwealth of Australia v John Fairfax & Sons* (1980) 147 CLR 39.

17 Spycatcher litigation: *A-G v Guardian Newspapers (No 1)* [1987] 1 WLR 1248 and *A-G v Guardian Newspapers (No 2)* [1990] 1 AC 109.

Commonwealth of Australia v Fairfax

In 1980 the Australian Government sought an injunction to restrain the disclosure of governmental information of a different nature, namely official communications relating to such matters as the then crisis in East Timor. Granting the injunction on the ground of confidence, Mason J (as he then was) echoed the approach of Lord Widgery. In a classic passage he said:

> 'The equitable principle [of confidentiality] has been fashioned to protect the personal, private and proprietary interests of the citizen, not to protect the very different interests of the executive government. It acts, or is supposed to act, not according to the standards of private interest, but in the public interest. This is not to say that equity will not protect information in the hands of the government, but it is to say that that when equity protects government information it will look at the matter through different spectacles'.[18]

Mason J borrowed Lord Widgery's spectacles. Quoting with approval the passage cited earlier from the judgment of Lord Widgery, Mason J explained that the approach of the court to an application for an injunction to restrain the disclosure of governmental information should be a restrictive one and that, whereas in the case of an application by a citizen it might be sufficient detriment to show that the disclosure of information relating to his affairs would expose his actions to public discussion and criticism, in the case of governmental information it was incumbent on the Government to establish specific detriment to the public interest.

Spycatcher

The reason why Mason J declined to grant the injunction sought by the Government in *Fairfax* was that the information had already been widely disseminated and so had lost its quality of confidence. For the same reason the English courts refused to grant the Attorney-General a final injunction in the *Spycatcher* litigation[19]: Mr Wright's 'disclosures' of his experiences in MI5 had received wide publicity (albeit mostly outside the jurisdiction) by the time of trial.

18 (1980) 147 CLR 39 at 51.
19 *A-G v Guardian Newspapers (No 2)* [1990] 1 AC 1.

The decisions in *Crossman* and *Fairfax* were cited with approval at every level of the *Spycatcher* litigation. In the Court of Appeal Bingham LJ (as he then was) noted the similarity between the approach adopted in the two cases, which required consideration of any other facet of the public interest contradictory of and more compelling than the interest in maintaining confidence. Bingham LJ pointed out that this approach accords with the limitation on the right of freedom of expression contained in Art 10(2) of the European Convention, which permits that right to be restricted where necessary in a democratic society for preventing the disclosure of information received in confidence [20].

The House of Lords in *Spycatcher* approved and followed both *Crossman* and *Fairfax*. No more than passing reference was made in the speeches to the European Convention on Human Rights. Lord Goff of Chieveley observed that he could see no inconsistency between English law on the subject and Art 10, save that, whereas Art 10, in accordance with its avowed purpose, proceeds to state a fundamental right and then to qualify it, the courts in England (where everybody is free to do anything subject only to the provisions of the law) proceed upon an assumption of freedom of speech and turn to the law to discover the established exceptions to it [21].

Subsequent developments

The approach to the confidentiality of information of a governmental or public nature, initiated in *Crossman*, was taken a stage further, again by Mason J. In *Fairfax* he had commented that it was unacceptable in a democratic society that there should be a restraint on the publication of information relating to government, when the only vice of such publication was that it enabled the public to discuss, review and criticise government action. If so, it seemed plain that the same principles would apply to attempts to enjoin information relating to local government and other public bodies [22].

Fourteen years later in 1994, Mason CJ (as he had become) was as good as his word. He refused to grant two public companies an injunction restraining the publication of commercially sensitive information, remarking obiter that in such a case a duty of confidence would arise only if it could be shown (as in the

20 [1990] 1 AC 1at 218-9.
21 [1990] 1 AC 1at 283.
22 *Commonwealth of Australia v John Fairfax & Sons Ltd* (1980) 147 CLR 39, 52.

case of governmental information) that the public interest demanded non-disclosure. The Chief Justice referred to the need in the public sector for 'compelled openness, not for burgeoning secrecy'[23].

As yet there is no English authority to similar effect (although in *Derbyshire County Council v Times Newspapers*[24] the House of Lords, for broadly analogous reasons, denied the right of a local authority to sue for libel). It remains to be seen whether an English judge would be persuaded, in a claim by a public authority to restrain disclosure of its confidential information, to superimpose a requirement that the utility must establish that that the public interest requires that it should be granted relief. Existing authority[25] suggests not.

But much may depend on the nature of the information sought to be protected: public companies possess commercially sensitive information (as do governments) and there seems to be no reason why courts should not protect such information from unauthorised disclosure without reference to the public interest. Most of the cases in the field of confidence relate to business data of one kind or another. There is little difficulty about establishing specific detriment. The court might view differently an application to prevent publication of undisclosed information relating, for instance, to the corporate governance of a public company or the policies of a public utility.

In *R v Shayler*[26] a former member of MI5 charged with offences under the Official Secrets Act 1989 claimed that he had signed the declaration under duress and maintained, optimistically, that it had been necessary in the public interest for him to reveal the information in question. Rejecting those contentions, Lord Woolf CJ referred with approval to the line of authorities flowing from *Crossman*. He accepted that the approach in those cases could be said to create a presumption as to the existence of a public interest defence, which must be rebutted by the public authority if it wishes to restrain publication. He added that such an approach is now buttressed by the Human Rights Act 1998.

23 *Esso Australia Resources Ltd v Plowman* (1994-5) 183 CLR 10.
24 [1993] AC 534.
25 *British Steel Corpn v Granada Television* [1981] AC 1096.
26 [2001] 1 WLR 2206, 2230.

A right of privacy at common law?

The equitable right to personal confidentiality, while perhaps a late developer, is now firmly entrenched in our law. It remains, however, a vexed and unresolved question whether under English law there is or should be a co-existing and free-standing right of privacy.

It is ironic that one of the first cases in which recognition was given to the existence of a right to what was described as 'personal privacy' occurred in a case concerned governmental information.[27] In his speech in *Spycatcher* Lord Keith of Kinkel, in the context of a discussion about the nature of the detriment which must be shown by a claimant in confidence cases, said:

> 'The right to personal privacy is clearly one which the law should in this field seek to protect.... As a general rule, it is in the public interest that confidences should be respected, and the encouragement of such respect may in itself constitute a sufficient ground for recognising and enforcing the obligation of confidence even where the confider can point to no specific detriment to himself. Information about a person's private and personal affairs may be of a nature which shows him up in a favourable light and would by no means expose to him to criticism. The anonymous donor of a very large sum of money to a very worthy cause has his own reasons for wishing to remain anonymous which are unlikely to be discreditable. He should surely be in a position to restrain disclosure in breach of confidence of his identity in connection with the donation. So I would think it a sufficient detriment to the confider that the information given in confidence is to be disclosed to persons whom he would prefer not to know of it, even though disclosure would not be harmful to him in any positive way'[28].

Those words are difficult to reconcile with the robust denial of any right of privacy under English law in *Kaye v Robertson*[29]. The conduct of the newspaper in that case demonstrated vividly that the absence of a remedy for invasion of privacy was a lamentable lacuna in English law: despite notices making plain that it was prohibited, photographs had been illicitly taken of a well-known television actor lying heavily sedated in his hospital bed suffering from serious

27 Earlier references to a right of privacy are to be found in the judgment of Lord Denning MR in *Schering Chemicals v Falkman Ltd* [1982] QB 1 at 21 and in the speech of Lord Scarman in *Morris v Beardmore* [1981] AC 446 at 464.

28 *A-G v Guardian Newspapers (No 2)* [1990] 1 AC 1, 255,6.

29 (1991) FSR 62, 71.

head and brain injuries. The photographs showed the scars to his head. The *Sunday Sport* proposed to publish the photographs together with a report of an interview with the semi-conscious actor.

The claim was brought in libel, trespass to the person, malicious falsehood and passing-off. No claim in confidence or privacy had been advanced because, as I understand it, the claimant's legal advisers wanted to protect their client from expensive and protracted litigation in uncharted legal territory. Lord Bingham of Cornhill, who was a member of the court, speaking extra-judicially[30], has said that a claim for breach of confidence could not have been successfully made, at any rate without doing impermissible violence to the principles on which that cause of action is founded: the complaint was not that information obtained in confidence was about to be misused but rather that Mr Kaye's privacy had been the subject of a monstrous invasion but for which the information would not have been obtained at all.

As to privacy, the members of the court were emphatically agreed that, regrettably, unlike US law [31], English law did not protect the privacy of an individual. A limited injunction was granted by the Court of Appeal in malicious falsehood restraining the newspaper from publishing the interview without making clear that it took place without the consent of Mr Kaye.

An earlier case which also suggested the need for a right of privacy was *Bernstein v Skyviews and General Ltd* [32], where the claimant in the absence of any recognised right of privacy was driven to rely (unsuccessfully) on the law of trespass to prevent aerial photographs being taken of his home. Griffiths J did, however, add that he was far from saying that the court would not regard constant surveillance of the plaintiff's house from the air as a monstrous invasion of his privacy which the court would restrain as an actionable nuisance.

In the event, surprising though it may seem in an era of increasing invasion of private lives by the tabloid press and others which generated a plethora of enquiries [33], the invitation extended by Lord Keith in *Spycatcher* to develop a

30 'Should there be a law to protect rights of personal privacy': lecture delivered to the Society of Liberal Democratic Lawyers [1996] EHRLR 450 at 461.

31 Leggatt LJ referred to *Barber v Time Inc* (1942) 159 SW 2d 831 and *Carson v Here's Johnny Portable Toilets Inc* (1983) 698 F 2d 831.

32 [1978] QB 479.

33 The Younger Report 1972 (Cmnd 5012); The McGregor Report 1977 (Cmnd 6810) and The Calcutt Report of 1990 (Cmnd 1102).

right to privacy was not taken up. A clutch of cases decided at about that time went some way to extend the right of confidence to cover information of a personal and private nature [34]. But the evolution of the law of confidence which appeared to be foreshadowed by the words of Lord Keith did not materialise. As late as 1997 Lord Nolan, in a case concerned with the installation by police of a listening device, commented that, under English law, there is in general nothing unlawful about a breach of privacy [35].

Judges appeared reluctant to extend the common law to protect privacy in circumstances where the law of confidentiality was for one reason or another not available. A committee under the chairmanship of Sir David Calcutt QC was set up in 1989 to consider, in the light of the excesses in which the media were at that time regularly engaging, whether there should be legislation to prevent invasion of privacy.

Almost exactly a century earlier, such excesses had prompted Warren and Brandeis to write their famous article for the Harvard Law Review. The First Amendment notwithstanding, they contended for the introduction of a privacy principle in American law. The immediate reason for the article was the behaviour of the local press at the wedding of Mr Warren's sister. The authors wrote:

> 'The press is overstepping in every direction the obvious bounds of propriety and of decency. Gossip is no longer the resource of the idle and of the vicious, but has become a trade, which is pursued with industry as well as effrontery. To satisfy a prurient taste, the details of sexual relations are spread broadcast in the columns of the daily papers. To occupy the indolent, column upon column is filled with gossip, which can only be procured by intrusion upon the domestic circle' [36].

The irony has been pointed out that 'though rooted in the English law of confidence, the American "privacy" torts have failed to germinate in England'[37]. Indeed the case has been made that they did not flourish in the US either [38]. The alternative method of protecting privacy by legislation was not immediately

34 See for example *Stephens v Avery* [1988] Ch 449.

35 *R v Khan* [1997] AC 558 at 581.

36 4 Harvard Law Review, 15 December 1890.

37 Wacks 'Privacy and press freedom' (1995).

38 David Anderson 'The Failure of American Privacy Law' in B Markesinis *Protecting Privacy* (1999).

adopted either. The Calcutt Committee, while acknowledging the problem about privacy and recommending a number of specific offences designed to limit it, concluded that it was not appropriate at that time to introduce a tort of infringement of privacy [39]. The government of the day accepted that recommendation.

Calcutt did lead to the setting up of the Press Complaints Commission. But it is open to question whether, at least until its amendment in 1998, following the merciless pursuit by the media of Princess Diana and her children, the Code of Practice of the PCC achieved any significant improvement in the respect paid by the media to the right of privacy.

Numerous private members bills were introduced into Parliament to protect personal rights of privacy. They all foundered. It appeared that the media had warded off the threat of what they perceived, probably correctly, to be an additional erosion of the right of freedom of expression. In 1995 the Government concluded [40] that, in the light of the industry's effort at self-regulation, there was no call for legislation.

True it is that in 1996 Laws J (as he then was), in the course of striking out an action for breach of confidence against the police for misuse of a photograph compulsorily taken of the claimant while he was in police custody, observed that it would be a breach of confidence for a photographer to use a photograph for an unauthorised purpose. He added:

> 'If someone with a telephoto lens were to take from a distance and with no authority a picture of another engaged in some private act, his subsequent disclosure of the photograph would in my judgment as surely amount to a breach of confidence as if he had found or stolen a letter or diary in which the act was recounted and proceeded to publish it. In such a case, the law would protect what might reasonably be called a right of privacy, although the name accorded to the cause of action would be breach of confidence' [41].

Since the essence of the complaint was that the photograph should not have been taken in the first place, it may be that the claim is more happily categorised as a claim in privacy rather than confidence.

39 Report of the Committee on Privacy and Related Matters, Cmnd 1102 (1990), para 12.5.

40 Privacy and Media Intrusion (Cmnd 2918).

41 *Hellewell v Chief Constable of Derbyshire* [1995] 1 WLR 804, 807.

The same may be said of the injunctions granted from time to time in the Chancery Division to prevent the taking of unauthorised photographs in circumstances where the court was able to find that there was reason to suppose that the photographer was aware that photography was not permitted [42]. But the ratio of these decisions was that the photographer, being aware of the prohibition, was impressed with an obligation of confidentiality. It so happens that in the two cases noted members of the public were present when the photographs were taken, so it may be doubted whether the information contained in the photographs had the necessary quality of confidence about it. These cases might also be thought to belong under the head of privacy, although that was not the ground of decision.

The right of privacy under Art 8

The lack of appetite for the introduction of a right of privacy by legislation, and the faltering development of a right of privacy as an offshoot of the law of confidence, were both overtaken by the enactment of the Human Rights Act 1998. By providing that it is unlawful for a public authority (including a court) to act in a way which is incompatible with a Convention right, the Act provided the impetus for a debate to take place whether the right of privacy contained in Art 8 of the Convention had become part of English domestic law.

Article 8 provides:

> '1. Everyone has the right to respect for his private and family life, his home and his correspondence.
>
> 2. There shall be no interference by a public authority with the exercise of this right except such as is in accordance with the law and is necessary in a democratic society in the interest of national security, public safety or the economic well-being of the country, for the prevention of disorder or crime, for the protection of health or morals or for the protection of the rights and freedoms of others.'

It is debatable whether the importation of Art 8 into our law was the optimum way of achieving the desired result. In a lecture delivered two years before the Human Rights Act became law[43], Lord Hoffmann expressed strong doubts as

42 *Creation Records Ltd v News Group Newspapers* [1997] EMLR 444; *Shelly Films Ltd v Re-examination Features Ltd* [1994] EMLR 134.

43 The Goodman Lecture, 22 May 1996.

to the suitability of employing the Convention as a vehicle for introducing into English law the protection of privacy. He expressed a preference that any English law of privacy should be 'a home grown affair, planted and tended on English soil'.

Although it was probably not what Lord Hoffmann had in mind, there do now exist several statutes which may be held to go some considerable way towards establishing a statutory right to privacy. Of these, potentially the most significant is the Data Protection Act 1998 [44]. The possible scope of this legislation is discussed in *The Law of Privacy and the Media*, edited by Michael Tugendhat QC and Iain Christie [45]. The view there expressed is that the introduction of express statutory rights for data subjects, in conjunction with statutory obligations on process servers, has conferred on data subjects a proprietary right in the information held about them.

It remains to be seen whether the DPA 1988 will make significant inroads on freedom of expression as it affects individuals in their daily lives. The threat that the Act was once thought to pose for the media has been largely removed by the decision of the Court of Appeal in *Campbell v Mirror Group Newspapers*[46]. While it was accepted that for the purpose of the Act publication (for example in a newspaper) did fall within the definition of 'processing' of data, the Court, adopting a purposive construction, held that the exemption contained in DPA 1988, s 32 applied not only to pre-publication processing of data but also to the publication itself. Otherwise, as Lord Phillips MR giving the judgement of the Court pointed out, the requirements of the Act would impose restrictions on the media which would radically restrict the freedom of the press.

The nature of the right to privacy

No discussion can take place about the desirability of introducing into English law a general right of privacy without clarification of the nature and extent of such a right.

44 Other such statutes include the Broadcasting Act 1996 (which establishes the Broadcasting Standards Commission); the Protection from Harassment Act 1997 and prospectively (by virtue of the exemptions from the right of access to personal data) the Freedom of Information Act 2000.

45 OUP, 2002, ch 5.

46 [2003] QB 633.

Defining the right is no easy matter. There is indeed, as Gleeson CJ has remarked, 'no bright line between what is private and what is not' [47]. The article by Brandeis and Warren, mentioned earlier, argued for the right to 'be let alone' and focused on the pain and distress caused by the publication of true but embarrassing facts. But in 1949 the Indiana Appellate Court proposed a wider definition to cover:

> 'the unwarranted appropriation or exploitation of one's personality, the publicising of one's private affairs with which the public has no legitimate concern, or the wrongful intrusion into one's private activities, in such a manner as to outrage or cause mental suffering, shame or humiliation to a person of ordinary sensibilities' [48].

The Court of Appeal has recently [49], subject to a cavil about the word 'highly', commended the following test of confidentiality suggested by Gleeson CJ in *Australian Broadcasting Corpn v Lenah Meats Pty Ltd* [50]:

> 'The requirement that disclosure or observation of information or conduct would be highly offensive to a reasonable person of ordinary sensibilities is in many circumstances a useful practical test of what is private'.

The sweep of the right has been widened by sub-dividing the concept into four separate torts: the unwarranted public disclosure of embarrassing private facts; illegitimate eavesdropping and other intrusions into a person's private space; depicting people in a false light and commercial exploitation of people [51]. It is to be noted that the right of privacy, in contradistinction to the right of confidence, does not necessarily involve the disclosure or publication of information: the mere taking of photographs without the knowledge or consent of the individual depicted may amount to an invasion of privacy even if no publication of them has taken place [52].

Professor Barendt has collected instances where European courts have intervened to protect privacy, including the right of anonymity in certain types

47 In *Australian Broadcasting Corpn v Lenah Game Meats Pty Ltd* [2001] 185 ALR 1.

48 *Continental Optical Co v Reed* (1949) 14 ALR 2d 743, cited by Brian Neill in 'Privacy: a challenge for the next century' in Markesinis (ed) *Protecting Privacy* (Clarendon Press, 1999) at 4.

49 *Campbell v Mirror Group Newspapers* [2003] QB 633 at para 48.

50 [2002] EWCA Civ 1373 at para 42.

51 Restatement (Second) of Torts para 652A (1976).

52 See *Campbell v Mirror Group Newspapers* [2003] QB 633 at paras 30-34.

of legal proceedings; information concerning a person's health or membership of or donations to churches or political organisations; intimate personal photographs; data protection rights and what the Americans call 'false light', that is, false portrayal, sham interviews and distorted photographs [53]. To this list one might add other instances, derived from the Consultation Paper of the Lord Chancellor in 1993, namely matters pertaining to a person's family and personal relationships and a right to be free from harassment or molestation. Information about a person's financial affairs would also generally qualify for inclusion [54].

This short account of the range of activity which might be covered by any right or privacy suffices to demonstrate the difficulty of delineating the types of information to be protected. It may be argued that such difficulty of itself militates against the introduction of a right of privacy to be superimposed on existing rights in confidence, defamation and under the DPA 1988. Moreover the broader the scope of the right of privacy, the broader the collision with the right to freedom of expression contained in Art 10.

Building incrementally on the right of confidentiality: the gradualist approach

Undoubtedly there do exist domestic authorities (some of which have already been mentioned) upon which the existing right of confidentiality could be incrementally constructed so as to construct an enlarged right which accommodates the rights which Art 8 is designed to protect [55]. Worthy of particular note in this connection, because they concern individuals' private sexual behaviour rather than the types of information with which the law of confidence is more typically concerned, are *Stephens v Avery* [56] and *Barrymore v News Group Newspapers* [57].

There is reason to believe that the European Commission itself, perhaps allowing a generous margin of appreciation, takes the view that the existing law of confidence affords sufficient protection of the rights of privacy contained in

53 Conference Reports: Freedom of Expression and the right to privacy, Strasbourg 23 September 1999.

54 But see *Fressoz and Roire v France* [2001] EHRR 1.

55 Collected in the judgment of Brooke LJ in *Douglas v Hello Magazine* [2001] QB 967, paras 65ff.

56 [1988] Ch 449.

57 [1997] FSR 600, Jacob J.

Art 8. In *Douglas v Hello*, Brooke LJ interpreted the rejection by the Commission of a complaint made by Lady Spencer about a photograph taken of her with a telephoto lens [58] as indicating that the Commission had been persuaded that in such circumstances English law provided a potentially satisfactory remedy in an action for breach of confidence [59].

Building on the existing right to confidentiality, judges would have been be well-placed, so the argument runs, to mould the nascent right of privacy so as to accord with evolving national moral and political views. Courts are already enjoined to develop the common law in a way which is compatible with Convention rights (including Art 8). Lord Woolf LCJ went so far as to say[60] that cases in confidence which pre-date the enactment of the Human Rights Act 1998 are 'largely of historic interest only'. Indeed he appeared in the same case to equate the duty to respect confidences with the duty to respect a person's reasonable expectation of privacy [61]. If the labels are interchangeable, why introduce a separate tort? Furthermore perceived deficiencies in the domestic law of confidence have to be considered in the light of other protection available against invasions of privacy, for example under the Data Protection Act 1998 or by virtue of media self-regulation.

Distinctions between the rights to confidentiality and to privacy

The argument against protecting privacy by means of the umbrella of a developing law of confidence presupposes that there are no distinctions of principle between the two rights such as to leave those who have suffered a substantial invasion of their right to privacy without a remedy.

The Court of Appeal in *A v B plc* [62], a case where a married footballer sought an injunction restraining disclosure of his sexual relationship with another woman, said:

> 'In the great majority of situations, if not all situations, where the protection of privacy is justified, relating to events after the Human Rights Act came into force, an action for breach of confidence now will, where this is appropriate, provide the necessary protection'.

58 *Earl Spencer v UK* 25 EHRR CD 105.
59 [2001] QB 967 at para 86.
60 *A v B plc* [2002] 3 WLR 542 at para 9.
61 [2002] 3 WLR 542 at para 11(ix).
62 [2002] 3 WLR 542 at 550.

It is true that a claim in confidence no longer depends upon the existence of a relationship between the confider and the recipient of the information: it is sufficient if the recipient knew or ought to have known of its confidentiality [63]. As Sedley LJ put it in *Douglas v Hello Magazine*[64]: 'The law needs to construct an artificial relationship of confidentiality between intruder and victim'. But there remain significant differences between the rights of confidentiality and privacy.

In the first place there are classes of information where information may be private although it lacks the quality of confidence. In *Privacy and the Media* [65], the following examples, culled from complaints adjudicated upon by the Press Complaints Commission, are given: a public figure's private address; photographs of a well-known novelist's child on a hotel beach; information that a woman has left her husband for another woman; and a photograph taken through a window from a public street with an ordinary camera. Other examples might be the religious or political beliefs of an individual; the identity of one's house guests; and the furnishing of one's home [66]. In all these cases, whether the individual concerned would have a reasonable expectation of privacy [67] would depend largely on the consequences for that individual of the invasion of his or her privacy. Worthy of note in this context is the width of the definition of 'personal data' protected by the Data Protection Act 1998, including as it does such matters as a person's racial or ethnic origins and previous convictions.

As pointed out above, the law of confidence is designed to prevent *disclosure* of information which is not publicly available, whereas the essence of a claim in privacy is *intrusion* or (as it is sometimes put) interference with the personal autonomy of an individual, even if no disclosure is intended or threatened. The victim of such intrusion may suffer injury to his or her feelings in the absence of any publicity being accorded to the private information. A case in point is *Wainwright v Home Office* [68], where visitors to a prison who had been subjected to strip searches sought damages for invasion of their privacy. Another

63 *Spycatcher (No 2)* [1990] 1 AC 109, per Lord Goff at 281; *Venables v News Group Newspapers* [2001] Fam 430 para 81, 111.

64 [2001] QB 967 at para 126.

65 Edited by Hugh Tomlinson QC (2002), para 1.10.

66 Tugendhat and Christie (eds) *The Law of Privacy and the Media* para 4.15, 4.19.

67 The test propounded by the Court of Appeal in *A v B plc* [2002] 3 WLR 542 at 551.

68 [2002] 3 WLR 405.

is *Campbell v Mirror Group Newspapers*[69] where the claimant expressly conceded that she did not pursue her claim for invasion of privacy and so made no complaint of the unauthorised taking of photographs of her outside the venue of a Narcotics Anonymous meeting.

Once confidential information enters the public domain, or, as Professor Gurry puts it[70], becomes accessible, any right of confidence is, generally speaking, lost for ever. Inaccessibility has been treated as a basic attribute of confidentiality[71]. But it is at least arguable that information which has been published can remain private and personal and so merit protection[72]. A second invasion of privacy may be no less hurtful than the original invasion and may be far more so[73]. The right to privacy should not be forfeited until the disclosure of the information, in terms both of the quality and the extent of the disclosure, reaches the point where the information can no longer be described as private[74].

Another problem about 'shoe-horning' the protection of privacy into the tort of breach of confidence relates to the position of the third party recipient of the information. Under the law of confidence the traditional approach, deriving from the doctrine of equitable fraud, has been that such a third party will come under a duty of confidence if as a matter of conscience he ought to have appreciated that the information was confidential. What the is the position of an editor who receives confidential information which he honestly but mistakenly believes it to be in the public interest to publish? In *Campbell v Mirror Group Newspapers* the Court of Appeal rejected the submission of the newspaper that in such circumstances it would not be guilty of breach of confidence[75].

69 [2003] QB 633 at paras 30-34.
70 *Breach of Confidence* (1984).
71 By Bingham LJ in *Spycatcher*.
72 This appears to have been the view of Ousley J in *MRA v BBC* [2002] EWHC, where previous publication was not regarded as a bar to a claim by a paedophile that his face should not be broadcast.
73 In *Spycatcher*, Lord Keith suggested that harm should be the test: [1990] 1 AC 109 at 260f-g.
74 Human Rights Act 1998, s 12(4) requires the court to have regard to the extent to which the information has become available to the public. But that applies only where the court is being asked to grant injunctive relief.
75 [2003] QB 633 at para 68.

A final possible distinction between confidentiality and privacy is that the former right applies only to information which is true, whereas the right to privacy of an individual may be invaded by the disclosure of facts about him or her which are untrue. This was the view expressed by Sedley LJ in *Financial Times v Interbrew SA*[76]. It is difficult to see how a quasi-proprietorial right of confidence could be asserted over information which is fictitious. By contrast the right of privacy, in the sense of personal autonomy or the right to be let alone, would be breached by the publication of untrue personal information; eg the falsity of the information would aggravate the injury.

These distinctions between the two rights are of more than academic interest. To the extent that they are differences of principle, it is difficult to see how the law of confidence can be adapted to give worthwhile protection to all aspects of the right of privacy.

The scope of the horizontal effect achieved by the Human Rights Act 1998

As has been seen, English judges have been hesitant about creating a common law right of privacy. Has the Human Rights Act 1998 rushed in where the judges feared to tread? Does the Act confer a right or privacy on the part of one citizen against another – in the jargon does it have horizontal effect? Surprisingly the answer to this question remains unclear.

It is a curious feature of the formulation of the right to privacy in Art 8 that, however unqualified the right appears to be in Art 8(1), what is prohibited by Art 8(2) is interference with the right 'by a public authority'. By contrast the Quebec Charter of Human Rights and Freedoms[77] makes clear that the right is intended to have horizontal effect. There is an historical explanation for the formula adopted by the Council of Europe: the Convention was agreed in the aftermath of the Second World War and was designed to ensure (in the words of Winston Churchill) that when there is a knock on the door in the early morning, it is the milkman. In other words the original purpose of Art 8 was to protect the citizen against the arbitrary exercise of the power of the state.

The wording of Art 8(2) of the Convention is reflected in the Human Rights Act 1998, s 6, which reads:

76 [2002] EWCA Civ 274.
77 1998 1 SCR 591, 613.

> 'It is unlawful for a public authority to act in a way which is incompatible with a Convention right'.

At first blush it might appear that the prohibition bites only on the state, that is, has only a vertical effect. But courts are public authorities. For a judge to deny a citizen relief in respect of a violation of his Convention right would or might be, so the argument runs, to 'act incompatibly' with that right. Professor Wade has expressed the view that:

> 'There is nothing to confine [the provisions of s 6] to cases brought against public authorities. I see no escape from the conclusion that [s 6] incorporates the scheduled human rights as equally applicable in all proceedings in the same sweeping way that European Union law is incorporated by section of the European Communities Act 1972'. [78]

Others, including Buxton LJ extra-judicially, have expressed a contrary view, pointing out that, while complaint can be made against a court, such a complaint has to be made by way of appeal or through judicial review proceedings. If the complaint is made on appeal, the appeal will be against the opposite party and not against the court and judicial review does not run against a court exercising its adjudicatory function [79]. In neither situation will the right achieve horizontal effect.

Professor Gearty, however, is of the opinion [80] that in litigation between private litigants (in which category he would include persons certain of whose functions are of a private nature [81]) the court is now bound to give effect to Convention rights. His argument is that courts are duty-bound not to act in a way which is incompatible with a Convention right. An act is for these purposes specifically said to include a failure to act [82]. So in determining whether or not to act (eg to grant a remedy in a case before it), courts will have to ensure that they do not act unlawfully by acting (or not acting) in a way which is incompatible with a Convention right. If in the course of submissions the court indicated an intention to disregard the Convention (eg by refusing an injunction to restrain the violation of a claimant's right to privacy), the claimant as the prospective 'victim' of its proposed conduct would be able to point to HRA 1998, s 7(1)(b)

78 'Human Rights and the Judiciary' JSB Annual Lecture 1998.
79 See HRA 1998, s 9(2).
80 'The Impact of the Human Rights Act' (1998).
81 See HRA 1998, s 6(3)(b).
82 See HRA 1998, s 6(6).

under which he or she is specifically empowered to 'rely on the Convention right or rights concerned in any legal proceedings'. There is, according to Professor Gearty, no reason why this point should not be taken in the course of the proceedings in which the possibility of the court acting unlawfully became apparent. If the judge was not dissuaded, the Court of Appeal would be entitled to substitute a lawful relief or remedy[83].

The wedding pictures

The issue whether the Convention right to privacy under Art 8 is available in private litigation not involving any public authority potentially arose for decision in *Douglas* [84]. In that case the claimants, both celebrated actors, who had granted exclusive rights to *OK!* magazine to publish photographs of their wedding, sought an injunction to prevent a rival magazine, *Hello*, from publishing photographs taken surreptitiously at the wedding. The litigation was therefore between private persons.

It does not appear from the report [85] that the argument was expressly advanced on behalf of the defendant that the court should not give effect to Art 8 in litigation between private persons. (As was pointed out, the case reached the Court of Appeal in a rush. This is likely to be typical of most privacy claims, and will not assist a reasoned evolution of the law in this area).

Brooke LJ noted the dilemma arising from the fact that the prohibition on interference with the right to privacy is directed at a public authority. For him the solution lay in the obligation undertaken by the contracting parties by virtue of Art 1 of the Convention to secure to everyone within their jurisdiction the rights and freedoms contained in the Convention. The wording of both Art 8 and HRA 1998, s 8 appear to be concerned to confer on individuals rights against the state and not against each other. But in a number of Strasbourg authorities, in particular *X and Y v The Netherlands* [86], the Court had held that the negative undertaking contained in Art 8, there was a positive obligation on contracting states to secure respect for private life. Moreover the Commission had apparently accepted that the English law of confidentiality provided sufficient protection for the privacy of the Countess Spencer (who had been

83 See HRA 1998, s 8(1).
84 [2001] QB 967.
85 [2001] 2 WLR 992.
86 (1985) 8 EHRR 235, 239-240.

photographed by means of a telephoto lens while walking in the grounds of a private clinic)[87].

By this route Brooke LJ felt able to conclude that the formula adopted in the HRA 1998 was designed to enable judges to develop the law so that it gives adequate recognition to Art 8(1) rights, including recognition of a horizontal right to privacy.

Sedley LJ tackled the horizontality issue head-on. He said[88]:

> '... we have reached a point at which it can be said with confidence that the law recognises and will appropriately protect a right of personal privacy ... the Human Rights Act requires the courts of this country to give appropriate effect to the right to respect for private and family life as set out in Art 8 ... by virtue of s 2 and s 6 of the Act, the courts of this country must not only take into account the jurisprudence of both the Commission and the European Court of Human Rights which points to a positive institutional obligation to respect privacy; they must themselves act compatibly with that and the other Convention rights'.

Later he accepted in terms the submission of counsel for the claimants that a horizontal effect was precisely the kind of incremental change for which the Act was designed[89]. He pointed out that HRA 1998, s 12(4), which requires the court to have particular regard to the right to freedom of expression, demonstrates the direct applicability of at least one article of the Convention as between one private party to litigation and another. At least according to the judgment of Sedley LJ, albeit in the context of a decision only that the claimants' case was arguable, the legal landscape has, as he said, changed.

In *Venables v News Group Newspapers Ltd*[90] the 18-year-old claimants, who had been released after serving the sentences passed for murders committed by them when aged only 10 years, sought injunctions to restrain various newspapers from divulging their whereabouts. The claimants relied on the right to life (Art 1) and Art 8. The newspapers asserted their right to freedom of expression under Art 10. Dame Elizabeth Butler-Sloss P held[91] that, since the defendant newspapers were not public authorities, Convention rights

87 [2001] 2 WLR 992 at para 105.
88 [2001] 2 WLR 992 at paras 109-112.
89 [2001] 2 WLR 992 at para 129.
90 [2001] 2 WLR 1039.
91 [2001] 2 WLR 1039.

were not directly enforceable against them. But the President went on to hold[92] that the court had a 'positive obligation' to provide machinery in order to protect the rights of the individual. Citing with approval the dictum of Sedley LJ as to the direct applicability of at least one article of the Convention in litigation as between one private party to litigation and another, the President accepted that she had to apply Art 10 directly. However she added the rider [93] that it did not appear to her that the court was obliged to create a free-standing cause of action based on the Convention. To that extent she appears to differ from Sedley LJ in *Douglas*.

Mrs Wainwright and her son claimed damages for the manner in which they were strip-searched by prison officers, which they said constituted an infringement of their rights of privacy. The conduct complained of took place before the passage of the HRA 1998 and in any case the defendant, the Home Office, was a public authority. In his judgment Buxton LJ expressed the view[94] that 'the difficult social balance' involved in defining the ambit of any tort of privacy was for Parliament and not judges to strike. He firmly rejected the notion, as did Mummery LJ, that the tort of invasion of privacy is one which exists in English law independently of the Convention. So to hold would be inconsistent with earlier decisions binding on the court [95].

Buxton LJ also emphasised that the Convention by its terms creates obligations only against the state. He said that he saw many difficulties about the contention that HRA 1998, s 6 creates private law rights in the same terms as Art 8. Lord Woolf LCJ expressed no opinion on the point (although he referred to the judgment of Sedley LJ in *Douglas* as 'most instructive').

The question whether the HRA 1998 creates a private law right of privacy arose for decision in *A v B plc*. The Court adopted what is best described as a pragmatic approach. Giving the judgment of the Court, Lord Woolf advised judges dealing with applications for interlocutory injunctions that it was most unlikely that any purpose would be served by seeking to decide whether there exists a new cause of action in tort which protects privacy[96]. But the judgment includes observations which suggest that, whether it be labelled privacy or

92 [2001] 2 WLR 1039 at paras 25-6.
93 [2001] 2 WLR 1039 at para 27.
94 [2002] 3 WLR 405 at paras 108-112.
95 *Kaye* (1991) FSR 62; *Malone v Metropolitan Police Comr* (1979) Ch 344 and *Khorasandjian v Bush* [1993] QB 727.
96 [2002] 3 WLR 542 at 550.

confidence, the right to protection will arise in a wide range of situations, 'whenever the party subject to the duty is in a situation where he either knows or ought to know that the other person can reasonably expect his privacy to be protected' [97]. The Court optimistically added: 'There must be some interest of a private nature which the claimant wishes to protect but usually the answer to the question whether there exists a private interest worthy of protection will be obvious' [98].

The question whether HRA 1998, s 6 has spawned a private law right of privacy unfortunately remains unresolved. It requires rapid resolution. If there is a private law right of privacy, there remains the thorny question how widely the right should extend. Should it, as Lord Bingham has suggested [99], 'be narrowly drawn, to give full effect to the right of free speech and the public's right to know'? If the right is to be narrowly confined, is there a risk that English privacy law will fail, as has been said to be the American experience?[100]

Reconciling Article 8 with Article 10: the collision between the right to privacy and the right to freedom of expression

At the heart of the problem of producing a balanced and workable definition of any right to privacy lies the indisputable tension between the right of privacy on the one hand and the exception to that right made in Art 8 (2), where necessary in a democratic society, 'for the protection of the rights and freedoms of others'. The right which is principally engaged is of course the right to freedom of expression contained in Art 10, which is subject to a corresponding exception.

The Convention itself provides no assistance how this tension is to be resolved. Where the rights collide, how is the judge supposed to decide which should yield to the other? In his Goodman Lecture Lord Hoffmann quoted Sir Isaiah Berlin:

97 [2002] 3 WLR 542 at 551.
98 [2002] 3 WLR 542 at 550.
99 'Should there be a law to protect rights of personal privacy?' [1996] EHRLR 450 at 461.
100 Professor David Anderson 'The failure of American privacy law' in Markesinis (ed) *Protecting Privacy* (Clarendon Press, 1999).

> 'The world that we encounter in ordinary experience is one in which we are faced with choices between ends equally ultimate, and claims equally absolute, the realisation of some of which must inevitably involve the sacrifice of others .... It is not merely in practice but in principle impossible to reach clear-cut and certain answers, even in an ideal world of wholly good and rational men and wholly clear ideas'.

As Lord Hoffmann observed, one cannot have freedom of expression without some sacrifice of privacy and vice versa. In *R v Central Independent Television*[101] he did not (as has been suggested) say that freedom of speech is always a trump card; what he said was that it is a trump card unless it is subject to clearly defined exceptions either of the common law or enacted by Parliament in accordance with its obligations under the Convention. Article 10(2) contains exceptions but are they clearly defined?

Moreoever, as Brian Neill has pointed out [102], privacy embraces wider issues than relations between individuals and the media:

> 'It is a mistake to consider privacy simply in the context of relations between individuals and the media. If consideration of the subject is concentrated on this aspect of privacy there is a danger that any analysis and certainly any public discussion will revolve around censorship and free speech. Properly understood, privacy is a much wider concept and is concerned with individual freedom and individual dignity and affects a citizen's relations not only with the media but with the state and with its fellow citizens as well as with companies or other entities which may wish to gain information about him to further their business interests'.

Although the Convention is silent on the question how to reconcile the rights under Articles 8 and 10, the Council of Europe has given guidance [103]:

> 'The Assembly reaffirms the importance of every person's right to privacy, and of the right to freedom of expression, as fundamental to a democratic society. The rights are neither absolute nor in any hierarchical order, since they are of equal value.

101 [1994] Fam 192, 202-204.

102 'Privacy: a challenge for the next century' in Markesinis (ed) *Protecting Privacy* (Clarendon Press, 1999) 22.

103 Resolution 1165 of 1998, para 11 and 12.

> However, the Assembly points out that the right to privacy afforded by Art 8 of the [ECHR] should not only protect an individual against interference by public authorities, but also against interference by private persons or institutions, including the mass media'.

That even-handed approach is not reflected in HRA 1998, s 12. Under the rubric 'Freedom of expression', the section deals with the potentially wide-ranging cases where the relief sought, if granted, would affect the right to freedom of expression. HRA 1998, s 12(3) provides that no such relief is to be granted so as to restrain publication before trial unless the court is satisfied that the applicant is likely to establish that publication should not be allowed. In other words, an arguable case is not enough [104]. Subsection (4) requires the court to have particular regard to the importance of the Convention right to freedom of expression and, where the proceedings relate to inter alia journalistic material, to the availability of that material to the public, to the public interest and to any relevant privacy code. The signs that this section was the product of lobbying by the media are not hard to detect.

In a loose sense the section appears to be intended to confer a superior status on Art 10 where it collides with other Convention rights. What is not so clear is how courts are supposed give effect to the superior status. What in practice is meant by having 'particular regard to' Art 10, especially when the court is also required to have particular regard to any relevant privacy code?

The self-regulatory bodies

Arguing the toss between the abstractions contained in Arts 8 and 10 is likely to provide judges, who are confronted with the problem, with uncertain guidance. The proof of the pudding is in the eating. In the course of time a body of authority will no doubt be built up which will provide on an empirical basis an indication when the right to privacy has to yield to the right to freedom of expression and, perhaps, vice versa.

Some assistance may also be derived from the stance adopted by the Press Complaints Commission and the Broadcasting Standards Commission in their respective self-regulatory privacy codes, to which the court is obliged by

104 A distinction which did not impress Sir Andrew Morritt VC in *Imutrans Ltd v Uncaged Campaigns Ltd* [2001] 2 All ER 385 at para 17.

the HRA 1998 to pay particular regard. (It has to be borne in mind, however, that the codes have no application to threatened publications, being concerned with publications which have taken place.)

The codes are of particular interest because they are presumably designed to list, for the guidance of editors, concrete instances where the right of privacy may be overridden in the name of the abstraction, freedom of expression.

Following its amendment in 1998, the PCC Code incorporated almost verbatim the wording of Art 8(1). Specific restrictions apply in certain defined circumstances, including for example a right to privacy in relation to details of physical or mental impairment and in places where there is a reasonable expectation of privacy. The PCC Code contains no blanket exception corresponding to Art 8(2). But it does list exceptions where in the public interest the right of privacy is abrogated: detecting or exposing crime or serious misdemeanour; protecting health; and public safety and preventing the public being misled by some statement or action of an individual or organisation.

The BSC Code is to similar effect, save that it refers to 'disreputable behaviour' which creates a materially larger exception than does 'serious misdemeanour'.

There is plenty of scope for debate what constitutes a misdemeanour and when it may be deemed 'serious', as there is for deciding when the public have been misled. Interestingly neither code includes an exception to those cases, the subject of much litigation in the US, where a journalist infringes rights of privacy in the course of news-gathering [105].

How in practice have judges so far resolved the tension between Articles 8 and 10

There is as yet sparse authority to guide judges how the balance between the right to freedom of expression and the right to privacy should be struck. This is in large part due to the fact that such decisions as there have been have tended, with the notable exception of *Venables* [106], to be interlocutory and, with the equally notable exception of *Douglas* [107], delivered on urgent applications

105 *Cohen v Cowles Media Cor* (1991) 501 US 663, discussed in David Schulz *Newsgathering as a Protected Activity* (OUP, 2000).

106 [2001] Fam 430.

107 [2001] QB 967.

for injunctive relief allowing insufficient time for the preparation of a fully reasoned judgment.

In *Venables* [108] the President held that the court was obliged to act compatibly with Convention rights and that the exceptions to the right of freedom of expression contained in Art 10(2) were wide enough to justify the court in preventing the disclosure of the identities and whereabouts of two child murderers. It made no difference that there was no pre-existing relationship between the parties or that the information in question was true. Although not in terms so described, the right being protected was indeed a right of privacy.

Although in *Douglas* the Court of Appeal ultimately refused an injunction on the ground that damages would be an adequate remedy, the reasoned decision is plainly an important one. Sedley LJ observed [109] that in litigation involving freedom of expression, it is necessary not only to have particular regard to the right to freedom of expression but also to have particular regard to among others the Convention rights to life and to privacy because of the limiting words to be found in Art 10(2) [110]. He also expressed the view [111] that the reputations and rights of others – not only but not least their Convention rights – are as material as the right of freedom of expression. There would appear to be no justification for conferring on Art 10 a status equivalent to that of the First Amendment in the US.

Some effect must be given to HRA 1998, s 12 but what effect? In *Douglas*[112], Brooke LJ described the right to freedom of expression as 'a powerful card' even if not the ace of trumps. Sedley LJ held that if the right is to be impeded it must be on 'cogent' grounds [113]. But it is not unfair to suggest that neither formulation has about it the precision necessary to enable citizens (or the media) 'to regulate their conduct' [114]. Dame Elizabeth Butler-Sloss P has said that to obtain an injunction against the media 'requires a strong case' [115]. How strong?

108 [2001] Fam 430.
109 [2001] QB 967.
110 [2001] 2 WLR 992, para 133.
111 [2001] QB 967.
112 [2001] QB 967.
113 [2001] QB 967, paras 49, 136.
114 *Rantzen v Mirror Group Newspapers* [1994] QB 670, citing *Sunday Times v UK (No 2)* (1991) 14 EHRR 229.
115 [2001] 2 WLR 1039 para 43.

Similarly Sir Andrew Morritt VC in *Imutran Ltd v Uncaged Campaigns Ltd*[116] held that HRA 1998, s 12(4) does not require the courts to place greater weight on freedom of expression than they already do, but it does require the courts to give it specific and separate consideration. The solution adopted in *Kelly v BBC*[117] was to say that those wishing to bring themselves within the exceptions contained in Art 10(2) must so establish 'convincingly' and by reference to 'proper evidence' rather than mere assertion. *Kelly* was, however, not a case where the conflict between Arts 8 and 10 arose directly for decision.

In *A v B plc*[118] a married professional footballer sought an injunction to prevent the *News of the World* from publishing accounts of his extra-marital sexual relations with two women. The judge upheld his claim and rejected the newspaper's claim that there was a public interest defence which would defeat his right to privacy. In the Court of Appeal it was acknowledged that Arts 8 and 10 pull in opposite directions. Lord Woolf stated[119] that a balance could be achieved by the courts 'if, when holding the balance, they attach proper weight to the important rights both articles are designed to protect. Each article is qualified expressly in a way which allows the interests under the other article to be taken in account'. But he added, as he was no doubt constrained to do by HRA 1998, s 12(4), that freedom of the press is 'a matter of particular importance', so that any interference with it has to be justified[120]. The injunction was discharged.

Was the judge wrong to conclude that publication would not be for the public benefit? The Court of Appeal observed[121]:

> 'Where an individual is a public figure he is entitled to have his privacy respected in the appropriate circumstances ... The public figure may be a role model whose conduct could well be emulated by others ... If you have courted publicity then you have less ground to object to the publicity which follows. In many of these situations it would be overstating the position to say that there is a public interest in the information being published.. It would be more accurate to say that the public have an understandable and so a legitimate interest in being told the information.

116 [2001] EMLR 563.
117 [2001] 2 WLR 253, 264, Munby J.
118 [2002] 3 WLR 542.
119 [2002] 3 WLR 542 at para 6.
120 [2002] 3 WLR 542 at para 11(iv).
121 [2002] 3 WLR 542 at para 11(xii).

> If this is the situation then it can appropriately be taken into account in deciding which side of the line a case falls'.

However talented and famous he may be on the football field, it is not immediately obvious what legitimate public interest (as opposed to prurient curiosity) there is in his activities in the bedroom. Should the right of privacy of celebrities be forfeited in circumstances where the private information has nothing to do with the reason for their celebrity [122]?

On the other hand it has been said that freedom of expression deters inappropriate behaviour[123]. Should those in the public eye be permitted to conceal their feet of clay? Does it make a difference that the information sought to be concealed has no bearing on those attributes which brought the individual concerned into the public eye? In *Campbell v Mirror Group Newspapers*, Lord Phillips commented:[124]

> 'For our part we would observe that the fact that an individual has achieved prominence on the public stage does not mean that his private life can be laid bare by the media. We do not see why it should necessarily be in the public interest that an individual who has been adopted as a role model, without seeking this distinction, should be demonstrated to have feet of clay'.

There are no more than a handful of first instance decisions which are worth mentioning. In *Mills v News Group Newspapers* [125] the claimant, a former model who subsequently married Sir Paul McCartney, failed to prevent *The Sun* from publishing details of a home she had recently acquired. The claimant feared for her physical safety if the address were to become public knowledge. The claim was framed in both confidence and privacy. The judge doubted the existence of a separate right of privacy but expressed the view that the day may not be far off when that deficiency would be remedied. Having taken account of the factors mentioned in section 12(4) of the Human Rights Act and the disavowal by the editor of any intention on the part of *The Sun* to publish the address unless it entered the public domain, the judge declined to grant an injunction.

122 Elias and Copple 'Freedom of Expression and freedom of Religion – some thoughts on the Glenn Hoddle case' (OUP, 2000).
123 *Ex p Kaim Todner* [1999] QB 966 at 977.
124 [2003] QB 633 at para 41.
125 Lawrence Collins J (Ch D) 4 June 2001.

The claimant in *Re A* [126] had been born a Siamese twin. An all-embracing injunction had been granted in the Family Division at the time of the application for permission to operate to separate her. Thereafter her parents negotiated a deal with two national newspapers for the publication of photographs of the child taken at that time. A's parents applied with the support of the two newspapers of the injunction to be varied so as to permit publication of those photographs. It emerged that, shortly before the application was made, another provincial newspaper had taken a photograph of A on the steps of a hospital but without her permission and using a long lens. The parents and the national newspapers applied successfully, after the provincial newspaper had published its photograph in an evening edition, to prevent further publication. The provincial newspaper applied to discharge the injunction. The judge declined to do so, holding that the claimant (or her parents) had a right to sell private photographs and that she had a reasonable expectation of privacy in relation to the photograph taken on the steps of the hospital. The court was unimpressed by the argument that such harm as might be suffered by reason of the publication of the photograph was financial (in that publication by other newspapers would have damaged the exclusivity of the rights granted to the two national newspapers).

Campbell v Mirror Group Newspapers [127] was unusual in that it went to trial. The judge held that the information that the claimant, Naomi Campbell, the fashion model, was receiving therapy for drug treatment was confidential and that its publication was not justified in the public interest. (As has been seen, he also held that she had a remedy under the Data Protection Act 1998.) By the time the case reached the Court of Appeal the issues had narrowed: Ms Campbell elected not to pursue her claim for damages for invasion of privacy. Even so, the Court of Appeal expressly acknowledged that Art 8 had a role to play in what had become a case framed solely in confidence. Lord Phillips said[128]:

> 'The Human Rights Act has had a significant impact on the law of confidentiality. On the one hand, when considering what information is confidential the courts must have regard to the Art 8 right to respect for private and family life. On the other hand they must have regard to the importance of freedom of expression, particularly where it is the media that seeks to exercise this freedom ...'.

126 Bennett J (Fam Div) 15 June 2001.
127 [2002] All ER (D) 177.
128 [2003] QB 633 at para 42.

He added that the courts are in the process of deciding on a case-by-case basis the principles by which the law of confidence must accommodate Arts 8 and 10.

The appeal in *Campbell* was allowed: it was held that disclosure of the fact of Ms Campbell's treatment for drug addiction was justified in the public interest. In a passage upon which the media will no doubt fasten, the Court commented[129]:

> 'Provided that publication of particular confidential information is justifiable in the public interest, the journalist must be given reasonable latitude as to the manner in which that information is communicated to the public or his Art 10 right to freedom of expression will be unnecessarily inhibited'.

The present position

Although there are dissentients, the preferred judicial route to affording appropriate recognition for the Art 8 right to privacy appears to be by developing the law of confidentiality. It is a trite observation that the genius of the common law (or in this instance equity) lies in its ability to develop and adapt to meet new circumstances. But is the law of confidence a suitable vehicle for importing a right of privacy into our law?

It may be that the right to privacy can be 'shoe-horned' [130] into the tort of breach of confidence. Doing so will, however, require substantial adaptations to the principles underlying the law of confidence as it is understood at present if the substantial distinctions between the two rights are to be ironed out. Proceeding on a case-by-case basis will inevitably mean that progress will be at a slow pace. The process is not assisted by the fact that, so far at least, the necessary development has taken place mainly in the context of cases between footballers and models and the tabloid press. In the meantime there will be continuing uncertainty.

It remains to be seen if the balance of judicial opinion will continue to be in favour of the conservative approach of developing the law of confidence rather

129 [2003] QB 633 at para 64.

130 A term used by Lord Phillips in *Campbell v Mirror Group Newspapers* [2003] QB 633 at para 69.

than introducing a free-standing right of privacy based on Art 8 and the Human Rights Act 1998. It is by no means obvious that the latter approach is open to the objection that it would be impossible adequately to protect the bastion of freedom of expression.

The law of contempt: the thalidomide contempt litigation in the domestic courts

In recent times the law of contempt has posed far less of a threat to freedom of expression. It was not always so.

In the late 1950s Distillers, a pharmaceutical company, started to market in the UK and elsewhere a sedative containing the drug thalidomide which had been developed in Germany. The drug proved to be particularly popular in the treatment of early morning sickness in pregnant mothers. In May 1961 a young Australian doctor encountered within the space of three weeks two cases of phocomelia, that is, deformity due to pre-natal injury to the foetus. Because of the rarity of that condition, he investigated whether there might be a common exogenous cause for the two cases and found that in each case the mother had taken thalidomide early in her pregnancy. The doctor notified Distillers and the drug was taken off the market.

Although the drug had been on the market for a relatively short period of time, several hundred children were born with terrible deformities. A number of actions were commenced against Distillers claiming, on behalf of some of the deformed children, damages for negligence. There were, however, formidable difficulties in proving that Distillers had been negligent. It was necessary to prove not only that Distillers knew or ought to have known that the drug was toxic (it had been thought to be non-toxic) but also that it would cross the placental barrier, if taken by a pregnant mother, and cause teratogenic damage to the foetus. Recognising these difficulties, some claims were settled on modest terms. But other cases surfaced leading to further claims for damages on behalf of 389 children. Their parents rejected settlement proposals as being inadequate.

It was against that background that the *Sunday Times* published articles which argued in general terms that liability should be absolute in such cases and that the then current level of damages was inadequate. Although the articles sought to exert pressure on Distillers, no action was taken in respect of them. But the

Sunday Times planned another article, based in part on Distillers' own documents, which argued the case in detail for saying that Distillers had been negligent and brought yet further pressure to bear on the company to settle the claims on generous terms. A draft of that article was submitted to the Attorney-General who decided to seek an injunction restraining publication on the ground that it would be a contempt.

In the Divisional Court [131] Lord Widgery CJ summarised the argument of Brian Neill for the newspaper as follows:

> 'Mr Neill's main argument is that, even if the authorities support the conclusion that it is a contempt of court to make any comment which involves a serious risk of interference with the course of legal proceedings, these rules are outdated and, being merely procedural, should be relaxed. He submits that the court's concern with a possible prejudice to the public mind has lost much of its force with the decline in jury trials, and that the increase in public interest in newspaper articles and broadcasts on current affairs has produced a new climate in which the news media have both the right and the duty to keep the public informed on matters of great public interest, even if some interference with the course of legal proceedings may result. He contends that in cases like the present there are really two competing public interests: one, the protection of the administration of justice, and another, the right of the public to be informed on the grave and weighty issues of the day, and he says that even if a case of contempt has been made out within the authorities to which we have been referred, the publication should not be punished or restrained if, on balance, the latter interest is the more important, in the circumstances of the particular case'.

Thirty years on it is easy to overlook the boldness of that submission: not only was it virtually unsupported by pre-existing authority, it went so far as to assert a right on the part of the media to inform the public even if that interfered with the administration of justice. The submission fell on stony ground: the Divisional Court acceded to the application for an injunction. The Court of Appeal (unsurprisingly, since it included Lord Denning MR and Scarman LJ) was more receptive to the newspaper's contention. Lord Denning held [132] that the case was unique and the comment in the proposed article was fair, so that the public interest in public discussion outweighed the prejudice which might

131 [1973] QB 710 at 725F.
132 [1973] QB 710 at 740A-F.

as a result be occasioned to Distillers. Scarman LJ expressed himself more broadly, referring to the very great interest which the public have in freedom of discussion [133].

The Attorney appealed. In the House of Lords Brian Neill repeated the argument that there was a balance to be struck between freedom of speech on the one hand and preventing interference with the administration of justice on the other. But his contention that, in holding the balance, greater weight should be given to the former, did not find favour with any member of the House. Lords Diplock and Simon of Glaisdale were prepared to allow that, if the discussion of topics of legitimate public interest has the indirect effect of bringing pressure to bear on a particular litigant to abandon his action, that must be tolerated because of the greater public interest in maintaining freedom of discussion on matters of public concern [134]. The House was, however, unanimous in holding that any publication which pre-judged the issues in pending litigation (as did the proposed *Sunday Times* article) would be a contempt. An injunction was granted and the article was spiked.

Reform of the law of contempt: the Phillimore Committee

Coincidentally a Committee under the chairmanship of Phillimore LJ (who was the third member of the Court of Appeal in the thalidomide contempt case) had since 1971 been considering whether changes were needed in the law of contempt. The thalidomide contempt litigation was concluded in the domestic courts before the Committee reported.

While recognising that the pre-judgment test for contempt introduced by the House of Lords injected greater clarity and certainty into the law of contempt, the Phillimore Committee preferred a test which made direct reference to the mischief which the law of contempt was supposed to suppress, namely the risk of prejudice to the due administration of justice.

The Committee further considered, in the light of the decision of the House of Lords, whether a general defence of public benefit should be introduced. In its Report [135] the Committee rejected the proposal on the grounds that it

133 [1973] QB 710 at 746G.
134 [1974] AC 273 at 310F-H, 313A-B, 314C.
135 Cmnd 5794.

would be difficult to define and productive of uncertainty. The Committee was unimpressed by the suggestion that in particular cases the public interest might outweigh the public interest in ensuring that the accused had a fair trial. The Committee did, however, recommend that the test of contempt should be whether the publication created a risk that the course of justice would be seriously impeded or prejudiced. That recommendation, if implemented, would in effect have done away with the notion of 'technical' contempt as Brian Neill had advocated in the thalidomide case.

English contempt law breaches the Convention

Following its defeat in the House of Lords, the *Sunday Times* brought proceedings against the UK in Strasbourg alleging breach of Art 10 of the Convention [136]. The argument before the European Court of Human Rights raised the vexed question how to reconcile the conflict between the right to freedom of expression contained in Art 10 and the entitlement to a fair hearing by an independent and impartial tribunal conferred by Art 6(1).

The argument for the newspaper echoed in Convention terms the submission which Brian Neill had made to the Divisional Court, summarised earlier, and repeated in the higher courts. The *Sunday Times* argued that the legitimate public concern about the thalidomide litigation was so great that in the particular circumstances of the case the right to freedom of expression should prevail over the perceived infringement of Distillers' right to a fair hearing under Art 6. The newspaper argued further that the restriction on its freedom to discuss the issues in the litigation was not 'necessary in a democratic society ... for maintaining the authority and impartiality of the judiciary' so as to come within the exception allowed by Art 10(2).

Those arguments were upheld by the court in Strasbourg. The Phillimore Committee had reported some years earlier in 1974 but (as is not unprecedented) the deliberations of the Committee had borne no legislative fruit. The judgment of the European Court of Human Rights provided the necessary impetus for Parliament to act. The Contempt of Court Act reached the statute book in 1981. The ancestry of two of the provisions of that Act can be traced to the argument addressed on behalf of the *Sunday Times* to the English courts in the thalidomide litigation.

136 *Sunday Times v UK* (1979) 2 EHRR 245.

The strict liability rule

CCA 1981, s 2 provides that criminal contempt by the publication of matter calculated to interfere with the fair trial of criminal proceedings is committed if and only if a substantial risk of serious prejudice to those proceedings is established. This marked the *quietus* for the concept of technical contempt which had been advocated on behalf of the *Sunday Times* in the thalidomide case.

When propounding the pre-judgment test in the thalidomide case, the House of Lords had in effect resuscitated the notion of technical contempt: it would be open to the court to find contempt proved notwithstanding the absence of any more than a small risk of prejudice to pending proceedings. From the perspective of the media the adoption of such a test was unacceptable because of the wide spectrum of publications which might be caught by it. It was cold comfort for editors to be told that historically fines were not imposed for technical contempts, if (as not infrequently happened) the respondent publisher was ordered to pay the costs of the technically contemptuous publication.

The enactment of CCA 1981, s 2 was for the media a welcome liberalisation of the law. Liability continued to be strict in the sense that it was unnecessary to establish that the publisher intended to interfere with the administration of justice or to cause prejudice. But the strictness of the rule is tempered, firstly, by the fact that it applies only to proceedings which are 'active' and, secondly, by a series of judicial decisions as to the meaning and effect of the linked concepts of 'substantial risk' and 'serious prejudice' in CCA 1981, s 2(2).

'Active' proceedings

The CCA 1981 identifies the point in time when proceedings are 'active' with the consequence that the strict liability comes into play. Thus criminal proceedings in England generally become 'active' upon the arrest or oral charge of the defendant. This, it might be supposed, provides the media, who are facing quasi-criminal liability, with the certainty to which they are entitled. The requirement in Art 10(2) of the ECHR that any restriction on the right to freedom of expression be 'prescribed by law' requires that the law should be 'formulated with sufficient precision to enable the citizen to regulate his conduct'[137].

137 *Sunday Times v UK* (1979) 2 EHRR 245, 271.

Nothing is as straightforward as it seems. A publication may be actionable as a contempt at common law even if it takes place before the proceedings are active: *A-G v News Group Newspapers* [138]. (The decision in that case was not surprising on its facts: the *Sun*, having offered to fund a private prosecution of a doctor for sexually molesting a young girl, published at a time when criminal proceedings were virtually certain, a story under the headlines 'He's a real swine' and 'Beast must be named says MP'.) In the main, however, CCA 1981, Sch 1 tells editors with suitable precision when they are on risk as to contempt.

Substantial risk

By CCA 1981, s 2(2) the strict liability rule applies only where there is a substantial risk of prejudice to the proceedings in question. In *A-G v English*[139] Lord Diplock, with whom the other members of the House concurred, held that 'substantial' was hardly an apt word to apply to 'risk', which was a noumenon, and that the two words in combination were intended to exclude a risk that is only remote. Judicial reluctance to tolerate even a slight risk of prejudice is understandable. It is however, questionable whether this construction of 'substantial' accorded with the spirit of the recommendation of the Phillimore Committee or even with the decision of the ECHR in *Sunday Times v UK*.

Some inroads upon the notion that anything other than a remote risk of prejudice will suffice were made in *A-G v News Group Newspapers*[140], where an injunction was sought to restrain the publication of an article to be published in the *News of the World* on the ground that it would prejudice the forthcoming trial of a libel action brought by the cricketer Ian Botham against the *Mail on Sunday*. That newspaper had made claims of drug-taking and sexual misbehaviour on a tour of New Zealand. The *News of the World* also wanted to regale its readers with allegations of sex and drugs, but this time on a tour of the West Indies.

Sir John Donaldson MR and Parker LJ explained that the test of 'substantial risk' and 'serious prejudice' are separate but overlapping. The degree of risk of the impact of a publication on a trial and the extent of any such impact may both be affected by the nature and form of the publication and how long it

138 [1989] QB 110.
139 [1983] 1 AC 116 at 141-142.
140 [1987] 1 QB 1.

occurred before trial. Although the libel proceedings were 'active' and despite the high profile of the claimant and the massive circulation of the newspaper, the application for an injunction was dismissed because the trial was not due to commence for 10 months, so that the risk of prejudice was insufficient.

In the same case Sir John Donaldson quoted with approval the words of Lawton J in a case involving the Kray twins decided many years before the enactment of the Contempt of Court Act [141]: 'The drama, if I may use that term, almost always has the effect of excluding that which went before'. So the unlikelihood that jurors, once seized of a case, will allow extraneous publicity to divert them from their task is another basis for holding that a sufficient risk of prejudice has not been made out.

Another route by which the court may escape the conclusion that the risk of serious prejudice is no more than remote is by reliance on the ability of the trial judge to direct the jury to decide the case on the evidence and to put out of their minds everything else. Thus in *Ex p The Telegraph plc* [142] Lord Taylor of Gosforth LCJ said that, in determining whether a publication would cause a substantial risk of serious prejudice, the court should credit the jury with the will and ability to abide by the judge's direction to decide the case only on the evidence before them. The consequence in that case was that the media were permitted to report fully the trial of certain defendants for importing the drug ecstasy tablets notwithstanding that other associated defendants were awaiting trial on identical charges and that in both the trials the prosecution case depended almost entirely on the evidence of the same alleged accomplice.

In assessing whether the threshold of substantiality has been crossed the court will take heed not only of the interval between the date of publication and the trial but also of the length of the publication; whether it is ephemeral; and whether it is likely to circulate in the area from which jurors are likely to be empanelled. These were among the factors which led the Court of Appeal in *A-G v ITN Ltd* [143] to dismiss a contempt motion in respect of a televised report of the arrest of two men for the murder of a special constable, which included the startling revelation that one of them had escaped from a jail in Belfast where he had been serving a life sentence for the murder of an SAS

141 (1969) 53 Cr App R 412, 415.
142 [1993] 1 WLR 980 at 987E.
143 [1995] 2 All ER 370.

officer. As Schiemann LJ was later to point out in *A-G v MGN Ltd* [144] a small risk multiplied by a small risk results in an even smaller risk.

Serious prejudice

By CCA 1981, s 2(2) the strict liability rule only bites where the risk that the course of justice will be 'seriously impeded or prejudiced'. Does this mean that a publication which prejudices pending proceedings is acceptable, provided only that the prejudice is not 'serious'? It might be supposed that in a civilised society, subject to a *de minimis* argument, no prejudice to the fair trial of an accused person is tolerable. That broadly reflects the opinions of most members of the House of Lords in the thalidomide contempt litigation. But Lord Diplock made clear in *A-G v English*[145] that 'serious' does not just mean 'real' but rather is descriptive of the extent of the prejudice or impediment to the course of justice which is a condition of liability under the strict liability rule.

The Human Rights Act 1998, s 3 requires CCA 1981, s 2 to be read and given effect to in a way which is compatible with Convention rights. It was this requirement which in *A-G v Guardian Newspapers Ltd* [146] led Sedley LJ (with whom Collins J with some hesitation agreed) to elevate significantly the criteria necessary to establish contempt. He said [147]:

> 'Although the material parts of the Human Rights Act 1998 are not yet in force, the history of the Contempt of Court Act 1981 makes it not only legitimate but necessary to construe and apply the latter so far as possible in conformity with the European Convention on Human Rights. The values which the Convention assigns to free expression and to fair trials are replicated in the New Zealand Bill of Rights and the Canadian Charter of Fundamental Rights and Freedoms, making the jurisprudence of all three instruments – the one European, the other two governing common law jurisdiction – of potential value to us. It is therefore interesting to find substantially the same concept of a localised balance of rights and interests, rather than a defeasible priority of the claims of justice, informing the decision of the European Court of Human

144 [1997] 1 All ER 456 at 461.
145 [1983] 1 AC 116 at 142.
146 [1999] EMLR 904.
147 [1999] EMLR 904 at 922.

> Rights in *Worm v Austria* [148] from which Collins J has already given full citations .... '.

From that preface Sedley LJ proceeded to hold that the test for contempt should be equated with the test to be applied in a criminal appeal based on publicity adverse to the appellant. The test being the same in each case, the self-evident difference is that risk has to be gauged prospectively in a contempt case and retrospectively in a criminal appeal. But, as Sedley LJ pointed out, before any criminal appeal can take place, the judge will have had the opportunity to direct the jury to ignore extraneous publicity. In many, if not most cases, such a direction will obviate the risk of a successful appeal.

The logic of the decision of the Divisional Court in *A-G v Guardian Newspapers Ltd* is that, where (as would usually be the case) the motion to commit is heard after the trial of the criminal defendant, it will often be possible for the alleged contemnor to avoid liability by reference to the direction which the trial judge either had given or would give to the jury in relation to the allegedly prejudicial material. If the words of Lord Taylor in *Ex p The Telegraph plc*, cited earlier, are taken at their face value, it is to be assumed that the jury will act on the judge's direction.

It may be that in practice proceedings for contempt under the strict liability rule will be brought only where the trial judge has felt himself constrained by the prejudicial publication to abort the trial. Even in those cases it will of course be open to the respondent to argue that, whatever the judge presiding over the criminal trial may have felt, the statutory criteria for liability under the strict liability rule are not satisfied.

A discussion of public affairs

Another provision in the CCA 1981 whose ancestry can be traced to the submissions of the *Sunday Times* in the thalidomide contempt case is to be found in s 5:

> 'A publication made as or as part of a discussion in good faith of public affairs or other matters of general public interest is not to be treated as a contempt under the strict liability rule if the risk of impediment or

148 (1997) 25 EHRR 454.

prejudice to particular legal proceedings is merely incidental to the discussion'.

This new defence reflects the argument for the *Sunday Times* that the importance of free speech requires that the restriction imposed by the law of contempt should not apply in those cases where the subject matter of the publication was of legitimate public interest. Two of the speeches in the House of Lords in the thalidomide contempt litigation recognised the desirability of the public interest in discussion of matters of public interest being permitted to prevail, even if impinging on pending litigation, at least where the public discussion was already under way before the proceedings were commenced.[149] The condition that the discussion be already under way, did not, however, find its way into the section.

The Phillimore Committee had considered whether there should be a general defence of public benefit. It recommended that no such defence should be enacted. The Committee did, however, recommend the introduction of a defence where the publication in question formed part of a legitimate discussion of matters of public interest and the risk of serious prejudice to particular proceedings was incidental and unintenional. This recommendation recognises (as does the defence introduced by CCA 1981, s 5) that there will be circumstances where a publication which creates a substantial risk of serious prejudice to the fair trial of an accused person will be immune from liability as a contempt.

The House of Lords was called upon to consider the effect of CCA 1981, s 5 for the first time in *A-G v English*[150]. In the course of a criminal trial of a general practitioner for murder by prescribing a drug and nursing regime which resulted in the death of his patient, who was a child suffering from Down's syndrome, the *Daily Mail* published a report of the election address of a journalist who had the previous year stood as parliamentary candidate. The address, which had received some publicity at the time of the election, suggested that it was common practice to let such babies die of starvation or otherwise to dispose of them. The Attorney-General applied to commit the editor and the newspaper.

The difficulties in deciding whether the defence under CCA 1981, s 5 is available stem from the use of the term 'discussion' and the phrase 'merely

149 [1974] AC 273, per Lord Reid at 296; and per Lord Simon at 321.
150 [1983] 1 AC 116.

incidental to'. The Divisional Court, finding the contempt proved, had held that a 'discussion' was confined to 'the airing of views and the propounding and debating of principles and arguments'. Lord Diplock pointed out that so narrow an interpretation of 'discussion' would emasculate the intended effect of the section. Newspapers cannot be expected to talk entirely of abstract generalities.

More problematic was the phrase 'merely incidental', which evidently derived from the judgment of Jordan CJ in *Ex p Bread Manufacturers*[151], a case which had featured prominently in the argument of Brian Neill in the thalidomide case and which had been cited with approval in that case by Lords Reid and Simon of Glaisdale. The Divisional Court had held that the risk of prejudice consequent on the publication of the *Daily Mail* article was not merely incidental to the public discussion because the article contained unnecessary assertions of fact that the doctor had done what the prosecution alleged he had done. Lord Diplock expressed the opinion that this approach was also too narrow: he considered the words 'merely incidental to the discussion' to mean no more than the risk was an incidental consequence of expounding its main theme. He rejected the notion that, in order to be incidental to the discussion, the contents of the article had to be necessary to the discussion.

CCA 1981, s 5 having been liberally construed, one would have expected that it would regularly provide the media with an escape route from liability for contempt. But, for whatever reason, cases on the section are few and far between. One such arose out of the memorable occasion when an intruder named Fagan broke into Buckingham Place and entered the Queen's bedroom[152]. He was charged with various criminal offences. Several national newspapers published largely factual accounts of the break-in and some of the articles mentioned Fagan's drug-taking. The articles were plainly prejudicial to his fair trial. But the safety of the Queen was plainly a matter of general public interest and the risk of prejudice was no doubt merely incidental. The respondents were perhaps fortunate to find that their factual accounts of Fagan's escapade qualified as 'discussions'.

CCA 1981, s 5 did not assist the respondent in *A-G v TVS Television Ltd*[153]. The programme, entitled 'The New Rachmans', was ostensibly a general discussion about unscrupulous landlords. But it focussed on an area where

151 (1937) SR (NSW) 249.
152 *The Times*, February 1983.
153 (1989) Times, 7 July.

prosecutions were pending against certain landlords for obtaining public money by deception. The court held that, whatever the intention behind the programme, the discussion contained in it was too closely related to the criminal proceedings for the risk of prejudice to qualify as 'merely incidental'.

A narrow construction was put on CCA 1981, s 5 in *A-G v Guardian Newspapers* [154], referred to earlier. A man named Kennedy was accused of stealing body parts from a hospital for what were said to be artistic purposes. In the course of his criminal trial (at which he argued that body parts were not capable of being stolen because they did not belong to anyone), the *Observer* published an article suggesting that Kennedy was a necrophile and a pervert.

The motion to commit the newspaper for contempt failed on the ground that a substantial risk of serious prejudice had not been established. But the court held that CCA 1981, s 5 would not have availed the newspaper because the risk of prejudice could not be said to be merely incidental to the discussion, since the subject matter of the article was the conduct of Kennedy which had led to his prosecution [155]. The requirement that there must be some reason or justification for the publication which is independent of the conduct or incident which led to the institution of criminal proceedings places a significant limitation upon the application of CCA 1981, s 5. The defence will not be available to a publication which discusses the wisdom of a criminal prosecution, no matter how great the public interest in the issues to which the prosecution gives rise. The case of *Fagan* may be regarded as having turned on what one trusts were its own special facts.

It would be wrong to write off CCA 1981, s 5 as a dead letter. But the number of cases where the statutory defence had been successfully invoked seem to be remarkably few. It is noteworthy, as the editors of the leading textbook on the law of contempt [156] point out, that judges displayed a willingness to restrain by injunction public discussion of the affairs of Mr Robert Maxwell because of its prejudicial effect on the pending proceedings against two of his sons and others, despite the manifest importance of the issues raised by his misconduct[157].

154 [1999] EMLR 904.
155 [1999] EMLR 904 at 921.
156 *Arlidge, Eady and Smith on Contempt* (2nd edn) para 4-296.
157 *R v Maxwell* (unreported, Phillips J, 6 March 1995; *A-G v BBC, Hat Trick Productions* [1997] EMLR 76 and *A-G v Steadman* (unreported, Bell J, 7 February 1994).

The legacy of the thalidomide contempt litigation

It is incontrovertible that the thalidomide contempt litigation provided the stimulus for some radical changes in the law of contempt of court by prejudicing pending proceedings. Liability remains strict. Otherwise the CCA 1981 was a liberalising measure. The media are no longer left in a state of uncertainty when the rule starts to apply. The concept of technical contempt has been consigned to history. The conditions for establishing liability for contempt under the strict liability rule are more onerous than was (and remains) the case under the common law. Recent authority [158] suggests that publications which take place during or shortly before a criminal trial will generally escape liability for contempt if the trial judge permits the case to continue. That in turn may cause the Attorney-General (who alone can institute proceedings under the strict liability rule) [159] to hesitate before initiating proceedings. CCA 1981, s 5 may be said to have proved something of a lame duck. But, all in all, the reforms set in train by the argument for the newspaper in the thalidomide case have largely eliminated the chilling effect which the law of contempt once had on freedom of expression.

The last word

These are but a handful of the questions which judges will have to resolve in the years ahead. In answering them they will do well to bear in mind what Brian Neill wrote in 1995:

> 'I hope and anticipate that once the Convention has been incorporated into English law the courts will become increasingly willing to give effect to the principles underlying it. In time therefore the dignity of the individual should assume a fresh importance and, though the freedom of speech and the freedom of the media will remain very powerful counterweights, I hope that in appropriate cases they will not be allowed to act the part of trump cards. There may be lessons to be learned from the jurisprudence of other countries that in this field as in others the courts must seek to balance conflicting rights and try to find the point of equilibrium'.

158 *A-G v Guardian Newspapers* [1999] EMLR 904.
159 Contempt of Court Act 1981, s 7.

Index